Inshallah Bangladesh

Praise for the Book

'Deep Halder has a keen understanding of the new Bangladesh, unencumbered by rigid templates of the past and old ideologies. In this book, he goes deep into the factors that led to the 5 August youth revolt against Sheikh Hasina: what were the military leaders and top officials up to in the hours before the street protests erupted; how Hasina ignored the early warning signs, underestimated the threats and refused to escape to safety; and who is whispering about a global conspiracy. Read this book for an intimate view of the flux that Bangladesh finds itself in today and how it is moving beyond Sheikh Mujib's dream.'

– **Shekhar Gupta**, founder and editor-in-chief, *ThePrint*

'What Bangladeshi journalist Sahidul Hasan Khokon went through after the fall of Hasina is not his story alone. It is the story of a country at war with itself, trying to wipe out its own history and the legacy of 1971. *Inshallah Bangladesh* is a must read for those interested not just in Bangladesh's future but the fate of the subcontinent itself.'

– **Manash Ghosh**, former resident editor, *The Statesman*, Delhi, who covered 1971 Bangladesh War of Independence

'With Bangladesh trapped in an existential crisis today, brought on by local and foreign conspiracy, this work provides hope to its people. *Inshallah Bangladesh* is a prayer for a return to decency. It is also a reaffirmation of the Bengali people's determination to recover, restore and re-establish the foundational principles of the nation-state they inhabit.'

– **Syed Badrul Ahsan**, former executive editor of *The Daily Star*, Bangladesh

Inshallah Bangladesh

The Story of an Unfinished Revolution

Deep Halder
Jaideep Mazumdar
Sahidul Hasan Khokon

JUGGERNAUT BOOKS
C-I-128, First Floor, Sangam Vihar, Near Holi Chowk,
New Delhi 110080, India

First published by Juggernaut Books 2025

Copyright © Deep Halder, Jaideep Mazumdar, Sahidul Hasan Khokon 2025

10 9 8 7 6 5 4 3 2 1

P-ISBN: 9789353459871
E-ISBN: 9789353454951

The views and opinions expressed in this book are the authors' own. The facts contained herein were reported to be true as on the date of publication by the authors to the publishers of the book, and the publishers are not in any way liable for their accuracy or veracity.

All rights reserved. No part of this publication may be reproduced, transmitted or stored in a retrieval system in any form or by any means without the written permission of the publisher.

Typeset in Adobe Caslon Pro by R. Ajith Kumar, Noida

Printed at Thomson Press India Ltd

This book is dedicated to Bangladeshi voices that refused to be silenced, before, during, after Hasina.

'I am against revolutions because they always involve a return to status quo. I am against the status quo both before and after revolutions.'

– HENRY MILLER
An Open Letter to Surrealists Everywhere (1939)

Contents

Preface   xi

SECTION I: SOCIETY

1. Hasina's Day Out   3
2. The General Who Betrayed Hasina   20
3. Bangladesh Turns Back the Clock   34
4. Rise of the Razakars   52
5. Mujib: The Man, the Myth   70
6. Why Young Bangladeshis Hate India   92

SECTION II: POLITICS

7. Good Hasina, Bad Hasina   107
8. A New Messiah?   124
9. Boys and Girls in King's Party   143
10. India's New Headache?   157

SECTION III: PEOPLE

11. A Hindu Homeland   175
12. No Country for Other Muslims   189
13. Can Cinema Save Bangladesh?   200
14. The Return of Secular Bloggers   216
15. No Woman, No Cry   234

Afterword   249
Notes   256
Acknowledgements   280
A Note on the Authors   282

Preface

The Day I Became an Anti-National

9 August 2024

11.30 a.m.–2 p.m., Dhaka to Faridpur

'Whose dead bodies are these?' I ask one of the ambulance drivers at the Shyampur bridge on the Dhaka–Mawa–Bhanga Expressway. Why do they call these vehicles that carry the dead freezing ambulances, I wonder. But what else can they possibly call them! The middle-aged man looks me in the eye and doesn't answer immediately.

There is a traffic snarl at the bridge, with five ambulances standing in a line, one after the other, along with cars, trucks, buses and bikes. Around a hundred student protestors have *gheraoed* the bridge. They are stopping vehicles, asking drivers and passengers to get down for questioning, frisking them, checking their luggage. They are escorting a few drivers and passengers down the bridge. To where, no one knows.

'There are bodies of eleven policemen in these five ambulances,' the driver tells me, his voice unwavering, bored, perhaps, by the delay in his journey.

'Where are you taking them?' I ask again.

'Too old, aren't you, to be a student protestor and asking so many questions?' he smirks at me.

'I am just an ordinary citizen trying to return home to Faridpur,' I manage a smile. I am riding pillion with my junior colleague, Mir Anees, who is on the saddle of his trusted bike that has taken him far and wide for many reporting assignments.

Today, it might just save our lives.

It has been four days since Bangladesh Prime Minister Sheikh Hasina flew to India. Madness has descended on my country – there is no government, no rule of law, no order, no sanity. There have been big celebrations at the fall of Hasina, and killings, rapes and maiming of the Awami League's – Hasina's party – leaders, workers and supporters, as well as anybody the student protestors and faceless mobs, moving from skinny alleys to paved streets, from unpaved village lanes to newly-built highways and bridges, breaking into homes and offices, deem anti-national. News of Hindu homes and temples being attacked across the country are pouring in.

Student coordinators, heroes of the revolution that ended Hasina's reign, are manning the streets, managing traffic, trying to separate the 'neo-nationalists' from the 'anti-nationals'. 'Anti-national' has become an umbrella term for anyone who was in Hasina's government or party, was an alleged beneficiary of her regime or was deemed to be in any way close to our neighbour, India.

I, Sahidul Hasan Khokan, professional journalist and writer for twenty years, having worked with some of the top media houses in Bangladesh and India – and till recently the Dhaka correspondent of the India Today Group – father to an eight-year-old boy, husband to a college teacher, have been branded 'anti-national'. My fault? I have extensively covered the Sheikh Hasina government and uncovered the nefarious designs of the Bangladesh Jamaat-e-Islami and its hard push for a radical Islamist nation.

In 2023, I was asked to become a member of the Awami League international affairs committee, given my vast experience covering the diplomatic relationship between Dhaka and Delhi. What had seemed like a new career path then, a gradual shift from journalism to diplomacy, has now become a clear and present danger for me.

Preface

I am escaping from my home in Dhaka with a rucksack on my back, 25,000 Bangladeshi taka and a few clothes. My wife and son are at a relative's place in Dhaka, but far from the neighbourhood where we lived for the last decade. My contacts in Bangladesh's military intelligence told me that I should leave my Dhaka home immediately, hide somewhere in the hinterland, throw away the SIM card in my phone so that I cannot be traced and try to have no contact with my family so that they do not come in harm's way.

'What have I done? Why do I have to run away like a fugitive from the law?' I had pleaded with a top officer of the Directorate General of Forces Intelligence (DGFI), Bangladesh's military intelligence unit, a source I had cultivated over the years.

'There is no law. Run before it's too late,' the voice on the other end had said, disconnecting the call.

I could have asked for help from the police or the military, but after the attacks on cops, the police stations are unmanned and the mob has been lynching citizens in front of the military.

After dropping off my wife and son the previous night, I had made a distress call to tell Anees to pick me up from home at 11 a.m. today. I had decided against driving out of Dhaka in my sparkling new Toyota Noah, on which I had spent a small fortune, as it would draw too much attention. Little did I know that I would never see it again! Anees picked me up from home, navigated the traffic snarls within Dhaka and reached the Dhaka–Mawa–Bhanga Expressway, the country's first expressway that had been operational since 2022.

We find ourselves stranded next to the ambulance, which, along with the four other ambulances behind it, is carrying bodies of slain policemen. The driver tells me they are transporting the bodies to their respective families in towns and villages. 'They have been hacked to death, some bodies have limbs missing, some have heads cracked open. Never seen policemen killed like this,' the driver tells me, lighting a bidi.

Four student coordinators approach us. 'Where are you headed?' they ask Anees, after telling both of us to take off our helmets. 'I am a reporter,' says Anees, 'and he is my senior in the profession. We are off to Faridpur on assignment.'

My heart skips a beat. Why did Anees say we are off for an assignment! What if they ask me to open my rucksack and find 25,000 Bangladeshi taka hidden inside a bundle of clothes? Who takes that kind of money to a reporting assignment? Anees and I should have discussed this before we set out and thought of a better excuse for carrying money and clothes.

The boys move towards me. 'What is your name? Which media house do you work for?' I bring out a press card that reads 'Sahidul Hasan Khokhon, Reporter, *Ekushey Songbad*'. It is a fake ID card I had printed last evening from the neighbourhood printer shop, anticipating such a moment. With Hasina gone, being associated in any way with India is as injurious to life and limb as being part of the Awami League ecosystem. The boys take a good look at the card as I feel my heart beats faster, my throat parched. At any moment they can ask me to open the rucksack and show them what is inside.

'Let them go,' one of them says.

Anees pushes the bike's start button.

Fifteen minutes pass as we zip through the expressway, praying no further 'check posts' manned by student coordinators come in our way. At the Dhaleshwari toll plaza in Munshigunj district, a group of *huzur*s – religious preachers – easily identifiable by their long beards, skull caps and short pyjamas, ask us to stop. We are asked again who we are and where we are headed. The same answer and the same fake press card. Allah saves us one more time as they indicate that we can carry on. As I breathe a sigh of relief, something catches my eye. The signboard at the Dhaleshwari toll plaza had read 'Bangabandhu Elevated Expressway Toll Plaza'. Now, there is a new cheap plastic signboard with the words 'Jatir Pita Hazrat Adam (AS) Toll Plaza'. Bangabandhu Sheikh Mujibur Rahman, the founding father of Bangladesh, has been replaced by Adam, the first human being on earth according to the Abrahamic faiths!

My Bangladesh has irrevocably changed.

We reach Faridpur town by 2 p.m. There are no interruptions on the way. Anees hasn't stopped for roadside tea or coconut water. We have exchanged no words.

2 p.m. Onwards

At sixty-six, Syed Modarres Ali Isa is a man of considerable influence not just in Faridpur district – Bangladesh's second largest district after Dhaka – but also in every nook and cranny of Bangladesh where the Bangladesh Nationalist Party (BNP) holds sway. Isa is not only the district president of the BNP's Faridpur unit, but also a central executive committee member of the party. Last evening, 8 June, Isa bhai, again an old contact since my reporting days, had made an unexpected call.

'Sahidul, are you okay?'

'Bhai, as okay as one can be given what's happening all around.'

'They are hunting for "Indian agents" and Hasina's people. I am scared you might be targeted. Come to Faridpur with your family.'

'Bhai, I do not know how to express my gratitude for such generosity. But I do not wish to be a burden.'

'Come over, Sahidul. Don't be stupid. People have gone mad. Just pack a bag and come,' Isa bhai had said.

Isa bhai had reasons to be worried about me. News had been pouring in of media offices being taken over by raucous mobs, journalists being heckled on streets and attacked inside homes on charges of being pro-Hasina, pro-India or both. The few like me who had doggedly reported on the rise of fundamentalism in Bangladesh even during the Hasina years were in graver danger.

My wife and I had decided to stay in separate places for the safety of the family. She would be in Dhaka with our boy and I would reach Faridpur and take shelter at Isa bhai's house.

'This is your house, Bhai. Make it home,' Isa bhai's wife tells me. 'You should have brought your family here with you.'

I tear up as I try to say something.

Bhabhi smiles and gently points me to a room. 'That's your room. Please freshen up. You must be hungry.'

The three-storied white house has an electronics shop on the first floor, sharing space with a women's clothing outlet. The second floor, where the Isa family stays, has three bedrooms and an expansive drawing room. The third floor has been rented out.

I freshen up, sit with Bhai and Bhabhi and Anees. Bhabhi has prepared quite a spread: two types of river fish cooked with spices, dal and steaming hot rice. Famished from the travel, we eat to our heart's content. Anees takes his leave after lunch. Isa bhai asks me to rest as he goes out to attend a party meeting. 'Do not go out and do not talk on the phone,' he tells me. I assure him I have thrown away my SIM card. He turns to Bhabhi and says that if anyone asks who I am, she should say I am his distant cousin who works abroad and is visiting.

'Do not let strangers come inside the house,' he tells her before leaving.

I go to my room, lie down on the bed and fall into a deep sleep in no time. I have hardly slept the last four nights.

The last thought on my mind? The face of my boy and the question he asked when we said goodbye to each other: 'Baba, when will you come back to me?'

I wake up to darkness. It takes me a while to remember where I am. The wall clock shows that it's 7 p.m. I feel like a having smoke, though I have not had a single one since I was detected with a brain tumour in 2020. It had taken almost three years and gamma knife surgery at AIIMS, Delhi, to heal me.

I come out of my room and request Bhabhi for a cup of tea. With the first sip, memories of what has been lost in the last four days since Hasina's fall come flooding back.

Preface

5 August had passed in a jiffy; too much had happened too soon for me to register it all. Sipping tea at Isa bhai's apartment, somewhat relieved at having found a temporary refuge, I look back at the day Bangladesh changed. I had woken up early on 5 August with a sense of unease and called my contacts in the army and the police to know how things were.

Student protestors demanding the resignation of Sheikh Hasina had clashed with the police and paramilitary forces. Reports had come in of horrifying deaths in these clashes, of students and citizens being shot, of policemen being attacked by mobs, stripped on the streets, lynched or burnt to death and hung from bridges. The news had disturbed me. As a Bangladeshi, I am not new to violent protests, terror attacks or political clashes. In the last fifteen years of the Sheikh Hasina government, there have many student protests. They have resulted in violent clashes with the police, injuries and deaths.

However, by the end of July 2024, WhatsApp forwards from colleagues, friends and neighbours reported thousands of student deaths. My own sources in the administration, police and military gave vague answers every time I called. 'Don't quote figures without verifying,' they told me each time. Who would verify the number of student deaths, I had asked. The calls went cold.

What had also bothered me in those dark days was that I could remember no time in the country's history – since the birth of Bangladesh – of police personnel being killed in this manner.

Were these killings done by students who wanted the end of Sheikh Hasina's dictatorial rule? Or was there someone else behind the protests? If so, who? How had a students' protest in response to the Supreme Court of Bangladesh reinstating a 30 per cent quota for descendants of freedom fighters turned into this? These questions had given me sleepless nights. None of it added up. I could sense a gap in the narratives being floated. Frantic phone calls to sources in the government, to student leaders, opposition party leaders, the police and the military had given no clear answers.

It is frustrating for a journalist to seek the truth and not find it. But Bangladesh, during July 2024, had entered the post-truth era.

August 2024 would bring hard truths back to Bangladesh.

I had woken up on 5 August with one prayer: Allah should stop any further bloodshed in my country. Not just student protestors, but also people from all walks of life, from every nook and cranny of Bangladesh, had threatened to descend on Dhaka and lay siege on Gonobhaban, Hasina's official residence. I dialled my contacts. Before I had gone to sleep the previous night, my contacts in the army had said that no lethal force would be used and that the army and paramilitary personnel would push back protestors who tried to lay siege on Dhaka. My morning calls revealed the exact opposite. From the four main entry points to the city, Jatra Bari, Uttara, Gaptoli and Babu Bazar, big crowds of protestors had entered the city and were moving towards Gonobhaban. All my reporting colleagues confirmed this, as did the news channels.

'Do not worry, they will be stopped well before they come near Gonobhaban,' my source at the DGFI told me. This was around 12.30 p.m. He added that the army top brass would shortly sit with members of all political parties and the student leaders of the mass movement against Hasina to reach a solution.

'Peace is just round the corner,' he assured me.

In hindsight, I would have perhaps got two-and-a-half hours of peace if I hadn't made one more phone call that afternoon.

In the life of a field reporter, sometimes sources become close allies, which can be both a good thing and bad. In this case, the Bangladesh army major I dialled had become a very close acquaintance who gave me very bad news as he picked up my call. He is still a serving officer and for his safety I shall withhold his name.

'Bhai, the army has betrayed Hasina.'

'What! Why? What does that mean?'

'I can only say that the army won't stop the crowds now.'

'What happens then? They will storm Gonobhaban?'

'There would be no one to stop them if they do. There will be mayhem in the city, bhai. *Apni safe thaken* [You stay safe],' he said.

I sat holding my phone for I do not know how long. At some point my wife came, asked me what was happening in the city, and what I would have for lunch. I do not remember what I told her or whether I said anything coherent at all.

At 3 p.m., an Awami League central committee leader texted me: 'It's over. *Apa* [elder sister, a term Hasina's close associates reserved for her] is flying away from Bangladesh.'

At 3.05 p.m., the world saw the dramatic visuals of a helicopter flying over Gonobhaban. And then the C-130J military transport aircraft took her to India.

Hasina left Bangladesh.

My world was crumbling.

How does one recount days lived in abject fear? I have interviewed survivors of massacres and political violence who have seen death at close quarters and shivered when asked to narrate what they witnessed. Over the years I have hardened as a person and learnt to separate fact from emotion. Looking back on 5 August and the days that followed, I forget the sequence of events that led to my flight to Isa bhai's house.

What happened immediately after the news of Hasina fleeing Bangladesh came up on TV screens? What happened the morning on or after 7 August? What did I do all day on 8 August as Bangladesh descended into darkness? At what hour on 8 August did I first think of fleeing Dhaka?

Was it when Bangladesh started committing patricide by urinating on, garlanding with shoes and finally pulling down the statues of Bangabandhu Sheikh Mujibur Rahman, the hero of the 1971 War of Independence and the founding father of the nation? I remember the first time I saw those visuals on TV – there would be many more such incidents in the coming days across the country – and how I had thrown up in fear and disgust.

My mind was a mess, and my memories jumbled like a jalebi's spirals. What I do recall is that I wanted to light a cigarette on

5 August immediately after seeing the visuals on TV of Hasina leaving, and had walked to the balcony of my second-floor apartment in one of Dhaka's oldest neighbourhoods, famously known as Puran Dhaka. Over the decade that I had lived there, I had fallen in love with its old-world charm that seemed untouched by the winds of change that had transformed some of the newer society blocks in the city.

There is a mosque right next to my apartment building, and another one barely 500 metres away, a Shiv mandir not far from it, a church in the next lane, and Muslims, Hindus and Christians live together as good neighbours. An Awami League party office stood right opposite my building. My local Member of Parliament (MP) Sayeed Khokon, councillor Haji Samsuz Zoha and many leaders from the Awami League top brass were regular visitors.

As I stood on my balcony, a small group of students came out of the madrasa next to the mosque that shares a boundary wall with my apartment building.

'*Nara-e-Takbeer*,' they shouted, followed by 'Allahu Akbar'.

Something was amiss, I had wondered. But what? These have always been their slogans. And then I saw they were carrying lathis and cans filled with a liquid which I couldn't immediately recognize.

'*Hoi hoi, roi roi, Sheikh Hasina gelo koi* [Where has Hasina fled]?'
'*Dhaka na Dilli? Dhaka, Dhaka!*'

The group had started shouting these slogans as more boys from the madrasa joined them. By now, some neighbours had come out onto the street to see what the commotion was about.

Two boys kicked open the door to the office building, which was locked from outside. And then they unscrewed the cans and started splashing the liquid on the office door, windows and signboards of Sheikh Mujib and Hasina.

I realized then what was in the cans. Petrol.

As I watched from the second-floor, the Awami League office building went up in flames. Before spraying it with petrol, some of the boys had broken into the office. Now they were laughing loudly as they carried away chairs, tables, a TV set and a few desktop computers.

'*Bharat er dalal ra husiyar, sabdhan* [Dalals of Bharat, beware, beware],' some of them shouted. The entire lane had, by then, become a sea of white skullcaps as smoke engulfed the building.

I think my wife had pulled me back inside the drawing room.

What had she told me? I forget now. Maybe she had said I should not draw their attention as I too could easily be branded Bharat's dalal, since I had covered Bangladesh for India Today and the Bengali news channel based out of Kolkata, Kolkata TV, for almost a decade.

I remember switching on the TV. There were visuals of a raucous mob entering Gonobhaban, ransacking its inner chambers, pulling down chandeliers, raiding the prime minister's closet.

'*Apa-r* bra,' a toothy young man had shouted before the TV cameras, laughing, displaying for the world the prime minister's undergarments. 'Turn off the TV now!' my wife had almost screamed. She had never been a fan of Hasina; she had been rather critical because of the allegations of large-scale corruption that had been levelled against her government for years, as well as the suppression of opposition voices. But that day, seeing the naked hatred on public display and the attempt to strip someone who had been the most powerful woman in the country till that morning of all dignity made my wife shudder and turn her face away from the TV screen in shame. There were tears in her eyes as she sat down beside me on the sofa. 'What have we done! What will happen to this country now?' she whispered.

I remained quiet.

When was it that I had redialled the major who told me that the army had betrayed Hasina? Was it the morning of 6 August or the evening? My memory fails me again. But I remember I had made that call after news of violence poured into my phone from across the country. Women being raped, houses being torched, people being hacked to death. Frantic calls had come in from colleagues in the hinterland running away to safety, Awami League contacts crying out for help, journalist friends from India wanting an exclusive story, asking me to fact-check the videos from Bangladesh they had been receiving on their phones.

But there was one call that made me tear up.

My former boss at India Today, Deep Halder, called with one question.

'Sahidul, are you okay?'

I couldn't answer. My voice was choked with tears.

'Boss ...' That was all I could say.

'Let me know if there is anything I can do, anything at all,' he had said, asking me if the Indian High Commission office building would be a safer space for me at such a time.

'No, boss, I will manage. I will let you know,' I remember saying.

With a heavy heart, I had called Nitai kaka. As the vice chairman of the BNP's central executive committee, a former state minister for law, justice and parliamentary affairs, and a Supreme Court lawyer, Nitai Roy Chowdhury is not a man of modest means. But apart from who he is, it was the familial bond I share with him that prompted me to make a distress call to him. Nitai kaka is from my village and is my father's childhood friend.

'What do I do now, Nitai kaka? Where do I go with my wife and son?' I had almost pleaded over the phone.

'What can I do, Sahidul? You should not have written those reports for Indian news outlets. You also shouldn't have been a part of the Awami League international affairs committee.'

'Kaka, it was something I had taken up to improve Bangladesh's relations with India. In almost every country, senior journalists on the foreign affairs beat are invited by governments to help in diplomatic affairs. Before me, senior journalist Ranjan Sen has been appointed first secretary (press) at the Bangladesh Deputy High Commission in Kolkata.'

'Well, you shouldn't have accepted their offer, Sahidul. What more can I say?' He hung up on me.

It is in times like these that relationships cultivated over decades come undone, when knowing powerful people from close quarters doesn't protect you from harm.

'Maybe Nitai kaka is right. You shouldn't have written those reports against the Jamaat-e-Islami or worked for Indian news outlets or become a part of the Awami League international affairs committee,' my wife said.

My boy simply asked, 'Baba, why can't I go out to play?'

Again, I had no answers.

An interim government headed by Nobel laureate Muhammad Yunus would take oath in Bangladesh at 8 p.m. on 8 August, Bangladesh Army Chief General Waker-uz-Zaman said at a press conference in Dhaka. 'A government will be in place. This madness will now stop,' my wife sighed in relief.

On 8 August, the major called again.

'Where are you, Bhai?'

'Home. Puran Dhaka.'

'Why!'

'Yunus will take oath. The worst is over.'

'How long have you been a journalist, Bhai? This will be a government controlled by the Jamaat-e-Islami. They will systematically target anyone associated with the Awami League, Dhaka journalists, free thinkers and "India-backers". Run!'

And so I had.

'Bhai, will you have pangas fish and bele fish curry with rice for dinner? The servant has got fresh catch from the river,' Isa bhai's wife asks, breaking my reverie.

'Yes, Bhabhi. Sounds delicious.'

The Next Ten Days

What do neighbours see when they peek inside your home? When they watch your family squabbles turn into murderous assaults, see you become your own worst enemy? From the relative safety of Isa bhai's house, I read how India and the rest of the world reported on Bangladesh going to war with itself. Some of those reports were disingenuous, some spread disinformation, some spoke of hope when there was none.

The Western media feted Chief Advisor Muhammad Yunus as the reformist who would bring Bangladesh out of the dark ages of Hasina's authoritarian rule and turn it into a secular, democratic country where the citizens would be empowered. What I saw instead was the release of the dreaded terrorist Jashimuddin Rahmani, chief of the banned militant outfit Ansarullah Bangla Team, on 26 August, barely weeks after Yunus took over the reins of the country on 8 August.

Not only had Rahmani spread his terror network within Bangladesh, but two terrorists linked to his outfit – Bahar Mia and Rarely Mia – were arrested at Guwahati railway station by the Assam Police in May.

However, before this news came out, terror winked at me through an email.

Disturbed as I was with the goings-on in the country and my separation from my family, Isa bhai and Bhabhi were making every effort to ease my mind. While Isa bhai would keep me engaged by talking politics, Bhabhi would lay out a big spread of basmati rice, fresh river fish cooked in mustard oil and homegrown spices, and thick red mutton curry.

Morning walks, *adda*s over chai, sumptuous meals and sleeping early were becoming routine when an email from an unknown sender, without a subject line, landed in my inbox. I opened it on Isa bhai's desktop and saw a screenshot of a 2015 article I had written for a local daily on a Pakistan-based terror outfit Lashkar-e-Taiba operative being arrested from Dhaka on charges of circulating fake currency and operating a terror module.

I had written the article a few days after the man was arrested; by the time the article was published, he had been released on bail. But after my article came out, it created a sensation in Dhaka, and he was rearrested. I called a contact in the cyber security cell of the Dhaka Metropolitan Police. 'Forward me the mail and delete it from your inbox,' he instructed me. A day later, he called back on my new number to say the mail had been sent to me from a Pakistani server.

My DGFI contact and Isa bhai both told me it was not safe for me to stay in one place. A witch-hunt was on for 'people like me'. 'Go somewhere close to the border and try to get out of the country,' the DGFI officer told me. I had been at Isa bhai's house for ten days. I called Anees and we set off again on his bike to a new hideout.

20 August–21 October 2024

At six-foot-something, Simul Khan, the BNP's local leader in Jessore district, is around fifty years of age and built like a prizefighter – except for a missing palm and a left leg amputated at the knee. This was the result of the violence unleashed under the last caretaker government in Bangladesh in 2007, infamously known in history books as One Eleven.

Khan and I first met before that, in 2003, when I did a story on gang wars in Jessore district and did not mention him in good light. Khan had threatened to kill me then. How I managed to save myself and come into his good books as he went from being gang lord to BNP leader is a story for another day. But now, Khan is my last resort because he controls the muscle on the streets in Jessore.

It is a homecoming of sorts. Khan and I have met each other with our families many times since our bitter beginning. Meeting him after months, tired after a long bike ride, I did not expect the knockout punch he delivered to my face. Through his question, not literally.

'Sahidul, are you a RAW (Research and Analysis Wing) agent?'
'Uncle, you are asking me this!'

Khan laughs his loud laugh. 'I know you are not, Sahidul. I know you are just a pesky reporter who pisses off everyone he meets. But Jamaat has been spreading this lie about you everywhere. The word has reached me,' he tells me. 'Do not worry. No one can come here and harm you. And if such a time comes, I shall let you know beforehand. Rest now.'

In the days that follow, the hospitality at Khan's matches the treatment I got at Isa bhai's house. But I lose both my sleep and my appetite as Bangladesh stares into the abyss. The fourth pillar is crushed by the heavy hand of the mob and the law. On 16 September, my dear friends and two of Bangladesh's most famous journalists, editor of *Bhorer Kagoj*, Shyamal Datta, and Muzammil Babu, managing director and chief editor of Ekattor TV, one of the biggest TV channels in Dhaka, are arrested. A mob accosts them and takes them to a police station, where the cops book them under spurious charges.

This would be the beginning of the clampdown on free press by the Yunus administration, along with the attacks on minorities and civil rights activists. The targeting, killings and arrests of Awami League workers and supporters hadn't stopped since the day the mob set fire to that office opposite my Dhaka house.

October brings back sweet memories of my village, where every year I sponsor the local Durga puja as a mark of respect to my Hindu neighbours. This year, I have no way of reaching there. Instead, news comes of my friend Haradon Roy, ward councillor of Rangpur city corporation, being hacked to death by student protesters for being Hindu and part of the Awami League.

'*Sabash*, revolution, sabash!' I cry out in pain.

But my troubles won't let me mourn my friend. Mid-October, Khan kaka tells me the CCTV camera outside his house has captured groups of men in skullcaps and kurta pyjamas in the dead of night, pointing to my room on the second floor of the house.

I call my contact at the DGFI. 'There is no place to hide inside Bangladesh, Sahidul. Wherever you go, they will find you. Khan may be able to save you from a mob, but not from rogue cops. Call your contacts in the Indian embassy and get a medical visa asap.'

Leaving the family behind was an idea that didn't sit well with me even then. But then my wife called, afraid, hardly able to speak through her tears. 'There is an online article on you that is being mass circulated. It is titled: "Khokon: The Indian Media's 'Trusted Insider'", with links of some of your articles for Indian media and your pictures with Indians, including Deep Halder during the launch of his book on Bangladeshi Hindus. Please go, go away from here and save your life. In this life or the next, we shall meet again. Inshallah.'

My last week in Bangladesh is spent making frantic calls, getting a medical visa from a contact at the Indian embassy for post-operative complications that I developed after my treatment, and calling contacts in the Border Guards Bangladesh (BGB) to ensure a safe passage for me from Jessore. Taking a flight is fraught with danger, as many people with valid visas are being arrested by airport immigration.

Interestingly, perhaps I never once worried about my impending visit to India or the time I would have to spend there in exile. I knew Sourav Sikdar and his wife Suchismita Sanyal – who I call my Indian family – would make sure my time in exile was spent in comfort and among people I love on the other side of the border. And it is not because of the fact that Sikdar is an influential politician in West Bengal, but because his forefathers are from the land which I call my country. Sikdar's grandfather Dr Dhirendranath Sikdar was my granddad Manik Fakir's closest friend. Neither Partition nor time has been able to wipe out the generational bond our families share.

Sikdar told me over a phone call that he would make every arrangement to escort me to safety from the border.

A journalist friend in Jessore, whose name I cannot disclose, takes me to Benapole border on 21 October 2024 at 12 p.m. A senior official of the Indian intelligence establishment had already spoken to top officials of the BGB to allow me safe transit. Sikdar had ensured this happens by calling up his contacts in India's security establishment. On Sikdar's instructions, I had called up a lieutenant colonel of the BGB who had assured me safe passage to India.

'Carry only a small rucksack,' he tells me over the phone.

And here I was, standing inside his office at the Benapole border, carrying just a rucksack.

The officer instructs my friend to leave.

'I will take it from here,' he commands.

I hug my friend, the only person apart from Khan kaka who I had trusted with my whereabouts in Jessore. We can't stop the tears. I have left my family behind; he is the only one close to my heart in Bangladesh to whom I can say goodbye.

'Do not worry. You will reach your destination,' the officer assures me, his tone cold, eyes fixed on mine. He tells me immigration police has become very strict in the past few months. There are also intelligence officers from various agencies who are checking papers of Bangladeshis in transit and detaining whoever they have to.

'If anyone among them decides to cross question you, leaving Bangladesh may become impossible even with a valid medical visa,' he tells me. I feel fear rising up my spine, but the officer tells me he has spoken to an immigration officer about me.

'One of my officers will walk with you to Zero Point where your passport will be stamped. Someone else will walk you to India,' the lieutenant colonel says. I nod a yes, what other option do I have now but to trust him.

The process will take some time, and the lieutenant colonel offers me lunch. I could hardly eat. 'Rest in my room,' he tells me after and leaves.

Rest? I smile to myself. My family, friends and colleagues, my entire life I was leaving behind. If I was leaving at all and not being detained a short while from now.

The lieutenant colonel comes back at 3 p.m., with him was a major in the BGB. I am told the major will take me to the crossover point at the border. I hand him my passport. 'When you walk with me, walk straight and talk to me as if you know me from before. It should appear you are one of us, a BGB officer in plain clothes,' he tells me.

We walk out of the lieutenant colonel's office, get into a security jeep and in about five minutes reach the border crossing zone. A soldier is waiting for us. He takes my passport and my rucksack. The major and I walk to Zero Point. As instructed, I begin talking to the major, who I have only just met. 'My boy loves toy cars you know. He also likes toy guns. But I scold him and tell him he should not have a gun.' I blabber. The major smiles. 'That's what I tell my boy too,' he says. I feel tears welling up, but I cannot allow them to come out. I keep smiling and talking, and pushing back tears and fear. The soldier comes back with my stamped passport and rucksack, hands it over to me.

'Best of luck,' says the major.

He has walked me to the point where Bangladesh ends and India begins.

I cross over from Benapole to Petropol, from Bangladesh to India. I turn back and whisper: 'I shall come back. No matter what it takes. And I will tell your story to the world. Inshallah Bangladesh. Till we meet again.'

Sahidul Hasan Khokon
June 2025
Delhi

Section I

Society

1

Hasina's Day Out

4 a.m., 5 August 2024

An alarm clock went off on the mahogany bedside table in Sheikh Hasina's bedroom on the first floor of the inner chambers of Gonobhaban.

The old clock was one of the few possessions of her slain father, Sheikh Mujibur Rahman, that Sheikh Hasina could retrieve from Bangabandhubhaban or Dhanmondi 32, Dhaka's most famous address, where her parents, siblings and other family members were gunned down in the small hours of 15 August 1975.

It had not left her bedside since then.

The alarm clock, a steel-bodied mechanical device whose dial had become sepia-tinted, was salvaged by Hasina when she was allowed entry into Bangabandhubhaban in the upscale and leafy Dhanmondi area of central Dhaka in July 1981, a full six years after the massacre of her family in that house.

The alarm clock was lying in a closet along with the personal papers and diaries of her father, which were published later as his memoirs. The alarm clock would accompany her on her trips around the world. After 4 August 2024, as she would be forced to change not just her zip code in Dhaka but also the country of her residence, Sheikh Hasina would open her eyes to its shrill wake-up call at the break of dawn at her South Delhi safehouse, where she had taken refuge.

But on 5 August 2024, Hasina reached out and pressed the alarm lever. She had had a fitful sleep for only three hours and had woken up weary and distraught. The turn of events in her country and the pressure on her to step down as prime minister and make way for an all-party or an interim government had left her physically and mentally tired.

Hasina got out of bed, freshened up and readied herself, like every morning, for the *fajr* (early morning) prayers. After the prayers, she stepped out of her private chambers. Her sister, Sheikh Rehana, who had been giving her company at Gonobhaban for the last three days, had also said her morning prayers and stepped out of her bedroom into the spacious living room on the first floor of the prime ministerial residence.

On other days, Sheikh Hasina would sit for a while in the living room, leaf through the morning newspapers and flip through the news channels before stepping out for a walk on the expansive and manicured lawns of Gonobhaban.

Her morning walk, in which she would be accompanied by her domestic helpers and bodyguards, would include visiting the poultry and cattle sheds at the rear end of the prime ministerial residence, and also a large kitchen garden on the premises.

Hasina was always an avid gardener and a strong advocate of growing fruits and vegetables in kitchen gardens. She had set an example by cultivating paddy, vegetables, fruits and herbs like turmeric and ginger in the premises of Gonobhaban.[1]

But this Monday, 5 August, was no normal day. Bangladesh had been losing its grip on sanity since early July. What started as an agitation against unreasonable quotas in government jobs for descendants of *mukti-joddha*s (freedom fighters of the 1971 War of Independence that birthed Bangladesh) had suddenly and somewhat inexplicably turned into a nationwide uprising against Sheikh Hasina and her party.

Hasina had been unable to get ahead of the crisis that had

engulfed her country. She had told her inner circle of ministers and advisors that she couldn't fathom how her citizens could have turned so quickly and intensely against her. After all, she had reasoned with them, she had been the very face of Bangladesh's economic upliftment and infrastructural development.

That inner circle had failed to communicate to the prime minister that she had become deeply unpopular across Bangladesh while she herself was so cocooned that she could not come to terms with the angry howls for her resignation reverberating throughout the country. Hasina had thought the storm would pass; after all, she had weathered many crises in her chequered political career as the tenth prime minister of Bangladesh from June 1996 to July 2001 and again from January 2009 to this day.

Listed among *Time*'s 100 most influential people in the world in 2018, and as one of the 100 most powerful women in the world by *Forbes* in 2015, 2018 and 2022, Hasina could still not see that the fires that had consumed her country this time would not only diminish her politically and reduce her legacy to cinders, but also snub out the historical relevance of her illustrious father who had been revered by generations of Bangladeshis as 'Bangabandhu'.

How a spark of dissent arising from a high court ruling restoring unreasonable and unpopular quotas for descendants of muktijoddhas became an inferno is a subject for another chapter.

For now, let's return to Gonobhaban on the fateful morning of 5 August, where an air of foreboding hangs heavy over the 3,600 square feet prime ministerial residence. Soon after Hasina had her morning tea, calls started pouring in. One after the other, she spoke to the chief of the Dhaka Metropolitan Police (DMP) Habibur Rahman, her principal secretary Mohammad Tofazzel Hossain Miah and senior leaders of her party.

Then Awami League General Secretary Obaidul Quader – the public face of the party as its principal spokesperson – informed Hasina over the phone that many senior leaders of the party had fled over the past sixteen hours, mostly to India and countries in

Southeast Asia, but some had also gone to the Middle East en route to Western countries.

Sheikh Hasina had, on the morning of 4 August, given blanket permission to all leaders and functionaries of the party who had become jittery over the alarming turn of events in the country to go abroad temporarily. 'Temporarily' because Sheikh Hasina still believed she could seize the day. She had told her party colleagues and the police and army top brass that firm action against agitators would quell the movement against her.

On the evening of 4 August, the DMP chief, army chief General Waker-uz-Zaman, senior administration officials like Cabinet Secretary Mohammad Mahbub Hossain and senior party colleagues, including Education Minister Mohibul Hassan Chowdhury, who had gathered at her residence, told her the tide was turning and she should leave the country till security forces could bring the situation under control.

Sheikh Hasina had flatly refused to even consider the proposal. She had asked the education minister how she could even think of fleeing her country at such a critical juncture. She had asked General Waker-uz-Zaman if he would stand firmly with her.

The general had said an emphatic 'yes'.

The four-star general is a distant relative of Sheikh Hasina – his mother-in-law Sarhanaz is a first cousin of Hasina's father, Sheikh Mujibur Rahman. General Waker-uz-Zaman's father-in-law, General Mustafizur Rahman, served as the ninth army chief of Bangladesh from December 1997 to December 2000 during Hasina's first tenure as prime minister (23 June 1996–15 July 2001).

General Waker-uz-Zaman is married to Sarhanaz and Mustafizur Rahman's daughter, Begum Sarhanaz Kamalika Rahman.

The General's 'yes' would come as a relief to Hasina.

But Bangladesh navy chief Admiral Mohammad Nazmul Hassan as well as Bangladesh air force chief Air Chief Marshal Hasan Mahmood Khan, who had also reached Gonobhaban on the evening of 4 August, told Sheikh Hasina that while they were firmly behind her, she would be well-advised to consider the proposal of leaving the country, or at least shift to the Dhaka cantonment immediately.

Sheikh Hasina remained firm. As prime minister and the daughter of the nation's founding father, there was no way she would abandon Bangladesh.

Instead, she discussed plans with General Waker-uz-Zaman and senior police officials on how to handle the mass protests against her regime. Hundreds of agitators had died, most of them victims of police firing. Cadres of the Bangladesh Chhatra League (BCL) had been patrolling the streets of Dhaka and other major cities, countering the protests in a heavy-handed manner.

In mid-July, when the protests against quotas in government jobs for descendants of mukti-joddhas were gaining momentum, the BCL cadres attacked and injured more than 350 students of Dhaka University and other institutions who were seeking a reform in the quotas.[2,3,4] A website, www.shohid.info,[5] lists the names of all martyrs (students and others) felled by police bullets and also allegedly killed by the BCL, along with the circumstances of their deaths. The BCL would be banned[6] later by the interim government headed by Mohammad Yunus, which would take over the reins of the country after the fall of the Sheikh Hasina government.

But on the evening of 4 August, Sheikh Hasina was told by the police chief yet again that there was a groundswell of anger against the government and using force would make matters worse. Hasina would stick to her assessment that the protests were baseless, and that they were being fuelled by external forces. Use of force would quell the protests, she insisted.

The three service chiefs, as well as others who were either present or were constantly in touch with the prime minister over the phone and video conferencing throughout the evening of 4 August and the morning after kept telling her that using force wouldn't help anymore.

Hasina had her arguments ready. The protests had nothing to do with the agitating students, they were political in nature and were being fuelled and controlled by external forces, she reasoned. She had been saying this ever since the protests gained momentum. She would insist that her government had already filed an appeal against the high court's 5 June 2024 order[7] that restored 30 per cent quotas for descendants of mukti-joddhas in government jobs. It was, after all, the high court order that had triggered nationwide protests.

But her government had moved quickly and filed an appeal before the appellate division of the Supreme Court challenging the quotas. That was in sync with the demands of the students. Things, however, had taken a turn for the worse when the apex court's six-member bench headed by the then Chief Justice Obaidul Hassan passed an interim order on 4 July upholding the high court order. But the Supreme Court said it would set a date for hearing appeals against the quotas and pass a final order eventually. The apex court also asked the agitating students to return to their classes.

The Supreme Court's order failed to calm the protestors and its appeal to them to return to their classes went unheeded. The protests went on and soon became an uprising against Sheikh Hasina, even though her government promised that it would present a strong case before the Supreme Court when it started the final hearing on the case.

The prime minister's contention was that the students did not appeal against the high court order and only carried on their agitation, while it was her government which filed the appeal against the high court order reinstating quotas. This, she held, showed that the anti-quota stir was a manufactured one. She also strongly believed that the fact that the students did not honour the Supreme Court's appeal to return to their campuses and classes proved that the movement was being controlled by other players.

When leaders of the anti-quota movement, which was being conducted under the banner of the Boisomyobirodhi Chhatra Andolan (Students against Discrimination [SAD]), started demanding her resignation from the end of the third week of July, she knew she had been right all through about the foreign hand behind the turmoil.

Hasina told her aides and colleagues in the government that the agitation needed to be handled through the use of force to get to the foreign hand.

On the afternoon of 4 August, the prime minister chaired a meeting of the National Committee on Security Affairs, which was attended by the three service chiefs, some senior ministers, her security advisor Major General (retired) Tarique Ahmed Siddique (brother-in-law of the prime minister's sister, Sheikh Rehana), the foreign and defence secretaries, the then police chief, Chowdhury Abdullah Al-Mamun, principal staff officer of the armed forces division, Lieutenant General Mizanur Rahman Shamim, the director general of National Security Intelligence (NSI), Major General Mohammad Hossain Al Morshed, the director general of DGFI, Lieutenant General Hamid Ur Rahman, the director general of BGB, Major General Mohammad Ashrafuzzaman Siddiqui, the director general of the Bangladesh Coast Guard, Rear Admiral Mir Ershad Ali, and Special Branch (SB) chief, Monirul Islam.

The mood in the room was sombre as reports of deaths and terrible acts of violence kept pouring in. A total of ninety-one people had died that day,[8] most due to police firing, but also in other acts of violence. The dead included sixteen police officers – fifteen at Enayetpur in Sirajganj district and one in Comilla's Eliotganj. Police stations across the country were attacked, looted and torched[9] and vehicles, public facilities and shops were burnt down by irate mobs.

What also caused great concern among the military brass was the fact that on 4 August, large mobs on the streets of the capital mingled with army soldiers and junior officers who were deployed on static duties on the streets. The people hugged and cheered the men in uniform, clicked selfies with them and even gave them flowers. The soldiers reciprocated with warmth. The army generals realized that their men could not be asked to take coercive action against the masses out on the streets anymore.

Those present at the National Committee on Security Affairs meeting on 4 August afternoon looked dejected. National Security Intelligence chief Major General Mohammad Hossain Al Morshed told the prime minister that things had spun out of control and the country was plunging into a civil war. The DGFI chief Lieutenant General Muhammad Hamid Ur Rahman said that a major conciliatory gesture on the part of the prime minister would be necessary to placate public anger.

The prime minister wanted to know what conciliatory gesture could be made. The men in uniform said it was up to her to figure it out politically. Some suggested that she could hand over the reins of the country temporarily to the president, Mohammad Shahabuddin, or some other 'neutral person' who could then form a caretaker government comprising representatives of all parties as well as civil society.

Sheikh Hasina summarily rejected the proposal. She said that she had been elected to power through electoral democracy and would not cede power to the undemocratic and anti-democratic forces that were engineering the protests.

There was some support for Hasina in the room still. The prime minister's security advisor Major General (retired) Tarique Ahmed Siddique concurred with her and said that the protests could easily be countered by force. He advocated strong action against all those who violated the curfew that had just been imposed. Some ministers present nodded in agreement. The police chief, Chowdhury Abdullah Al-Mamun, said that the killing of policemen in Sirganj and Comilla had shaken his force. But, he added, his force was disciplined and would carry out whatever orders were issued to them.

A ban was proposed on internet and social media sites like Facebook and Instagram, and messaging apps like WhatsApp and Facebook Messenger. These measures were approved and a blanket ban imposed.[10,11] A three-day general holiday (5–7 August) was declared to keep people indoors.

Even as the meeting was in progress, news came in that Asif Mahmud, a coordinator of the SAD, which by now was also being called the Anti-Discrimination Students' Movement (ADSM), had declared that the 'long march to Dhaka' scheduled for 6 August had been rescheduled to 5 August.[12]

The news set alarm bells ringing and the prime minister asked the police and security agencies to draw up plans to prevent the entry of people into Dhaka the next day.

Once again, some of the army generals and senior officials present at the meeting told the prime minister that using force to thwart the march would only worsen the situation and lead to a civil war. They suggested that the prime minister, as an immediate measure, call the leaders of the ADSM for talks at Gonobhaban right away.

Sheikh Hasina brushed the advice aside. She said what she had said many times before – that the anti-quota movement was a manufactured one, the students were being misled, external forces were at play and the country was under threat. At such a time, she implored, all forces should join hands and protect the sovereignty of Bangladesh.

After the meeting, Sheikh Hasina issued a statement asking people to obey the curfew and remain indoors. She also called the protestors 'terrorists' and 'arsonists'. 'Those who are carrying out violence are not students but terrorists who are out to destabilise the nation. I appeal to our countrymen to suppress these terrorists with a strong hand,' she said.[13]

Some of those present in the room, like the DGFI and NSI chiefs, the Coast Guard chief and the foreign secretary, left the meeting even though it remained inconclusive. Informal consultations, however, continued and everyone kept close tabs on developments and the fast pace of events.

Sometime later in the evening, the police chief told Sheikh Hasina that his force would require backup from the army because reports were coming in that lakhs of people were moving towards Dhaka from different parts of the country. He told the prime minister that the police were tired after being on duty on the streets for over a month and were low on morale. The police were also running short of ammunition.

The prime minister asked the army chief to redeploy troops and station them at all entry points into Dhaka as well as around other important addresses. General Waker-uz-Zaman told the prime minister point-blank that while troops would be deployed on the streets of Dhaka, as they had been on Sunday, they would not open fire or take any coercive action against the agitators.

A stunned Sheikh Hasina wanted to know why the troops would not take coercive action against protestors who would violate curfew orders. The army chief replied that many retired army officers and soldiers, as well as their family members, and also family members of many serving officers and troops, were participating in the anti-quota stir. His troops would not open fire on them or harm them in any way. Orders to do so would damage the morale of the force and may even trigger a revolt within. He told the prime minister he had already told his top officers earlier that day that army soldiers would not fire upon or take any punitive action against protestors.[14]

General Waker-uz-Zaman told Hasina that one of his predecessors, General (retired) Iqbal Karim Bhuiyan, and some retired senior officers had held a press meet earlier in the day urging soldiers to return to their barracks.[15] That had resulted in a lot of unease among the soldiers and officers deployed on the streets of Dhaka and he (the army chief) was getting calls and texts from his senior colleagues as well as retired officers to stop the army from being used against the people of the country.

Some retired officers, the most prominent among them being Brigadier General Mohammed Shahedul Anam Khan (who took to journalism after retirement and is an associate editor of Bangladesh's largest circulated English daily, the *Daily Star*), had already declared on 4 August that they would hit the streets of the capital in defiance of curfew.

The prime minister had no choice but to accept the army chief's decision. She called up the police chief, who had left Gonobhaban by then and was attending a late evening meeting with his top officers. The police chief told her that plans were being finalized to block the entry of people into Dhaka and protect important public buildings, including the Jatiya Sansad Bhaban (parliament building) and Gonobhaban.

Sheikh Hasina asked the army chief to ensure the presence of his troops in armoured personnel carriers on the streets of Dhaka to act as deterrence. General Waker-uz-Zaman consented, but reiterated that his troops would be static and would not take any coercive action against protestors.

Her visitors eventually left Gonobhaban, and Sheikh Hasina and her sister, Sheikh Rehana, had a quiet dinner around 11.30 p.m. Calls were still pouring in from the police, army, intelligence and civil administration officers. Sheikh Hasina took all calls and finally went to her bedroom well past midnight. Sheikh Rehana, who had been at Gonobhaban since 2 August to help her sister navigate the crisis in the country, had also stayed up till past midnight.

Neither knew that it would be their last night in Gonobhaban.

4–7 a.m., 5 August 2024

The morning began with a barrage of phone calls. Calls started coming in for the prime minister from Awami League leaders and senior officials in the home and defence ministries. All had one thing to report to Hasina.

Dhaka was under siege.

7 a.m.–12 p.m., 5 August 2024

The prime minister's principal secretary Mohammad Tofazzel Hossain Miah arrived at Gonobhaban, followed soon after by her security advisor Major General (retired) Tarique Ahmed Siddique. They were joined by the home secretary and a few other officials.

The NSI and DGFI chiefs also called and shared their inputs on the worsening situation in the country, especially in Dhaka.

The prime minister instructed the NSI chief to collect more details on the mood on the streets and how effective the police had been since early morning to control the crowds. The NSI chief called back within half an hour and told Sheikh Hasina that he had bad news. The mood on the streets of Dhaka was explosive and the people's anger was being fuelled further by the news published in most morning newspapers of a sixteen-year-old student, Golam Nafiz, who had been shot at by the police at the Farmgate area of Dhaka around 4.30 p.m. on 4 August. The police had loaded a badly injured Nafiz on a rickshaw and asked the rickshaw puller, Nur Mohammad, to take him to a hospital. Nafiz was lying on the footrest of the rickshaw while being transported to a nearby hospital.[16]

Photos of the injured young man being taken to the hospital in such a cavalier fashion had been published in the front pages of most newspapers and evoked shock, disgust and deep loathing for the Awami League government headed by Hasina. The newspapers also reported that the rickshaw carrying Nafiz was denied entry to a nearby hospital by Awami League activists.

Nur Mohammad had then taken his rickshaw towards Indira Road, crossed it and taken the road on the western end of Sher-e-Bangla Nagar Park to get on to Khamarbari Road. It was there that he ran into a crowd of ADSM activists who, on seeing a profusely bleeding Nafiz, put him in an autorickshaw and took him to Shaheed Suhrawardy Medical College Hospital about 2.5 kilometres away.

Golam Nafiz was declared dead on arrival. The Shaheed Suhrawardy Medical College Hospital is about 400 metres from Gonobhaban.

Major General Morshed told the prime minister that public anger had peaked and there was no way she would be safe inside Gonobhaban any longer. He told her that he had received credible intelligence inputs that protestors were planning to storm

Gonobhaban. General Morshed told her she should start getting ready to leave immediately.

Many others, including Cabinet Secretary Mohammad Mahbub Hossain, the NSI and DGFI chiefs, Special Branch Chief Monirul Islam and other senior police, army and civil administration officials kept coming into and going out of Gonobhaban. All of them brought grim news and told the prime minister that huge crowds had broken through police barricades and were moving towards Shahbagh, Mirpur Road and other prominent addresses in the city.

Tarique Ahmed Siddique had started contacting senior officials in India from Sunday evening. He was making contingency plans for the prime minister in case things got out of control. India would be the safest and nearest destination for her. He got word on Sunday night itself that India would be willing to provide safe refuge to Sheikh Hasina. In fact, India – which had been warning Sheikh Hasina that the anti-quota stir was getting out of hand and some external forces were directing the movement – had also offered to provide refuge to her in case of any emergency.

This offer was made on 2 August. On Monday morning, top officials from India's intelligence agencies and the country's security apparatus reached out to Dhaka and spoke of contingency plans to evacuate Sheikh Hasina. The Bangladesh army and air force chiefs, as well as the NSI chief, were abreast of these developments.

12 p.m., 5 August 2024

Army Chief General Waker-uz-Zaman reached Gonobhaban along with the navy and air force chiefs. They went straight into the prime minister's office chamber where Sheikh Hasina was closeted with others and told her she would have to leave Gonobhaban. They told her that her safety could no longer be guaranteed if she remained at the prime minister's residence. The army chief was insistent that she pack her bags and leave immediately.

Even as he was speaking with the prime minister, he started getting calls on his phone that a huge crowd had gathered around Mirpur 10 roundabout, less than 7 kilometres from Gonobhaban. Army troopers and policemen had rolled out barricades topped with barbed wire to stop the mob from going down Begum Rokeya Avenue that would lead straight to Gonobhaban.

The Special Branch chief informed the prime minister that huge crowds were also gathering in other parts of Mirpur, about 6 kilometres away from Gonobhaban. And then reports started pouring in of the buildup of more crowds at Mirpur, Farmgate, Shyamoli, Tejgaon and Dhanmondi, all areas around Gonobhaban.

12.30–1.30 p.m., 5 August 2024

Reports of crowds breaking through barricades, and army troopers firing blanks to disperse them at Mirpur started pouring in. A heavy but brief shower dispersed the crowds, but only for a short period. Senior police and army officers started making frantic calls to Gonobhaban, warning that it was no longer possible to stop the crowds from moving towards the prime minister's residence.

General Waker-uz-Zaman again told the prime minister that there was no time to lose and she would have to leave Gonobhaban immediately. The Bangladesh Air Force chief, Air Chief Marshal Hasan Mahmood Khan, said two transport aircraft had been kept ready at the Tejgaon air base and also at the Bangladesh Air Force (BAF) base at Kurmitola next to Hazrat Shahjalal International Airport to fly her out of the country to India.

Permission had already been given by Indian aviation authorities for any aircraft carrying the Bangladesh prime minister to enter Indian airspace.

Sheikh Hasina was not convinced that she needed to leave Gonobhaban. The service chiefs and others in the room implored her sister, Sheikh Rehana, to convince her. Hasina was adamant. A call was placed to the prime minister's son, Sajeeb Wazed, who lives in Falls Church City, Virginia, USA. Sajeeb spoke to his mother, asking her to leave Gonobhaban and fly to India. Sheikh Hasina continued to refuse, telling everyone gathered at Gonobhaban that she would rather die than flee her country.

1.30–2 p.m., 5 August 2024

Around 1.30 p.m., a call came in from a top official in India whom Sheikh Hasina knew well. It was a short call. The official told Sheikh Hasina that it was already too late and if she didn't leave Gonobhaban immediately, she would be killed. He also told her that she should live to fight another day.

As the call ended, General Waker-uz-Zaman told Hasina that if she didn't leave immediately, she would be endangering not only her own life, but also that of all those present at Gonobhaban, including the Special Security Force (SSF) soldiers and officers guarding the prime minister's residence. The SSF provides proximate security to top VVIPs in Bangladesh.

Reports started coming in that crowds were advancing towards Begum Rokeya Avenue through which Sheikh Hasina would have been evacuated to Tejgaon air base. The Tejgaon air base is just about 2.5 kilometres, or a five-minute drive, from Gonobhaban. Huge crowds had also formed near Mohakhali Flyover and Manik Mia Avenue behind the Jatiya Sansad Bhaban and were advancing towards Gonobhaban. This information precluded all plans to evacuate Sheikh Hasina and take her by road to the Kurmitola BAF base, about 13.5 kilometres from Gonobhaban.

The BAF chief, Air Chief Marshal Hasan Mahmood Khan, had foreseen this and made contingency plans and kept an Mi-17 helicopter of the Bangladesh air force ready.

Sheikh Hasina finally relented around 2 p.m. when it was clear that huge crowds of people were just a couple of kilometres away from Gonobhaban.

The storming of Gonobhaban was now inevitable. Hasina wanted to record a speech before leaving. The army chief and others around her put their foot down: It was a now or never situation.

1.30 p.m.–end of day, 5 August 2024

Sheikh Rehana literally pulled her sister into an SUV that had been waiting to whisk them to the helipad. A couple of close aides of the prime minister had packed a few suitcases with her clothes and other personal belongings. The pilots of the Mi-17 chopper were asked to start the engine and get ready for take-off immediately.

Sheikh Hasina and Sheikh Rehana boarded the helicopter along with a few SSF guards. At 2.23 p.m., the helicopter lifted off from the Gonobhaban grounds and headed to Tejgaon air base where a C-130J Super Hercules aircraft of the Bangladesh air force was waiting. As soon as the Mi-17 helicopter landed at Tejgaon at 2.35 p.m., the prime minister and her sister were transported to the BAF transport aircraft which had its engines running. The aircraft took off from Tejgaon at 2.42 p.m. into the overcast skies, broke through the cloud cover and entered Indian airspace over Malda in West Bengal after about twenty minutes. The take-off coincided with another short spell of showers.

A couple of fighter jets of the Indian air force (IAF) escorted the huge transport aircraft, its call sign AJAX1431, carrying the Bangladesh prime minister and her sister all the way to the IAF base at Hindon in Ghaziabad where the aircraft landed at around 6 p.m.

Hasina was received by National Security Advisor Ajit Doval, a man she knew well, and senior Indian military officials.

It had proved to be a narrow escape.

Barely twenty-five minutes after the Mi-17 helicopter carrying Sheikh Hasina and her sister lifted off from the helipad at Gonobhaban, a huge crowd of protestors who had gathered at the gates of the prime minister's residence broke through and headed for the main red-brick-facade building. The army soldiers who had been manning the barricades outside Gonobhaban did not resist or make any attempt to stop them.

Once inside the prime minister's residence, the mobs – mostly students, but also the general crowd – went on a rampage, breaking glass and furniture, smashing fine porcelain dinner and tea sets, looting the larder and Sheikh Hasina's personal belongings and taking off with paintings, books, artefacts, mirrors and anything they could lay their hands on.[17]

The SSF personnel guarding Gonobhaban also had a narrow escape. They had been instructed by General Waker-uz-Zaman, who oversaw the evacuation of the prime minister and left in his SUV for the Ministry of Defence (just a minute's drive away from Gonobhaban) immediately after the chopper took off, to guard Gonobhaban. But as soon as the mobs started breaking through the barricades, they sensed grave danger. The SSF guards had a considerable stockpile of sophisticated firearms. They quickly locked the arms in a small vault in the basement at the rear of Gonobhaban and fled to the nearby Jatiya Sansad Bhawan through a rear gate. Barely five minutes after they left, the mobs were rampaging through Gonobhaban.[18]

That Monday afternoon, 5 August 2024, brought the curtains down on Sheikh Hasina's controversial reign of fifteen years and seven months. And it opened yet another chapter of killings, retributions and strife in Bangladesh's blood-soaked history.

As the sun set on 5 August 2024, Bangladesh trudged through the road to perdition.

(The detailed reconstruction of the events at Gonobhaban during the last twenty-four hours of Sheikh Hasina's stay is based on extensive interviews with members of her personal staff, members of the National Committee on Security Affairs, a senior staff officer of Bangladesh, Army Chief Waker-uz-Zaman, two former Awami League ministers, officers of the NSI and Special Branch and two top Bangladesh police officers. Most of them are now in hiding in India, and those who remain in Bangladesh spoke to us on the phone.)

2
The General Who Betrayed Hasina

'It was Waker-uz-Zaman who betrayed my prime minister!'

'The Bangladesh army chief?' We baulked at the statement.

'Yes, the man himself. Related to Sheikh Hasina through his wife, Begum Sarahnaz Kamalika Rahman, Waker backstabbed the honourable prime minister. If he hadn't done so, Sheikh Hasina would have still been in Bangladesh, that fake students' revolution would have been quashed long ago and South Asia would not have plunged into such bloody chaos.'

We looked at the man in front of us in stupefied silence. A short distance away, in the coffee shop of the Delhi luxury hotel where we were having this conversation in the middle of June 2025, a young couple was talking excitedly. Relieved that they could not overhear our conversation, we turned to the man in front of us who had just dropped a bomb.

Asaduzzaman Khan Kamal was a veteran leader of the Bangladesh Awami League and had been home minister for two consecutive terms in Sheikh Hasina's government. We knew Khan had taken refuge in India some time last year after Awami League ministers, leaders, workers and supporters faced the brunt of both the mob and the law enforcement agencies that now reported to a new dispensation.

On 2 October, the Bangladesh press had reported that Khan was spotted in Eco Park, one of Kolkata's best-known leisure and recreational green spaces, but that Bangladeshi police had no evidence of his legal exit from Bangladesh. 'It can be confirmed that neither the former minister nor the others mentioned have legally left the country,' Additional Inspector General of Police (acting) Shah Alam had told the press. By then, Khan had been named in several cases related to killings during the ADSM in July and August 2024.[1]

The report created an uproar in Bangladesh after a Bangladeshi private television channel put out a report that Khan was seen at the park with former Awami League leader and MP Ashim Kumar Ukil, along with his wife, Apu Ukil, and several others from the party.

Under pressure, Shah Alam confirmed that several people had legally left Bangladesh shortly after the fall of the Sheikh Hasina regime. 'On the 6th and 7th of August, a few people left. At the time, no restrictions were in place. Former police officer Abdul Kahar Akand is among those who legally departed,' he told the press.[2]

We had been trying to reach Khan through our Awami League contacts who were now staying in Kolkata, but no one confirmed Khan's whereabouts. Months passed, and suddenly on one muggy June morning, an old Awami League contact called to ask if we were in Delhi and if we would like a quick conversation with Khan at a hotel in central Delhi whose address he would share closer to the time of the interview.

And here we were, in front of Asaduzzaman Khan Kamal, arguably the second-most powerful minister in the Sheikh Hasina administration after Hasina herself. We had interviewed Khan before, once in Delhi and several times in Dhaka at his residence in the posh Dhanmondi area. We had always found him nattily dressed like an upper-crust Bengali gentleman, in a starched white kurta and pyjama.

That day, though, he was dressed in formals. He wore a striped shirt and dark trousers, his eyes as silently watchful as they were before. There used to be a joke back in the day in Dhaka press circles about Khan. Ask him for an official reaction on anything under the sun, an incident of crime, mob violence in some part of the country or a political clash somewhere else, and Khan would have a standard reply: 'I have come to know about the incident. I am looking into it. The law will take its course.'

Today, Asaduzzaman Khan Kamal was in a mood to say much more.

And we were all ears.

'You know, looking back, I feel the end of the Sheikh Hasina government in Bangladesh bears an uncanny resemblance to the killing of Abhimanyu, son of Arjuna and Subhadra, in the great Kurukshetra war in the Hindu epic Mahabharata.'

'You have read the Mahabharata, sir?'

Khan laughs. 'Why wouldn't I. It is not your story alone! Like Abhimanyu was trapped from all sides and then felled in the war by his own, Waker tied up with the fundamentalist forces in Bangladesh to bring Hasina down. The Jamaat-e-Islami Bangladesh had brought all radical forces together before this. Do not forget that the radical Islamist parties in Bangladesh had often violently disagreed with each other in the past over ideological reasons and their interpretation of Islamic laws. But to bring down the Hasina government, they all came together under the guidance of the Jamaat-e-Islami,' Khan told us.

We had taken out our notebooks and were feverishly jotting down every word Khan was saying. The evening tea and snacks that had been served to us in the meantime had gone cold.

Khan took a sip from his cup and continued.

'It was a perfect CIA [Central Intelligence Agency] plot hatched over a long period of time to overthrow Hasina. We did not know the CIA had Waker in its pocket.'

'But why would the CIA want to destabilize an elected government in Bangladesh, sir?'

'Two reasons. The first is to not have too many powerful heads of state in South Asia. Modi, Xi, Hasina. How would the CIA operate if such strong leaders rule the subcontinent? American interests are best served with weaker governments. But there was a more immediate reason. St Martin's Island,' Khan says.

'What about the island, Sir?'

'Don't you remember the reports?'

Located in the northeastern part of the Bay of Bengal, St Martin's Island was approximately 9 kilometres south of the Teknaf coast in Cox's Bazaar (a beach town on the southeast coast of Bangladesh), and 8 kilometres west of northwestern Myanmar. The island was ideally positioned to facilitate surveillance in the Bay of Bengal, which had gained strategic significance in recent years due to China's assertive push in the Indian Ocean region.[3]

Beijing had been increasingly investing in the Bay littoral countries to gain a foothold in the Bay under the banner of its flagship Belt and Road Initiative. In 2023, a year before Hasina's fall, a notable development in the area drew world attention. It was Beijing's assistance in building Dhaka's first submarine base, the BNS Sheikh Hasina, off the coast of Cox's Bazaar. Inaugurated in 2023, the base opened the possibility of China operating submarines in the Bay of Bengal. In the same year, reports came of Beijing maintaining an intelligence facility on Myanmar's Coco Island, near the Strait of Malacca – a critical chokepoint for Beijing, as nearly 80 per cent of its energy imports passed through it. Analysts argued that China's expanding presence in the Bay was the baseline for an expanded maritime role in the wider Indian Ocean region and the Indo-Pacific. This ran contrary to US interests in the Indo-Pacific region, which aims to limit Beijing's influence.[4]

Eleven days after the fall of the Sheikh Hasina government, on 5 August 2024 in Bangladesh, Indian geostrategist and columnist Brahma Chellaney wrote for *Open* magazine in a column titled 'The New Great Game': 'It was on June 21, 2023 that Hasina openly raised the St Martin's issue, telling a news conference at her official residence in Dhaka that if she were to "lease the island of St Martin's to someone, then there would be no problem" with her staying ensconced in power. But, she added, such a lease "won't happen" on her watch.

'The US sought to build close defence ties with Bangladesh by urging the Hasina government unsuccessfully to sign the General Security of Military Information Agreement and the Acquisition and Cross-Servicing Agreement. But the US has never acknowledged wanting to lease St Martin's, a small island that is closer to Myanmar than to Bangladesh's coast.

'There are already around 750 American military bases spread across at least 80 countries. The US may be seeking to expand its strategic foothold to new areas where its presence is non-existent or weak, including the Bay of Bengal.

'St Martin's, with its vantage location just eight kilometres from the Myanmar coast, could serve as a US listening post. Such a listening post, however, would be more useful for electronic surveillance of sanctions-battered Myanmar and friendly India than America's sole challenger at the global level, China.'[5]

On 11 June 2025, Indian press reported on Hasina's Facebook live address to Awami League members. Hasina alleged that interim government advisor Muhammad Yunus was backing a proposed 'Rohingya corridor' in a bid to 'sell' St Martin's Island and undermine Bangladesh's access to the seas. 'Selling the nation, selling and undermining our access to the sea is what he (Yunus) is doing. This Rohingya corridor is a ploy to sell St Martin's Island and undermine our access to the seas,' Indian media quoted Hasina as saying in the speech streamed live on Facebook.[6]

'Indian press is reporting this now, but the prime minister had warned us much before the fall of our government in Bangladesh that the US is trying to push her out of power as it wants the St Martin's Island,' Asaduzzaman Khan Kamal told us.

'What we did not know was that General Waker-uz-Zaman was on their payroll. Our primary defence intelligence agency, the Directorate General of Forces Intelligence of Bangladesh, as well as Bangladesh's principal civilian intelligence agency, the National

Security Intelligence, did not warn the prime minister that Waker had decided to betray her. Maybe their top bosses were also involved in this plot. How won't they be! After all, the army chief himself was a principal plotter!

'You know, it's funny. Waker took charge as the Bangladesh army chief only in June 2024. On 5 August, he forced Hasina to leave Bangladesh. It seems his first secret assignment was to overthrow the very leader who chose him as the army chief. Waker's father-in-law, General Mustafizur Rahman, had served as the chief of army staff of the Bangladesh army from 24 December 1997 to 23 December 2000. Rahman is Sheikh Hasina's uncle. And Waker's wife, as you know, is Hasina's cousin. That is why they say in politics you are often done in by your very own!' Khan smiled ruefully.

'But what about the public anger against Sheikh Hasina in Bangladesh? All those innocents killed during the June–July agitation, students shot in cold blood, children killed as collateral damage?'

'Let me tell you what happened then,' Khan leaned forward on his sofa, his voice louder. We looked around to check if the couple was still around. They had left, the coffee shop was empty, except for the servers hovering at a distance.

'Pakistan's spy agency, the Inter-Services Intelligence [ISI], had been working closely with the Jamaat. In fact, some ISI-trained men had infiltrated the ranks of Jamaat and they were instrumental in killing policemen in late June. Did you not read the reports of policemen being killed and hung from bridges during the agitation?' Khan asked us.

Bangladesh's leading newspaper, *Prothom Alo*, reported on 18 August 2024 that forty-four policemen died during the violence over the student mass uprising that led to the toppling of the Awami League regime. A *Prothom Alo* report had quoted the media department of the police headquarters to put out a list of the police members who died during the protests. 'The police headquarters said that these cops were killed between 20 July and 14 August. Twenty-five policemen died on 5 August and fifteen on 4 August. Apart from that, two members died while undergoing treatment on 20 August and one each on 12 and 14 August,' the report said.[7]

'When you kill so many policemen, there would be mayhem on the streets. As home minister, I was in charge of the police in Bangladesh. In that mayhem, the top police bosses had told me it was not the students who were killing policemen but the ISI-trained men who had infiltrated Jamaat and were hiding among the crowd of student protestors. It was a well-laid out plan, you see.'

Why did he not do anything to stop the madness?

'I had rushed to Prime Minister Hasina many times during the June–July agitation. Only to be told by her that the army chief has assured her he would be able to manage the ever-growing crowd of agitating students. When I told Waker in the presence of the prime minister that ISI-trained men were doing the dirty job of killing policemen and the police had to open fire in retaliation, Waker had told me his men in uniform will "handle the situation".'

So the CIA wanted Hasina out and it got General Waker-uz-Zaman in their pocket, who in turn plotted with the Jamaat and other fundamentalist forces in Bangladesh to infiltrate a students' revolt against Hasina in order to remove her from power? Isn't this too much of a stretch?

'Is it?' Waker smiled. 'Do you not know how America operates even after your Operation Sindoor?'

We had no answer to this. Khan carried on.

'I am witness to Waker's betrayal. In fact, I saw him turn the knife inside the honourable prime minister. Late evening on 4 August, there was a high-level security meet to assess the situation on the ground. Agitators had threatened to enter Dhaka from across Bangladesh and storm Gonobhaban. At the prime minister's residence, there was me, Waker, the navy chief, the air force chief, the Dhaka Metropolitan Police commissioner, the chief of the Rapid Action Battalion (the counterterrorism unit of Bangladesh, under the command of Bangladesh Police) and the chief of the BGB. I had told the prime minister that police would man every entry point into Dhaka so that no agitating crowd could enter the city from outside. Waker told me in front of Sheikh Hasina that the people had lost faith in the police because of the violence on the streets and that it would be best to let the army stop agitators at entry points.'

'Did the army chief not say that evening that violence would not be used against agitators?'

'Yes, he did,' Khan said. 'But Waker said there was no need to open fire and injure more agitators, but the army personnel on the ground would ensure that no agitator enters Dhaka. I was not convinced. So in the room I had proposed that my policemen would man Gonobhaban. Waker had said there was no need for that also. As he would ensure that the army would not allow anybody near the prime minister's residence. Sheikh Hasina had trusted Waker that evening. You know what happened the next day.'

Khan was not alone. Sitting next to him throughout the entire meeting were two young Awami League MPs, Tanvir Hasan Munir and Saiful Islam. They had been silent after the initial exchange of pleasantries.

Now, Munir asked us: 'Where will you use this conversation?'

'We are writing a book on what happened to Bangladesh after the July Revolution. We would want to write about this interview in the book.'

'Don't call it a revolution!' Asaduzzaman Khan Kamal snapped.

'But, sir, even if we are to believe there was a larger plan to pull the rug from under Hasina's feet, there were students and citizens genuinely angry with Hasina who took to the streets.'

'Yes, there were. But the "revolution" was a well-laid-out plot with one aim and one aim alone: to overthrow the prime minister. And haven't you been reading about the leaders of the so-called students' party [the National Citizen Party (NCP) was formed in February 2025 by leaders of the ADSM that had spearheaded the uprising against Hasina] and the Jamaat-e-Islami being close allies? In fact, many of these student leaders were secretly members of the Jamaat-e-Islami. You know about Abu Sayed, right? The poor boy who lost his life in the agitation was a member of the Jamaat's students' wing. Bangladesh was taken for a ride by this fake revolution,' Khan said.

'On an aside, sir. Throughout our interview you have been referring to Sheikh Hasina as prime minister and not former prime minister. Why is that?'

'She is still Bangladesh's prime minister. She never resigned. Yunus lied to the country about the resignation letter. There is none.'

Khan and the two MPs got up to leave.

'Don't misquote me,' he said as we shook hands.

We assured him we wouldn't.

As we walked him to the elevator, Asaduzzaman Khan Kamal turned to us.

'Write every word I said. The world needs to know the truth about General Waker-uz-Zaman.'

A General Goes into Hiding

A week after our meeting with Asaduzzaman Khan Kamal at the Delhi hotel, we were on the phone with a former three-star general of the Bangladesh army, now dismissed from service. We had been strictly told that his name, official designation while he was in service and his current country of residence could not be disclosed.

'Members of my family still serve in the Bangladesh armed forces,' he told us.

The former general told us he was in the cantonment on the day Hasina left Bangladesh. 'It was on that day I got to know that my chief of staff, Waker-uz-Zaman, had betrayed not only the prime minister but the country itself.'

Why did he say so?

'You know there are generals in the army who are still loyal to Hasina and are deeply pained by what is happening to Bangladesh but are too afraid to speak out because of General Waker. They care for their careers and do not want to be dismissed like I was in September last year along with some other senior officers in the army,' the former general told us.

'On 5 August, our soldiers who were manning the entry points to the city were overwhelmed by the large crowds that started pouring in. When they called for backup from the army control room, none came. I and several other top officers directed soldiers in our command to reach various spots. We had no idea there was an internal sabotage. And that the chief himself had ensured that the army does not stop protestors from entering Dhaka or storming into Gonobhaban.'

When did he know that General Waker had instructed the army to stand down?

'After Sheikh Hasina left for India, it was openly discussed among top officers in the cantonment. The chief had kept only those generals he trusted in the loop.'

The former general told us it would take him days to fully grasp the magnitude of General Waker's 'betrayal'. 'In the army we train cadets to become tough men, to not display signs of weakness even when staring at extreme adversity. But when the mob started pulling down statues of the great Sheikh Mujib, the father of our nation, I could not stop my tears. I am the son of a *mukti-joddha*. My father had fought against the Pakistan army as a guerrilla soldier to free this country. And today, this country has embraced Pakistan again. Pakistani army generals are visiting Bangladesh military bases on regular intervals. What can be more shameful than this.'

Why was he dismissed from the army?

'I think General Waker had been keeping an eye on me for some time. I, and several other officers, were dishonourably discharged in September last year for conduct unbecoming of the army. I left the country soon after or else the military police would have picked me up, I guess,' the former general said.

'You know the general is a smart man. He knows how to balance between Indian interests and American interests. There was a plan from the interim government to engineer small incidents of flare-ups along the border with India to divert attention away from the political turbulence inside Bangladesh. Yunus's political graph has really come down in the last few months and all the political parties are getting impatient for the next round of elections.

'What I have heard from my contacts within the government and also the junior officers loyal to me and still serving in the army is that Yunus had discussed and given final touches to the plan to engage the Indian security forces in close consultation with the National Security Advisor Khalilur Rahman and with the army's quarter-master general, Lieutenant General Mohammad Faizur Rahman, around the same time that India had launched Operation Sindoor against Pakistan. The plan had the nod of the ISI and the Pakistan army as it would give Pakistan operational advantage to have India engaged on two fronts. But the general quashed the move.'

But isn't it a good thing as far as India is concerned?

'Yes, it is. But do not be mistaken in believing that Waker is India's friend. He is sharp enough to know he should not weaken his own position by engaging with the Indian army and thereby angering India only to strengthen Yunus. India should never trust a man who betrayed his own prime minister.'

So what was the Yunus administration's plan during Operation Sindoor?

'The plan was to get the BGB to adopt an overtly aggressive stance along the Indo-Bangladesh border and thereby trigger a confrontation with India's Border Security Force. The plan also involved deploying army units at some rear areas along the border to provide backup for BGB troops.'

The former general told us that this would not have been difficult to execute as the BGB had, soon after the political change in Dhaka on 5 August 2024, adopted an aggressive posture along the international border with India and started objecting to the erection of fences and even other constructions on the Indian side of the border.

'General Waker knows his army's strengths and weaknesses. He knows our army can't take on the Indian army even with Pakistan's help right now.'

And what were his own plans?

'I cannot return to Bangladesh. Not until General Waker is there as army chief. I don't trust that man after what he did to the country.'

More than a Conspiracy Theory?

Our meeting with Asaduzzaman Khan Kamal and the phone call with the dismissed general had left us in a state of shock. The theory of an American hand in Hasina's ouster was not a new one. It had been spoken about many times in India by strategic experts and Bangladesh watchers. But the explosive statement we heard on the Bangladesh army chief was a new one. It was widely believed that General Waker had saved Hasina's life from the murderous mob that entered her house not long after she left Bangladesh. He had done so, it was commonly believed, by giving Hasina enough time to flee. The fact that the general himself played a key role in her ouster, as claimed by Asaduzzaman Khan and the dismissed general was news to us.

As far as the 'US hand' theory is concerned, it seems even vocal supporters of the July Revolution have started believing in it. One of Bangladesh's best-known poets, philosophers and rights activists, Farhad Mazhar, had been a vocal critic of Hasina and Bangladesh's Constitution, and his book, *Gono-ovyutthan o Gathan* (Mass Uprising and Constitution, 2023), had a big influence on the student leaders who led the July Revolution.

On 2 July 2025, Mazhar spoke to Bangladeshi daily *Samakal* and rued the recent events in the country that led to Bangladesh's downward spiral. 'When the mob attacks *mazhar*s (*dargah*s, considered un-Islamic by hardline Islamist organizations) one after the other, no steps are taken to contain those attacks. Instead, poets and writers are being sent to jail for putting out literature in public domain. One the one hand, citizens' rights are being trampled upon and on the other, the democratic demand to build Bangladesh from scratch is being dismissed. In the name of reforms, the old Constitution and the old order are being protected. The mass uprising that we witnessed was nothing but a US-backed regime-change operation. American economist and public policy analyst Jeffrey Sachs has said as much in his article "Accusations of US Regime-Change Operations in Pakistan and Bangladesh Warrant UN Attention",' Mazhar told *Samakal*.[8]

And what had the Columbia University professor said in his 19 August 2024 article that came out fourteen days after the fall of the Sheikh Hasina government in Bangladesh?

Jeffrey Sachs said on 27 March, former Pakistan Prime Minister Imran Khan 'brandished the cypher', and told his followers and the public that the US was out to bring him down. On 10 April 2022, Khan was thrown out of office as the parliament acceded to the US threat.

'We know this in detail because of Ambassador Khan's cypher, exposed by Prime Minister Khan and brilliantly documented by Ryan Grim of The Intercept, including the text of the cypher. Absurdly and tragically, Prime Minister Khan languishes in prison in part over espionage charges, linked to his revealing the cypher,' he wrote.

According to Sachs, the US appears to have played a similar role in the recent violent coup in Bangladesh. He said Prime Minister Hasina was ostensibly toppled by student unrest, and fled to India when the Bangladeshi military refused to prevent the protestors from storming the government offices. Yet there may well be much more to the story than meets the eye.

Indian press reports have quoted Hasina to claim the US brought her down. Hasina has said that the US removed her from power because she refused to grant the US military facilities in a region that is considered strategic for the US in its 'Indo-Pacific Strategy' to contain China. While these are second-hand accounts by the Indian media, Sachs believes, they track closely several speeches and statements that Hasina has made over the past two years.

Sachs wrote that on 17 May 2024, the same Assistant Secretary Liu who played a lead role in toppling Prime Minister Khan, visited Dhaka to discuss the US Indo-Pacific Strategy among other topics. Days later, Sheikh Hasina reportedly summoned the leaders of the fourteen parties of her alliance to make the startling claim that a 'country of white-skinned people' was trying to bring her down, ostensibly telling the leaders that she refused to compromise her nation's sovereignty. Like Imran Khan, Prime Minister Hasina had been pursuing a foreign policy of neutrality, including constructive relations not only with the US but also with China and Russia, much to the deep consternation of the US government, Sachs wrote.

According to Sachs, in the cases of Pakistan and Bangladesh, the UN Security Council should seek the direct testimony of Prime Minister Khan and Prime Minister Hasina in order to evaluate evidence that the US played a role in the overthrow of their governments. 'Each, of course, should be protected by the UN for giving their testimony, so as to protect them from any retribution that could follow their honest presentation of the facts. Their testimony can be taken by video conference, if necessary, given the tragic ongoing incarceration of Prime Minister Khan,' he wrote.[9]

Maybe the America-backed regime change in Bangladesh was more than a conspiracy theory after all. But Bangladesh army chief Waker-uz-Zaman betraying Sheikh Hasina to serve American interests, as Asaduzzaman Khan Kamal and the former general alleged, was indeed a revelation. We wondered what his baiters within Bangladesh who called him an 'Indian agent' and demanded his ouster would have to say about this.

3

Bangladesh Turns Back the Clock

Sheikh Hasina's ignominious departure from Bangladesh barely half an hour before murderous mobs stormed Gonobhaban immediately set in motion the process of erasing the contributions of the Sheikh family – Bangabandhu Sheikh Mujibur Rahman and his daughter Sheikh Hasina – from the country's collective memory.

Sheikh Mujib, widely regarded as the 'father of the nation' and popularly known by the honorific 'Bangabandhu', became the target of the agitators' anger. Mujib was first addressed as 'Bangabandhu' (friend of Bengalis) by popular student leader Tofail Ahmed[1] at a massive rally at Dhaka's Race Course Maidan (known as Suhrawardy Maidan now) on 23 February 1969.[2]

The rally, attended by over 10 lakh people, was held to celebrate the withdrawal of charges against Mujib and many others in the infamous Agartala Conspiracy Case[3,4] following the 'mass uprising of 1969'.[5] At that rally, Tofail Ahmed addressed Mujib as 'Bangabandhu' to wide public acclaim, and the title has survived to this day.

But the widespread public anger against Sheikh Hasina and her government that led to the outpouring of public anger against her in June–July 2024 transformed into rage against Bangabandhu and a fiercely angry determination to obliterate his name, memory and contribution towards freeing Bangladesh from the shackles of Pakistan.

To begin with, Bangabandhu's statues and busts all over the country were pulled down and destroyed, murals that featured him were defaced, and his bungalow at Dhaka's upscale Dhanmondi[6,7] where he was gunned down along with his family members in the early hours of 15 August 1975,[8] was vandalized and burned. Till recently, the 32 Dhanmondi address was a revered national shrine and a memorial to Sheikh Mujib, also housing the Bangabandhu Memorial Museum. It was razed to the ground by activists of the Boisomyobirodhi Chhatra Andolan (or SAD) and Islamists on 5 February 2025.[9,10]

Houses and properties of Awami League leaders, functionaries and supporters, and those held 'guilty of association' with the party, were attacked, vandalized and destroyed, party offices were razed to the ground, and most Awami League members who could not flee the country were either killed or jailed.

Apart from the physical obliteration of statues, murals and structures associated with Bangabandhu, the interim government headed by Mohammad Yunus, installed on 8 August 2024,[11] has made systematic efforts to erase Bangabandhu from the nation's memory.

In January 2025, the interim government ordered the removal of chapters highlighting Sheikh Mujib's contribution to the country's independence from school textbooks.[12] New school textbooks credited Ziaur Rahman, the founder of the BNP, and not Sheikh Mujib, as the principal player in the 1971 liberation war.[13]

In early December 2024, the interim government issued a notification stating that Sheikh Mujib's portrait would not be printed on 20, 100, 500 and 1,000 taka denominations.[14] The printing of new banknotes was ordered, and old notes bearing Bangabandhu's portrait were withdrawn from circulation. The country's central bank stopped issuing new, already printed currency notes that had Sheikh Mujib's portrait. That resulted in an estimated loss of about 15,000 crore taka[15] and a severe shortage of currency notes.

The interim government issued a notification on 3 June 2025, scrapping a 2022 Act (passed by the erstwhile Sheikh Hasina government) that reaffirmed Sheikh Mujib's honorific as 'father of the nation' (*jatir pita*). The new notification did not refer to Mujib as '*jatir pita*' while referring to the 1971 liberation war and the role of freedom fighters (mukti-joddhas) in it.[16] This notification equated Sheikh Mujib with other freedom fighters.

Under the Bir Mukti-Joddhas (brave freedom fighters) category, the 2022 Act included members of the 'Mujib Bahini', one of the several guerilla outfits that waged insurgency against West Pakistani troops, as 'freedom fighters'. But the 3 June 2025 notification made no mention of 'Mujib Bahini', and this meant that surviving members of the outfit and family members of surviving and deceased members of the outfit would no longer be able to claim benefits.

This 'Mujib Bahini' was formed with the help of Indian agencies[17] to fight the West Pakistani army, and it comprised mostly activists of the Awami League and the Chhatra League (the student wing of the Awami League). Sheikh Mujib's nephew, Sheikh Fazlul Haque Moni, was instrumental in the creation of this militia that carried out many operations to incapacitate the West Pakistani army and its Islamist affiliates: the Razakars, Al-Badr and Al-Shams.

These are a few examples of the larger attempt to rewrite the country's history and downplay the role of Sheikh Mujib and the Awami League, and even downplay the genocide of Bengalis (both Muslims and Hindus) launched by the West Pakistani army and its Islamist affiliates before and during the liberation war. This rewriting of history,[18,19] hope the architects of the project, will pave the way for Pakistan's rehabilitation in the minds and hearts of future generations of Bangladeshis, allow Islamabad to regain the influence that it lost in Bangladesh during Sheikh Hasina's rule and also facilitate the formation and strengthening of a Beijing–Dhaka–Islamabad axis.

The Jamaat-e-Islami, which has long been accused of collaborating with the West Pakistani army in 1971 and even participating in the genocide of Bengalis[20] under Operation Searchlight,[21] as was described by the then US Consul General in Dhaka, Archer Blood, in what came to be famously called the 'Blood Telegrams',[22] has got a fresh lease of life under the Mohammad Yunus–led interim government and has been a vocal proponent of the history rewriting project which will also whitewash its role in the 1971 war.

In addition, the Jamaat and the country's Islamists want to tone down and even erase India's role in the 1971 liberation war;[23] the Jamaat now says it was never against the country's independence movement, but was against India's involvement in the movement. This involvement, it says, led to Indian hegemony over Bangladesh and, hence, it argues that the history of the 1971 war ought to be rewritten.

The BNP has been uncomfortable with this project of rewriting the history of the 1971 liberation war and downplaying the genocide by the West Pakistani army. Bangladesh Nationalist Party secretary general Mirza Fakrul Islam Alamgir, a widely respected senior politician, said at an event organized by the Forum for Bangladesh Studies in Dhaka in December 2024 that the 1971 war against West Pakistani occupation and the exploitation of East Pakistan should never be forgotten.[24]

To be fair, this rewriting of the history of the 1971 liberation war is not new in Bangladesh. Change of regimes in the past have triggered similar exercises. That's because the first twenty years of Bangladesh's nationhood were very tumultuous. Sheikh Mujib and almost his entire family were wiped out in a coup led by army officers in the early hours of 15 August 1975. The reins of power passed into the hands of a succession of military rulers, the longest-serving among them being Lieutenant General Hussain Mohammad Ershad who also founded the Jatiya Party.

The first proper elections in the country were held in 1991 and brought the BNP, founded by Lieutenant General Ziaur Rahman, to power. It started writing school textbooks ascribing primacy to its founder in the 1971 war. Ziaur Rahman, who was a young major in the Pakistani army, led a revolt by Bengali army officers against the (West) Pakistani army soon after Sheikh Mujib's arrest on the night of 25 March 1971. That was the night the infamous Operation

Searchlight was launched by the (West) Pakistani army to eliminate all those opposed to West Pakistan and demanding independence. Sheikh Mujib stayed behind bars during the entire duration of the liberation war and was released from a Pakistani prison only on 8 January 1972, nearly a month after Pakistan had surrendered to Indian forces in Dhaka on 16 December 1971. Ziaur Rahman was the first to declare independence in a series of broadcasts from Swadhin Bangla Betar Kendra (Independent Bangla Radio Station) between 27 and 29 March.

Ziaur Rahman was a 'sector commander' of the Bengali nationalist army (called the Bangladesh army), and he then assumed command of the 'Z Force' and played a major role in the offensive against the West Pakistani army.[25,26] He is considered a war hero.

Soon after Mujib's assassination on 15 August 1975, Ziaur Rahman became the army chief (on 24 August). He, however, is widely believed to have had no role in the coup against Sheikh Mujib. He took over as Bangladesh's president in April 1977 and continued in the post till his assassination in another coup on 30 May 1981. Though a military dictator, Ziaur Rahman was popular because he carried out many reforms, stabilized the economy, initiated major infrastructure projects, tried to establish the rule of law, allowed multiparty democracy and made efforts towards a free press and free speech. His supporters, and the BNP, say that Ziaur Rahman's role as an active commander of liberation forces in the 1971 war places him on the same pedestal, if not higher, than Sheikh Mujib.

This found reflection in the history textbooks written during the five-year rule of his widow, Khaleda Zia, from 20 March 1991 to 30 March 1996. History was written highlighting the role of Ziaur Rahman and giving him primacy in the liberation war. While Sheikh Mujib was not kept out, the names of other Awami League leaders like Tajuddin Ahmed and Syed Nazrul Islam, who also played very important parts in the liberation movement, were given equal prominence. And the contributions of Moni Singh who led the Communist Party of Eastern Bengal, Siraj Sikdar of the Purbo Banglar Sarbohara Party (East Bengal Proletarian Party) and Abdul Hamid Khan Bhasani of the National Awami League were also highlighted.

When Sheikh Hasina came to power in June 1996, she ordered the rewriting of all history texts to make her father, Sheikh Mujib, the central figure in the liberation movement while whittling down or even obliterating the role and contributions of others. The history of the liberation movement became, a Mujib-centric one. At the centre of this 'correction' of history was a civil society organization by the name of Ekattorer Ghatak Dalal Nirmul Committee (Committee to Root Out Collaborators and Agents of the West Pakistani Forces in the 1971 Liberation Struggle). This organization was born out of the acute resentment of many who had participated in the liberation movement against those who had collaborated with the West Pakistani regime. These 'collaborators' had been rehabilitated by successive military rulers, including Ziaur Rahman, after Sheikh Mujib's assassination and had even held important posts during military rule.

But in their zeal to name the collaborators and reverse efforts to whitewash their crimes, the committee, which included Awami League leaders, put Sheikh Mujib on a pedestal and belittled the role of other freedom fighters. Ziaur Rahman's role as the foremost military commander of the rebel army, which often incapacitated West Pakistani forces and played a critical role in helping Indian forces defeat the West Pakistani army was nearly obliterated from history textbooks. Sheikh Mujib was glorified and the contributions of all others whittled down. Even the success of military operations against the West Pakistani army was attributed to Sheikh Mujib, who was in solitary confinement at Central Jail Mianwali in (West) Pakistan's Punjab province from March 1971 till January 1972. Incidentally, Bhagat Singh and his comrades were also incarcerated in the same prison during the Indian independence movement.

All these 'corrections' were undone once again when the BNP

returned to power in October 2001. The 'rewriting' of history textbooks, especially the ones taught in schools and colleges, was carried out with a vengeance between 2001 and 2006 under Khaleda Zia's prime ministership. The role of Sheikh Mujib in 1971 was drastically downplayed and the revised textbooks said he (Sheikh Mujib) had not played any role in the liberation war since he was behind the bars for its entire duration. It was Ziaur Rahman who led the armed struggle against the West Pakistani forces, and he was projected as the prime hero of the war. Mujib's role was reduced to that of a mere bystander.

The Jamaat-e-Islami was an ally of the BNP in the coalition government and had driven the 'history revision' exercise in its own interests. Renowned historian Mumtajuddin Patowary, who taught at many universities in the country, details the whitewashing of the role of the Jamaat and other Islamists in the country's liberation war in his book *Pathyapustaka Muktijuddher Itihas Bikriti* (Distortion of History in Textbooks).[27] While doing so, the Islamists also perverted the role and contribution of Sheikh Mujib, who, while not having participated actively in the liberation war, definitely inspired it and had given leadership to the movement for recognition of Bangla as an official language of Pakistan. It was this language movement that grew into a movement for ending the hegemony of West Pakistan over East Pakistan, and ultimately led to the independence movement and the liberation war. There can be no doubt that Sheikh Mujib was one of the – if not *the* – prime leaders of the freedom struggle right from its inception as a language movement. The Jamaat and other Islamists of the country, whose ties with Pakistan were always strong – and these ties are out in the open now – had a vested interest in playing down Mujib's role in the freedom struggle. But they didn't stop at that; a concerted campaign was launched to deny the genocide and pass off the horrific atrocities committed on East Pakistan's Bengali populace as the inevitable 'collateral damage' during an armed conflict.

The whole 'revision' process repeated itself, once the Awami

League under Sheikh Hasina returned to power in January 2009. It must be explained here that the intervening period of twenty-six months from end-October 2006 (when Khaleda Zia stepped down at the end of her tenure) to 6 January 2009 (when Sheikh Hasina was re-elected to power) saw a military-backed interim government in power unconstitutionally. Bangladesh had a system of caretaker governments to oversee elections ever since the country's first free and fair elections were held following the resignation of military ruler Hussain Muhammad Ershad in December 1990 due to a mass uprising led jointly by the Awami League and the BNP. It was Ershad who initiated the system of a caretaker government comprising apolitical figures from the higher judiciary, bureaucracy, etc., to conduct parliamentary elections after the end of the tenure of an elected government. He had, while stepping down from power on 6 December 1990, appointed a caretaker government headed by Justice Shahabuddin Ahmed (he later served as Bangladesh's president from 1996 to 2001) to conduct free, fair and credible elections.

Two subsequent caretaker governments – the first under former chief justice Muhammad Habibur Rahman that held power for eighty-five days and oversaw parliamentary polls in May–June 1996, and the second under former chief justice Latifur Rahman that was in office for eighty-seven days and which conducted parliamentary elections in September–October 2001 – fulfilled their mandates.

But the next one that stepped in after the tenure of the BNP government headed by Khaleda Zia ended in October 2006 became controversial. It was headed by the then President Iajuddin Ahmed (who was the country's president from September 2002 to February 2009) instead of the then Chief Justice K.M. Hasan, as had become the norm (of chief justices heading the caretaker administrations to conduct elections). The Awami League alleged that the BNP had influenced the appointment of Iajuddin Khan as head of the caretaker government in order to manipulate the elections. Violent protests broke out all over the country against the caretaker government, and the elections scheduled for January 2007 were cancelled, allegedly at the behest of the country's military brass who replaced Iajuddin Ahmed with Justice Fazlul Haque (who served for only a day), and then Fakhruddin Ahmed , a renowned economist and former governor of the Bangladesh central bank. A limited state of emergency was imposed and the military brass wielded all the power behind the facade of a civilian caretaker government. The top leadership of the Awami League and the BNP were jailed and corruption charges brought against them. All political parties launched movements against the military-backed Fakruddin Ahmed government, and these protests became so intense that Ahmed was forced to announce parliamentary elections in December 2008. These elections brought Sheikh Hasina back to power in January 2009. In late June 2011, the Awami League government passed the Fifteenth Constitutional Amendment Bill that abolished the system of caretaker governments.[28]

Getting back to the revision of history, after Sheikh Hasina's return to power, the exercise was launched with renewed vigour. Hasina appointed commissions to obliterate the role of Ziaur Rahman and the rebel army in the liberation war, and gave primacy not only to her father but also to the mukti-joddhas – the army of civilian volunteers trained and equipped (with arms and ammunition) by India – over the rebel army (of which Ziaur Rahaman was a commander) in the 1971 war. Much to the anger of the BNP and the Islamists, the revised textbooks also acknowledged India's role in the 1971 war. That was anathema to Bangladesh's Islamists, given their fraternal ties with Pakistan and its Islamists. The Awami League government named hundreds of public buildings, roads, bridges and facilities along with government welfare schemes after 'Bangabandhu'. Scores of statues of Sheikh Mujib were erected across the country and his portraits became mandatory fixtures in government offices and public spaces. Murals featuring Bangabandhu came up in many parts of the country, schoolchildren started taking oaths in his name, and programmes celebrating his life became mandatory and regular affairs in schools, colleges, universities and government organizations. Bangabandhu became a ubiquitous presence in Bangladesh. So much so that people started resenting Bangabandhu's memory being forced down their throats as well as the deliberate downplay of the role of others in the independence movement.

This overdose of Mujib administered to Bangladeshis, coupled with the other failings of Sheikh Hasina – misgovernance, corruption, stifling of dissent, crackdown on opposition and denial of any space to opposition parties, gross human rights abuses, etc. – led to widespread anger against her and, by association, her father. The Islamists took advantage of this and, immediately after Sheikh Hasina fled Bangladesh, started erasing all physical memories of Sheikh Mujib.

The toppling of Bangabandhu's statues and the defacing of his murals were symbols, powerful ones at that, of the larger project to permanently wipe off Sheikh Mujib from not only the nation's history, but also its collective memory. By portraying him as a stooge of India who became a willing tool to break up Pakistan so that New Delhi could establish a permanent hegemony over Bangladesh, the Islamists are trying to widen the fissure between India and Bangladesh.

But their primary aim, as stated earlier on in this chapter, is to rehabilitate Pakistan in the hearts and minds of Bangladeshis and establish a firm bond based on Islam between the two countries. For that to happen, the genocide of 1971 has to be completely erased from textbooks and from the nation's public memory.

As part of the efforts to, once again, rewrite the nation's history, the Mohammad Yunus–led dispensation in Bangladesh seems to have given a free hand to Islamists. What is meant by Islamists here are not just the skullcap-and-kurta-clad bearded radicals espousing jihad, rule of the sharia and Islamic rule over the Indian subcontinent and the world; they include the suit-and-tie-clad bureaucrats, academics and intellectuals and the army officers in uniform who mask their radicalism with sophistry and obfuscation, often espousing the need for a Western-style liberal democracy where free speech is not curtailed. These two sets of people have deep mutual ties and work concertedly on a common agenda that includes promoting Pakistan's interests in Bangladesh.

A good example of the ground gained by Islamist, pro-Pakistan forces in the aftermath of the uprising that unseated Sheikh Hasina from power in August 2024 was the commemoration of Muhammad Ali Jinnah's seventy-sixth death anniversary at the National Press Club in Dhaka on 11 September 2024.[29] Urdu songs and couplets praising Jinnah were recited and sung, and speakers advanced the argument that without Jinnah and his 'towering achievement' of carving Pakistan out of India, Bangladesh would not have existed.

Mohammad Samsuddin, convenor of the Nagorik Parishad (one of the organizations that led the uprising against the Sheikh Hasina government) that metamorphosed into the Jatiya Nagorik Party (NCP), said at the event: 'If Bangladesh had not been part of Pakistan in 1947, we would have been in the same position as Kashmir today, with the Indian junta holding weapons to our necks. Bangladesh gained independence because of Pakistan, which Jinnah helped create.' Others spoke on the same lines at the event that was attended by the Pakistani deputy high commissioner Kamran Dhangal, Pakistani students studying in Bangladesh and leading Islamist figures.

An event of this nature would have been unthinkable till 5 August 2024 when Sheikh Hasina had to flee the country. Jinnah has been a reviled figure in Bangladesh since he was the one who imposed Urdu on the Bengali-speaking people. This imposition of Urdu was the first step in Pakistan's ruling class – comprising mostly politicians from Sind and Punjab provinces – imposing hegemony over East Pakistan. The imposition of Urdu was fiercely resisted, and spawned the language movement demanding that Bengali be given the same status as Urdu. The brutal suppression of the language movement by West Pakistani forces birthed resistance among the Bengalis and ultimately led to the freedom movement and liberation of Bangladesh from West Pakistan. To hold an event to celebrate Jinnah's life, and that too at a prominent venue in Dhaka in the presence of Pakistani diplomats and citizens, sent out an important signal: that the project to 'correct' history and whitewash Jinnah, the brutal reign of the West Pakistanis over East Pakistan for a little over twenty-four years and the war crimes and genocide of Bengalis during Operation Searchlight in 1971 was firmly on course. Though none from the interim government attended the event, there was no doubt that it had the full backing of the Mohammad Yunus dispensation.

'To celebrate Jinnah and Urdu is to completely reverse the ideals of the freedom movement and turn back the clock. This is diabolic and amounts to a sinister denial of history and of the trauma that we as a nation suffered for twenty-four years [from 1947 to 1971] under those brutal rulers from West Pakistan. Jinnah can never be rehabilitated in our minds and hearts; he was the first to reject our aspirations and initiated attempts to force us to abandon our Bengali identity. Jinnah is the reason why we broke away from West Pakistan and liberated ourselves. Urdu is the language that led to the breakup of Pakistan. We fought for Bangla, and to see paeans to Jinnah sung in Urdu drives a knife through our hearts,' said historian Rubul Ahmed Arefin. Arefin's father, a civil servant, was killed by West Pakistani soldiers during the 1971 liberation war.

This event in Dhaka to observe Jinnah's death anniversary was held to gauge the public mood and see if it evoked a backlash. But even though many, especially secular civil society members, were outraged over the event, they mostly kept their anger private and shied away from issuing statements or publicly opposing this attempt to rehabilitate Jinnah. That's because any expression of opposition could be easily used by the Islamists and their backers in the interim government to brand the opponents as Awami League supporters. Since August 2024, being labelled an Awami League supporter has inevitably attracted physical attacks, destruction of properties and arrest and incarceration on trumped-up charges of murdering people who participated in the July–August uprising against Sheikh Hasina.

'We were seething, but we kept our anger concealed. Expressing any anger would have been very dangerous. Everyone is scared for their lives. A reign of terror persists and all voices have been throttled. They accuse Hasina of stifling dissent, but they [the present set of rulers who include those who led the uprising] are far worse,' said Arefin.

The observance of Jinnah's death anniversary was followed by high-level exchanges between Bangladesh and Pakistan. Senior Pakistani army officers, including those from the ISI, visited Bangladesh and were feted by the Yunus dispensation,[30] triggering grave concern in India.[31] The Bangladesh army's senior Lieutenant General S.M. Kamrul Hasan visited Pakistan and met Pakistani army chief General Asim Munir and other top army officers of that country on 14 January 2025.[32,33] Lieutenant General Hasan is a prime proponent of closer military and strategic ties between Bangladesh and Pakistan and is known to be an Islamist.

In another sign of the deepening ties between Bangladesh and Pakistan, Mohammad Yunus met Pakistan Prime Minister Shahbaz Sharif twice over a period of four months in the latter half of 2024. The two first met at the sidelines of the UN General Assembly session in New York on 25 September 2024.[34] That meeting evoked concerns in India because Yunus called for the revival of the South Asian Association for Regional Cooperation (SAARC), a forum that New Delhi had been ignoring because of Pakistan's proclivity to use it to highlight bilateral (Indo-Pak) issues and also due to Pakistan derailing many attempts to forge trade and transit ties between SAARC members.

The two met once again in Cairo on the sidelines of the D-8 summit on 19 December 2024[35] and decided to strengthen bilateral ties and step up trade and technical cooperation between the two countries. Yunus, once again, reiterated his commitment to revive SAARC. A day after this meeting, the second cargo ship from Pakistan docked at Bangladesh's Chittagong port.[36] The two countries renewed direct maritime links after forty-seven years when the first Pakistani cargo ship from Karachi docked at Chittagong on 13 November 2024.[37]

There have been regular exchanges between the two countries since then and the visit of trade, military and other delegations, including reciprocal visits by academics, journalists and civil society members. Even social media exchanges between the two countries have intensified in recent months.

So strong is the commitment to erase history and whitewash the brutality, genocide and war crimes committed by West Pakistan that Bangladesh's then foreign secretary, Jashim Uddin, was severely reprimanded by Yunus and 'foreign advisor' (the de factor foreign minister) Touhid Hossain for demanding an apology from Pakistan (for the 1971 war crimes and genocide) and reparations amounting to $4.52 billion as Bangladesh's share of the pre-1971 assets during a bilateral consultation with his Pakistani counterpart, Amna Baloch, in Dhaka on 17 April 2025.[38] Pakistan's refusal to tender an apology for the war crimes and give Bangladesh its due share from the division of assets (foreign aid received by undivided Pakistan, unpaid provident funds to Bengali employees of the Pakistan government, savings instruments including fixed deposits belonging to Bengalis in Pakistani banks and $200 million given by international donors for the 1970 cyclone that devastated East Pakistan) has been a sore point with Bangladeshis since 1971. Pakistan has steadfastly turned down Bangladesh's requests to resolve these issues. The Bangladesh foreign secretary's reiteration of the demand for an apology and reparations angered Islamabad, which reportedly conveyed to the interim government in Dhaka that raising such contentious issues would hamper the forging of close ties between the two countries.

Jashim Uddin was asked to step down from his post on 21 May 2025 when he voiced his strong opposition to a proposal to establish a 'humanitarian corridor' through Bangladeshi territory to supply aid (including arms) to the Arakan army. This proposal was forwarded by the US and was actively backed by Pakistan. Bangladesh National Security Advisor Khalilur Rahman was an ardent proponent of this project. But Jashim Uddin opposed it and had to pay a price for that.[39,40]

Bangladesh has also become a willing partner in the China–Pakistan project of establishing a trilateral axis between the two countries. The first meeting of this proposed trilateral axis was held at Kunming, the capital of China's southwestern Yunnan province, on 19 June 2025.[41,42] Though this trilateral axis is ostensibly aimed at 'deeper cooperation including infrastructure, connectivity, trade, investment, healthcare, agriculture, maritime affairs, ICT, disaster preparedness, and climate change', there is little doubt that the actual objective is to forge close strategic ties between the three countries. This has grave and adverse security implications for India[43] and will pave the way for deep ties between Bangladesh and Pakistan, midwifed by China.

So how successful will the attempts to turn back the clock and undo the liberation war by making Bangladesh a close ally of Pakistan be? Dhaka watchers in Delhi say that though the Islamists and pro-Pakistani elements in Bangladesh may be powerful now, the 'spirit of 1971' will make a strong comeback.

Preeti Saran, former secretary (east) in India's Ministry of External Affairs (MEA) believes the secular and moderate forces in Bangladesh who uphold the spirit of the liberation war will rise again. 'It's difficult to say what will happen ultimately, but I'm sure the Islamists won't be in power in Bangladesh for very long,' she said.

'Bangladesh has had a chequered history. Within four years of its independence, Sheikh Mujib was assassinated and since then, there have been periodic and intense efforts to downplay his contribution. There is a dual version of the country's history and the liberation war with one version highlighting the heroism of Sheikh Mujib and placing him on a pedestal and the other downplaying him and highlighting the role of others. The situation is still fluid in Bangladesh, but I will not say that the current efforts to turn the clock back will succeed,' she said.

'The Awami League now suffers from a bad reputation due to the alleged misdeeds of Sheikh Hasina, but the party still has strong grassroots support and will not be relegated to the margins. The large constituency of mukti-joddhas and those who believe in the spirit of the liberation war will not sit idle; they will reassert themselves. Bangladesh will witness some dramatic changes, and those may happen very soon,' the former diplomat, who has deep knowledge of and close links with Bangladesh, said.

Former Indian high commissioner to Bangladesh Veena Sikri is also of the same view. While acknowledging that vigorous efforts are on to reverse history and make Bangladesh an Islamist ally of Pakistan, she feels they won't succeed.

'Bangladesh was the victim of a deep-seated regime-change conspiracy hatched by the Pakistani deep state and the Biden administration. Pakistan's proxy in Bangladesh is the Jamaat-e-Islami which is being clever and acting behind the scenes by manipulating Mohammad Yunus. The Jamaat was hoping that its project to foster close strategic ties between Bangladesh and Pakistan would succeed, especially since they were complementing it by trying to forge a strong anti-Indian sentiment in the country. But they haven't got people on their side. They've come up against a solid flank of opposition from many civil society organizations, political parties and prominent intellectuals. The spirit of the (1971) liberation war is still strong in Bangladesh, and those who believe in the ideals that fuelled the country's freedom struggle won't let Pakistan stage a comeback in Bangladesh. We have seen this in the past also when the BNP–Jamaat government tried to facilitate Pakistan's back-door entry into the country and how people foiled those efforts,' said Sikri.

Sikri said that Mohammad Yunus has lost a lot of credibility over the last twelve months. 'The indiscriminate arrests of political opponents and non-political dissenters, filing false cases against people, the interim government's failure to control inflation and arrest the country's economic downslide, the breakdown of law and order and rising crimes against women, the Islamization of society and polity are factors behind the fast dwindling popularity of Yunus. His stand-off with the army chief General Waker-uz-Zaman has also harmed him. At the same time, the Awami League's vote bank is more or less intact. Yunus does not have the mandate or the credibility to ban the Awami League and the feeling is growing that parliamentary elections cannot be held under Yunus's supervision,' Sikri added.

Bangladesh expert and senior journalist Jayanta Roy Chowdhury, who is an editor at the *Secretariat*, a New Delhi–based journal focused on international trade, strategic affairs and policy matters, believes that the current dominance of Islamists and pro-Pakistan elements will end. 'One must understand that the loudest or shrillest voices get heard, but that doesn't mean the others are acquiescing. There is this vast silent majority in Bangladesh who do not approve of what's happening in the country,' he said.

'The efforts to erase history or rewrite the events of 1971 and whitewash the role of the Razakars [collaborators of the West Pakistani forces] won't succeed because apart from the Awami League which still retains the support of at least 30 per cent of the country's populace, the BNP also draws its ideology from the 1971 liberation war and cannot disown the stellar role played by its founder [Ziaur Rahman] in that war,' he said. He pointed out that the pro-Pakistani elements have always been present in Bangladesh, and the country has witnessed a constant struggle between those elements and the pro-1971 forces. 'It is quite likely that the pro-Pakistani forces will get defeated. After all, it is difficult to draw sustenance from a failed state like Pakistan,' he added.

But some scholars, like anthropologist and author Rami Niranjan Desai is less hopeful. Desai is alarmed over the 'erasure of the secular nature of Bangladesh' under Mohammad Yunus. Desai, a distinguished fellow at the India Foundation (a leading right-wing think-tank in India), feels there is little chance of Bangladesh's reversal to its earlier avatar (under Sheikh Hasina). 'The Islamist radicalization of Bangladesh is irreversible. Islamist forces that have taken over the country will be hard to dislodge. It is not just Pakistan which has a lot of influence in Bangladesh right now; even Turkey has established its influence over the country. The youth of the country are being radicalized, and a lot of money and weapons are flowing in. Thanks to the growing influence of Pakistan and Turkiye, Bengali nationalism is on the wane, and irreversibly so. It takes only one generation to wipe out all memories of the past. The present generation of young men and women in Bangladesh have no lived-in memories of the 1971 liberation war and its horrors (the atrocities and genocide by West Pakistani forces). They learn about it from textbooks, and if textbooks are altered, as is happening now, to erase Sheikh Mujib's role and the atrocities committed by West Pakistan, as well as the brutal subjugation of East Pakistan by West Pakistan from 1947 to 1971, then the present and future generations will never learn what happened in the country. If the downslide of Bangladesh into a radical Islamic country run by radicals is to be arrested, a split among the radicals and Islamists has to be engineered. But who is going to do it, and how, and when?' she wonders.

The answer to Desai's question may well hold the key to the future of Bangladesh.

4

Rise of the Razakars

What was the man in the white shirt and dark trousers thinking?

The photographer was trying to take a perfect shot of a line of tanks that had rolled down the square to scare off pro-democracy agitators who had been at it for over a month.

And out of nowhere came this unknown man, carrying what looked like shopping bags, and messed up the composition of the frame. Perched on the sixth floor of the hotel balcony, which gave him a vantage point of the square, the sudden appearance of the man angered the photographer.

Who was this man? From the balcony, the photographer saw the man stand directly in front of the lead tank, even as the tank stopped and tried to go around him.

The man mimicked the tank and moved with it, blocking its path again.

Anger turned to amazement as the photographer watched the man get up on the tank and attempt to talk to whoever was inside.

'I was about a half mile away from the row of tanks and so I could not really hear much,' the photographer would say later.

The unknown man was finally pulled away by onlookers, not before the photographer had taken his picture. No one got to know who he was and whether he lived to tell his story. But he became a symbol, a symbol of the ordinary man standing up to power.

Jeff Widener, photographer with the Associated Press, would immortalize the unknown man as the 'Tank Man' who challenged the might of the Chinese state in Beijing's Tiananmen Square.

The day was 5 June 1989.[1]

Thirty-five years after the 'Tank Man' in Tiananmen Square, China, Abu Sayed rose against authority in Rangpur, Bangladesh.

On 16 July 2024, Abu Sayed was among the angry protesters who took on the police in front of Rangpur's Begum Rokeya University.

Unlike the 'Tank Man', the world would get to know who Abu Sayed was. He was young. He was a student at Begum Rokeya University. He had participated in the SAD movement that went from demanding an end to quotas after the Supreme Court of Bangladesh reinstated a 30 per cent quota for descendants of freedom fighters, to a clarion call for the dismissal of the Sheikh Hasina government.

Abu Sayed dared the state, arms outstretched.

On 16 July 2024, like the 'Tank Man', Abu Sayed stood ahead of other protesters, directly in the line of fire of the policeman in front of him. Videos of what happened next, captured by multiple media outlets, would show police officers firing rubber bullets at him, injuring the twenty-five-year-old student.

Abu Sayed fell to the ground. Fellow protesters rushed him to the Rangpur Medical College Hospital. Doctors on duty declared him dead on arrival.

The youngest of nine children and the only one to pursue higher education, Abu Sayed aspired to become a civil servant and uplift his family. His brother, Ramjan, said the family had lost its 'only hope'. Ill and bedridden, his father, Makbul Hossain, could not afford treatment. The family had sacrificed everything for Sayed's higher education, with the hope that he would bring them prosperity.[2]

'We could not save his life. Blood was pouring from his nose. The clashes between us and the police caused a delay in getting him to the hospital,' Anjan Roy, his friend, would tell the press later.[3]

Yet, Abu Sayed would become immortal. A photograph of him, arms outstretched, daring the police to shoot him, would fire the students' movement against Hasina's hard power, and cross borders to find resonance among students, artistes and celebrities.

In Calcutta, actors Swastika Mukherjee and Anindya Chatterjee, singer Sahana Bajpaie, music composer and director Indraadip Das Gupta would publicly cry out for Abu Sayed and voice support for the protesters in Bangladesh.

In an emotional post on social media, Indraadip Das Gupta wrote: 'Life will remember you, brother. With power comes responsibility, a truth often forgotten and overridden today. Shame on you, Governance. In absolute solidarity with the Bangladeshi student community.' Mourning Abu Sayed, Swastika Mukherjee wrote a poem: 'The field becomes heavy as mist descends/ The route march fades towards the horizon/ Is that a Krishnachura fallen by the roadside/ I bend down, pick it up in my hands/ Your severed head, Timir.'

Sahana Bajpaie shared a status from Calcutta journalist Arka Bhaduri's Facebook wall with the hashtag '#InSolidaritywithBangladesh'. 'Just before his death, Abu Sayed wrote on social media about his idol, Rajshahi University teacher and martyred Professor Shamsuzzoha, who was killed in police firing in 1969 during a student protest. In the mass uprising that took place that year, he sacrificed his life trying to protect students from the bullets of Pakistani soldiers.'[4]

No one scrolled down to see who else were Abu Sayed's idols.

Neither did we.

A month after Abu Sayed's death, we were invited to a closed-door meet at one of Delhi's top think-tanks to discuss the events unfolding in Bangladesh. The Hasina government had fallen by then, and so had her father Sheikh Mujib's statues, pulled down by violent mobs that went around smashing and burning anything that reminded them of the Awami League and what it stood for.

Inside the large lecture room at the think-tank, we were sworn to the Chatham House Rule that read: 'When a meeting, or part thereof, is held under the Chatham House Rule, participants are free to use the information received, but neither the identity nor the affiliation of the speaker(s), nor that of any other participant, may be revealed.'

Also present at the meet were two former Indian ambassadors to Bangladesh, two retired lieutenant generals of the Indian army, some leading strategic affairs commentators and a top intelligence official, now retired, who said India should be worried about the growing cult of Abu Sayed. And not get swayed by Abu Sayed's admiration of martyred Professor Mohammad Shamsuzzoha and be deceived into believing that the young Abu Sayed stood for the ideals of the 1971 War of Independence.

'Abu Sayed's Facebook posts showed a deep sense of mission. He drew strength from Islamic history, jihad and martyrdom. He was a fan of Jamaat-e-Islami's preacher-leader Moulana Delwar Hossain Sayeedi, a convicted war criminal in 1971. Do you guys know that in 2013, the International Crimes Tribunal in Bangladesh found Sayeedi guilty on eight out of twenty counts, which included murder, rape and religious persecution?' the retired official told the roomful of us; we were shocked by what he had just revealed.

But why was he keeping a tab on Abu Sayed's Facebook account? 'The intelligence community in India was keeping tabs on all the leaders of this so-called students' revolt against Hasina. Abu Sayed suddenly became this Che Guevara figure. We had to dig deeper about him. He was part of Bangladesh Islami Chhatrashibir, the de facto male student wing of Bangladesh Jamaat-e-Islami. And Sayed was not the only one. The movement was backed by the Jamaat from the start. Or should I say the agitation against quota was just an excuse to overthrow Hasina and hand the country back to her radical detractors,' he said.

'Hasina had been warned about this,' he added.

To the litany of questions we directed at him next, he shook his head to say 'no comments'.

But he was right.

Hasina knew about the danger lurking in the shadows of the posh Gulshan neighbourhood of Dhaka.

She knew much before the rise and fall of Abu Sayed.

Banned Film, Buried Truths

'You know snow isn't a problem in most Islamic countries. But, ISIS.'

Faraaz Hossain cracks this joke in the film *Faraaz*, which you can watch on Netflix if you are in India, but not if you are in Bangladesh. The Bangladesh High Court had banned it on 20 February 2023.

The order directed the Bangladesh Telecommunication Regulatory Authority to prohibit the streaming of *Faraaz* on domestic online platforms. This was because the film is much more than a silly joke. It is based on real people and real events. Events that point to truths so terrifying that perhaps Bangladesh, under Sheikh Hasina's rule, did not want to revisit them.

But what Hasina did not know then was that turning her face away from those truths would have terrible consequences for Bangladesh as well as India, a country it shares its 4,096-kilometre-long international border with, the fifth-longest land border in the world.

So, what was *Faraaz* about?

On the night of 1 July 2016, at around 9.20 p.m. Bangladesh time, five militants took hostages and opened fire on the Holey Artisan Bakery in Dhaka's Gulshan area. The militants entered the bakery with crude bombs, machetes and pistols, and took several dozen people hostage, foreigners and locals. In the immediate response, while Dhaka Metropolitan Police tried to regain control of the bakery, two police officers were shot dead by the assailants. Twenty-nine people were killed, including twenty hostages (seventeen foreigners and three locals), two police officers, five gunmen and two bakery staff members. The Islamic State of Iraq and the Levant claimed responsibility for the incident and released photographs of the gunmen, but Bangladesh's Home Minister Asaduzzaman Khan said the perpetrators belonged to the Jamaat-ul-Mujahideen.[5]

What shook the world was not just the daring nature of the attack in this upscale residential neighbourhood of Bangladesh's capital city that houses embassies and the who's who of the country, but the identity of the attackers.

All five were in their late teens or early twenties, and had been to the best private schools and universities in Bangladesh and abroad. They were Nibras Islam, Rohan Imtiaz, Meer Saameh Mubasheer, Khairul Islam and Shafiqul Islam. Nibras Islam was known as 'fun-loving, in and out of love, and had attended Monash University in Malaysia and returned because he didn't like it in Monash'. Nibras's father was a businessman with two houses in Dhaka, and one of his uncles was a deputy secretary to the Bangladesh government.[6]

In the first week of January 2024, we were in Dhaka to cover the national elections that were to bring Hasina back to power for a historic fourth straight term in office. At the residence of an Awami League MP who had invited us and some local journalists for dinner, we met an investigative journalist from one of Bangladesh's most prestigious newspapers. Little did we know that a few months' later, both the MP and the journalist would have to flee to India after the fall of the Hasina regime!

But that evening, the senior journalist, who had covered the Gulshan attack for his paper, told us: 'Bangladesh has had a history of violence. As a journalist I have been on the internal security beat for a long time and covering incidents of terror attacks had hardened me as a person. But the Gulshan attack crushed me and most of those like me who have kept the flame of a secular Bangladesh burning in our hearts. If the minds of Anglicized boys from affluent families, who have been sent to posh, private schools, and who lead privileged lives, could be hacked by terror groups operating from outside the country, what hope does Bangladesh have.'

The film *Faraaz* is about the events of 1 July 2016. The titular character is based on a real person who went into Holey Artisan Bakery that evening and didn't come out alive.

One of the terrorists was twenty-one-year-old Rohan Imtiaz, whose father, Imtiaz Khan Babul, was an Awami League politician. 'I never saw him reading or accessing any jihadi material. We have a common computer,' Babul would later say in an interview to CNN.⁷

'But he had a mobile. I don't know whether he was reading jihadi material through that. Someone must have planted these thoughts in his head.'

While the five terrorists were put down by Bangladesh's elite commandos, the response of the Hasina government in general to the mushrooming of terror was often called into question, before and after the Holey Artisan Bakery attack.

And it was not limited to banning a film.

'The lack of a clear state policy when it comes to secularism has helped accelerate the rise of fundamentalism, extremism, and anti-West sentiments in Bangladesh,' Shafi Md Mostofa, assistant professor of World Religions and Culture at Dhaka University's Faculty of Arts, wrote in for the Diplomat on 8 September 2020.⁸

Mostofa believed to what extent Bangladeshis were 'secular' to begin with was a matter of considerable debate, although by secularism in Bangladesh one means pluralism of religious faiths as opposed to the more expansive definitions of the term.

He wrote that though Bangladesh declared itself a secular state with its birth in 1971, and that secularism was chosen as one of the four pillars that were to guide official policy, Bangladesh's polity could not come to a well-defined position as to what kind of state it would be. Under Bangabandhu Sheikh Mujibur Rahman, he said, secularism faced an initial setback when the Education Commission of 1973 found that the majority of the country's citizens were in favour of religious education. 'From 1975 onward, after Bangabandhu's term in office, Bangladesh has yet to fully settle on the principles that would govern it. This has led subsequent regimes to play around with political Islam as well as secularism,' Mostofa wrote in the *Diplomat*.

Mostafa pointed out that the original constitution was changed in 1978 with the instalment of the phrase 'absolute trust and faith in the Almighty Allah' by the Ziaur Rahman government in order to replace secularism as a state principle. Rahman's government also built fraternal relationships with countries in the Middle East. The military dictator who followed Reahman, Hussain Muhammad Ershad, went one step further to declare Islam as the state religion in 1988. These military regimes, according to Mostafa, resorted to religion to legitimise their power, which they had usurped unconstitutionally. The subsequent democratic regimes since 1991 also followed the path of expedient politics and opportunism. These regimes also failed to ensure basic human rights, political stability and economic sustainability, and establish transparent institutions. Rather, corruption in Bangladesh grew, the country fell behind on the Human Development Index and cronyism became rampant.

The Bangladesh Awami League, once again came to the power in January 2009 with the promise to restore the 1972 Constitution. Mostafa believes they partially did so through the 15th Amendment to the Constitution in 2013 but they kept Islam as the state religion. There are questions around why this was the case, and what stopped the government, still in power, from restoring the provisions of the 1972 Constitution. Moreover, he pointed out, the Hasina government acknowledged the 'Qawmi Dawrah' degree (an Islamic religious qualification) to be equivalent to the Master's degree, enacted the Digital Security Act in 2018 to prosecute those deemed to be hurting religious sentiments, started building 560 'model mosques,' and corrected textbooks to fulfil demands of the 'Hefazat,' a coalition of several Islamist parties.

Alongside, there had been a constant pressure on successive governments to regularize Urdu, the same language that was rejected for Bangla when East Pakistan became Bangladesh. The process began with the constitutional amendment in 1975 that replaced the phrase 'Bengali nationalism' with 'Bangladeshi nationalism'. The number of madrasas kept going up as the decades passed. Research shows that between 1950 and 2008, the number of madrasas increased from 4,430 to 54,130. Between 1991 and 2000, 15,000 new madrasas sprang up across the country. This includes both Qawmi and Aliya madrasas. The Qawmi madrasas increased thirteen times and Aliya eleven times in the sixty-year span.[9]

The Hasina government controlled the Aliya madrasas with funding, prescribing syllabi and management. Hence, the process of modernization was in the hands of the government. The Qawmi madrasas were not regulated by the government. They adopted their own syllabus that followed a predominantly religious content emphasizing Arabic, Persian and Urdu language studies. These madrasas were financed by various sources such as religious and individual donations, expatriate Bangladeshis' contributions, especially from Middle Eastern countries, and frequent donations from charity-based Islamic organizations.

Off the record, Dhaka journalists told us that Aliya madrasas in Bangladesh tended to have political associations with the Bangladesh Jamaat-e-Islami. However, there was another interesting finding that revealed that students and teachers at Qawmi madrasas were also affiliated with political parties, both Islamist and otherwise.

On 18 August 2005, a report of a bomb explosion was published in the *Daily Star*. Interestingly, the report has now been taken down from their website. A source in the Dhaka Press Club office told us many old news stories are being forced to be taken down from news websites unders pressure from the current Yunus administration.

It read: 'In an unprecedented scale of terror attacks, a banned Islamist militant group yesterday simultaneously blasted at least 459 time-bombs in 63 of 64 districts across the country.'

Bangladeshi madrasas in particular drew global attention with the blasts. This series of suicide attacks even killed local judges and lawyers.

In Dhaka to cover the 2024 elections, we also met Nitai Roy Chowdhury, who was then and still remains the vice chairman of the central committee of the BNP, and a former state minister of the Ministry of Education, Ministry of Youth and Sports and Ministry of Law, Justice and Parliamentary Affairs. Roy Chowdhury is also among the few Hindus who were associated with the BNP and now the Awami League. Our interview with Roy Chowdhury went thus:

The Awami League says Sheikh Hasina is the only hope for Hindus in Bangladesh. As a top leader of the BNP, what do you have to say?
Nitai Roy Chowdhury: I can give you many examples to show that most of the anti-Hindu policies have been taken during the Awami League rule. The Enemy Property Act was renamed the Vested Property Act in 2013, but the intention remained the same. It is inherently anti-Hindu in nature. Across Bangladesh, Awami League leaders have misused this act and seized Hindu property. This is one example. There are many.

Roy Chowdhury went on to say that 'a political discourse has been created in Bangladesh to show Hasina as a secular leader. She is not. Do you have any idea that the list of liberation war heroes in Bangladesh is filled with people who never participated in it? Hasina must be aware of the fact that there are leaders and family members in the Awami League who played an active role in the Shanti Bahini (which fought the war in favour of West Pakistan during 1970–71). Doesn't she know her party shelters former Razakars as well? She surely does'.

But what about your own party, the BNP? Would you admit it is a communal party?
Nitai Roy Chowdhury: I will tell you this. The BNP is not a communal party and the Awami League is not a secular party!

Well, that is wordplay. The BNP has joined hands with the Jamaat. How can Hindus possibly trust them?
Nitai Roy Chowdhury: As a senior party member, I would say this was a party decision. My own view is it was not a good decision. Going with Jamaat did not go down well with Hindus and many open-minded people.

If you had fought the coming elections, which you didn't (the BNP boycotted the 2024 polls), would the BNP have upheld secular values?
Nitai Roy Chowdhury: We would have. We had released a twenty-seven-point memorandum. One of the most important points is *'Dharma jar jar, rastro sobar'* (Religion belongs to individuals, state belongs to everyone).

What Nitai did not tell us that day was the Awami League government's flirtations with the Hefazat-e-Islam. The Hefazat-e-Islam was set up by cleric Shah Ahmad Shafi in 2010. In 2009, when the Sheikh Hasina government came up with reforms including inheritance rights for women, Shafi protested against those reforms. The law was watered down as a result.

'In 2013, when bloggers and atheists gathered in Shahbagh Square pressing for equal rights for all genders, a secular Constitution and system of governance, they clashed with members of the Hefazat who marched their own protesters into Dhaka. This led to clashes between Sheikh Hasina's Awami League and Hefazat and over fifty people were killed,' *ThePrint* wrote on 31 March 2021.

As per *ThePrint* article, 'At the time, the Hefazat's thirteen-point charter included demands like reinstating faith in the Almighty in the Constitution. While Bangladesh was committed to secular principles in its Constitution after its independence, in 1972 the words "Bismillah-Ar-Rahman-Ar-Rahim" were inserted in the Preamble by then President Zia ur Rahman. This was subsequently removed along with another small subsection that had been added to the Constitution by General Ershad when he was president in the 1980s, in the form of the Eighth Amendment, which said Islam will be the religion of the state.'

The Hefazat did not stop at that. It also demanded that 'restrictions should be lifted on mosques and cultural programmes, capital punishment for blasphemy, etc. It wanted statues and busts removed from Bangladesh as statues promoted idolatry – except inside Hindu temples'.

'Sheikh Hasina pandered to the Hefazat and supported their cause to remove a Greek goddess statue in Dhaka,' *ThePrint* reported.

'Hasina's government also supported the Hefazat when they opposed the removal of the Eighth Amendment from the Constitution. This case was in the court and the Hefazat-e-Islam led a movement against it and it does look like Sheikh Hasina government bent over backwards to accommodate it and the court then dismissed the case on a technicality,' the article said.

'In 2017, Hefazat also wanted Bangladesh to launch a jihad on Myanmar to liberate Rohingyas from Rakhine. While Shah Ahmad Shafi was not anti-Indian, he was a conservative Islamist. His son Anas Shafi is believed to be friendly with the Sheikh Hasina government. The Sheikh Hasina government also indulges him, which might be something that she is paying for now because in the process what has happened is that a new Jamaat-e-Islami has come up.'

The article went on to say that it was this new conservative force, which the Sheikh Hasina government had flirted with in the past, which had become her government's Frankenstein.

'The Hefazat-e-Islam, the force behind the current protest, are the new Islamist conservative force in Bangladesh with which Sheikh Hasina's government has flirted with at some point … But it's a mistake that all democratic governments make in trying to control one set of extremists. They often play with the other set that looks less worse (but) in the course of time, they all become Frankensteins,' *ThePrint* said.[10]

On 18 November 2022, Indian Home Minister Amit Shah and his Bangladesh counterpart Asaduzzaman Khan had met in Delhi for the third 'No Money for Terror' ministerial conference on counter-terrorism financing.

We met Asaduzzaman Khan the same evening for a quick interview at the Taj Palace Hotel, where he was staying with his entourage, and asked him how the Sheikh Hasina government wanted to address the fear that Bangladesh Jamaat-e-Islami is going from strength to strength. That surely was bad news not just for Hindus in Bangladesh, who are often the target of Jamaat, but also for the ruling Awami League which publicly stood for secular and democratic values.

'Jamaat Shibir [Jamaat camp] is opposed to the very independence of Bangladesh. They gave birth to the Razakars and the Albadr Bahini [a paramilitary force composed mainly of Bihari Muslims which operated in East Pakistan during the Bangladesh Liberation War, under the patronage of the Pakistani government]. It is they who targeted and killed the intellectuals of Bangladesh. At present they are banned from participating in the politics of Bangladesh and trust me their number is getting smaller by the day,' Asaduzzaman Khan had told us.

'We have curbed extremism in Bangladesh considerably. The Awami League is committed to a democratic and secular Bangladesh,' he had added.

There is no way of knowing how Asaduzzaman Khan would have answered us if he could have gazed into a crystal ball that evening and seen that less than two years later, his leader Sheikh Hasina and a big chunk of the Awami League ministers, leaders and workers, including himself, would have to flee Bangladesh. Would he as home minister have tackled the problem of radicalism better?

Could he have?

The New Razakars

Let us return to that evening at the Awami League MP's house in Dhaka, in the first week of January 2024, where we met the investigative journalist who had been covering terror in his country. He had told us that if it ever came to such a pass that Jamaat became powerful in Bangladesh, he would have nowhere to hide.

His worst nightmare came true after Hasina's fall, as Jamaat flexed its radical muscles across Bangladesh.

We met him again, this time at the legendary Flurys tearoom in Kolkata's Park Street, a week after the Bangladesh Jamaat-e-Islami leaders held a meeting with top Qawmi scholars of the country, where participants voiced enthusiasm about establishing a country based on Islamic rules under the leadership of Jamaat chief Dr Shafiqur Rahman.

In a report headlined 'Qawmi Scholars Endorse Islamic State under Jamaat Leadership', Bangladeshi news portal *Dhaka Tribune* wrote on 21 August 2024: 'At the meeting, Jamaat Ameer Dr Shafiqur said: 'From now on, we are all for each other. We will all be united like a wall made of lead. I apologize to you if I have hurt you in the past. I hope you will forgive us.'

The meeting was a coming together of radical Islamist forces in Bangladesh and hailing Jamaat as the Big Brother.

In its report, *Dhaka Tribune* quoted Maulana Moniruzzaman Qasemi of Jamia Madania as saying: 'We are talking about unity. But we were already united. We drifted apart for some time. We were all oppressed. Now we all have to work together again. The largest Islamic party in Bangladesh is Bangladesh Jamaat-e-Islami. I have met the Jamaat Ameer many times. He is very humble. Therefore, I believe he is the one who can make us all stand on one platform.'

The scariest statement in the meeting came from Mufti Azharul Islam, a top leader of the Hefazat. 'We all have been able to unite at the call of Bangladesh Jamaat-e-Islami; for that, we are thanking God. According to my knowledge, the Jamaat-e-Islami amir fasts every Monday and Thursday. Although it is not right to praise anyone directly, I still want to share this. In my opinion, it will be possible to form an Islamic state through him.'[11]

Sharing a pot of first flush Darjeeling tea and a plateful of Flurys' famous pastries, strawberry cubes and rum balls, the investigative journalist told us that while an Islamic State might still be some years away, radicalism had entered the bloodstream of Bangladeshi society.

'And the Muhamad Yunus administration is doing nothing to arrest this trend,' he said.

There was no way to refute his allegation.

The Yunus government was sworn in on 7 August 2024. Mufti Jashimuddin Rahmani, chief of the dreaded Ansarullah Bangla Team, an Al-Qaeda-inspired militant outfit now known as Ansar al Islam, was released from the Kashimpur High Security Central Jail in Gazipur on 26 August 2024. A Dhaka court sentenced him to five years in prison in the murder case. In addition, he faced a total of four cases, including those under anti-terrorism and information and communication technology laws.[12]

This was not an exception. A few months later, on 28 May 2025, former acting secretary general of Jamaat-e-Islami Bangladesh A.T.K. Azharul Islam was acquitted by the appellate division of the Bangladesh Supreme Court, overturning the death sentence handed down by the International Crimes Tribunal for war crimes. On 30 December 2014, the International Crimes Tribunal had sentenced A.T.K. Azharul Islam to death for three charges and imprisonment for three other charges. The charges involved collaborating with the Pakistani army for the abduction, confinement, torture, murder and rape of fellow citizens during Bangladesh's liberation war in 1971.

One of the charges covered his actions between March and December 1971, when victims were abducted and confined in Rangpur Town Hall, used as a 'rape camp' where victim 'MK' was repeatedly raped and tortured.

Out of jail, A.T.K. Azharul Islam thanked the students, saying they made his freedom possible through toppling the Awami League regime on 5 August 2024. 'It was the students who took to the streets and shed their blood, mobilising the people against all the oppression and tyranny of the 15-year fascist government. Through the movement they built on the streets, the fortress was demolished and Bangladesh gained independence anew.'[13]

'There is no stopping the radicals now,' the investigative journalist had told us at Flurys. 'You know the one big radical influence among

Bangladesh's youth apart from the Jamaat? It is the emergence of Zakir Naik and his videos. In sharp suits and crisp English, Naik told the Bangladeshi youth it is possible to look modern while being radical,' he said.

In Bangladesh, he said, Naik's sermons found new life – translated into Bengali, shared in tea shop *adda* sessions, broadcast across Facebook feeds. When Digital Bangladesh emerged, in came the idea of Digital Jihad, powered by Digital Razakars.

'Young men, modern in appearance, armed with hashtags and Naik's rhetoric, began to claim this identity. They wore torn jeans and flaunted smartphones, but spoke of Islamist supremacy and dreamt of Islamic State. The Razakar of 1971 wore a uniform – skullcaps and short pyjamas, now, it's a smile and a device,' the journalist said. 'How do you recognize then who is the next Abu Sayed? Or the attackers of yet another Holey Artisan Bakery?'

We posed the investigative journalist's question to Iranian activist-writer Anita Kamali, who researches the rise of Islamic radicalism in South Asia. Kamali now stays and works from Auroville in Pondicherry. Over a WhatsApp video call, Kamali told us the real threat to democracies like Bangladesh comes from theocracy or a religious understanding of the world. 'It took centuries to move from divine will to human progress, from fear of afterlife to fear of death. The tragedy is that with the rise of Islamic radicalism, we are now reversing to divine will and fear of death,' Kamali told us.

Yes, Bangladesh's Digital Razakars fear the afterlife, Bangladeshi independent film-maker and writer F.M. Shahin told us over the phone. Shahin is one of the few public figures in Bangladesh today to say what he feels about the rise of radicalism in society.

'You know what else they fear and despise? The ideals of the 1971 War of Independence, Sheikh Mujibur Rahman, and India, in no particular order,' Shahin told us. 'The Digital Razakars are everywhere. In college campuses, in coffee shops, freshly recruited in private and government jobs, in media and NGOs. There is no escaping them. They come out to bring down the house of Mujib or gather to call for the ban on the Awami League and then they go back to their daily lives, to their social media feeds and their WhatsApp groups to talk about Islamist supremacy. It's a scary new world.'

The Keen Fundamentalist

When a Dhaka-based journalist friend gave us the contact of Shoriful Islam, we did not know how far the conversation would go. Shoriful Islam, forty, is a Bangladeshi garments exporter who told us at the very outset that he was not interested in the politics of self-aggrandizement. Over the video call, the bespectacled Islam sounded agreeable, friendly even. Islam told us that the last fifteen years of Sheikh Hasina's rule had forced many like him to live in fear, to never express their minds without fear of reprisal.

'I had to constantly change my address. I was a member of the BNP and vocal about my disregard for Hasina and everything she stood for. Way back in 2001, when the BNP came to power, I had to accept the post of joint secretary of the student's union of the party. But during the Hasina years, I saw the BNP for what it was, a party of opportunists where senior leaders do not care for the cadre,' Islam said.

For Islam, it is the strength of the cadre that determines what a party or organization is about. 'Look at Abu Sayed. He bravely faced bullets, gave his life for the July Revolution. That is what the Bangladesh Islami Chhatrashibir teaches you,' Islam said, a smile on his face now.

So Abu Sayed was with the Bangladesh Islami Chhatrashibir (The retired intelligence officer at the Delhi think-tank had said so)? 'Yes, he was,' Shoriful Islam confirmed. 'Abu Sayed was a "Sathi (Partner)",' he said.

What is a 'Sathi'? 'There are four stages at the Bangladesh Islami Chhatrashibir. 'Somorthok' (or Supporter), 'Kormi' (Worker), 'Sathi'

(Partner) and finally 'Sadashya' (Member). Abu Sayed was a Sathi,' Islam said.

And how does he know this? 'Chhatrashibir leaders have already confirmed this,' Islam said and shared a video clip with us of Shibir leader Jahidul Islam saying on camera that Abu Sayed was one of them.

The day the Hasina government fell, on 5 August 2024, Shoriful Islam joined the Jamaat-e-Islami. 'I have been a fan of the organisation for a long time. Their discipline, their dedication and their sincerity of purpose are mine too now,' Islam said. 'The July Revolution was in essence a revolution led by the Jamaat-e-Islami and the Bangladesh Islami Chhatrashibir. We controlled the media, and we controlled the narrative. Few could figure out that it was Chhatrashibir that was behind the July Revolution.'

With a chuckle, Shoriful Islam told us the story of the young Sadik Qaiyum. A debate champ in Dhaka University, Qaiyum was officially a member of the Bangladesh Chhatra League, the student wing of the Awami League. In a crisp shirt and a tie, with the easy confidence of a natural debater, Qaiyum would argue for democracy and hardly ever talk about religion. Till the Awami League government fell and he came out as a senior functionary of the Chhatrashibir who had infiltrated the ranks of the BCL.

'For fifteen years we were pushed back by Hasina. We had to join other political organizations, students' unions, hide who we are. Now, she has fallen and we have come out in the open. We will write Bangladesh's future. Inshallah.'

5

Mujib: The Man, the Myth

In 1971, Khaleque Biswas fought for the freedom of Bangladesh not from the trenches with a rifle, but as a staff writer for the *Freedom Fighter*, a weekly newspaper published from the old part of Dhaka. The paper closely followed the exploits of the Muktibahini, the guerilla force that had picked up arms against the West Pakistani army and was fighting a pitched battle for freedom. In the absence of the great Sheikh Mujibur Rahman, who was jailed in Pakistan for treason, the paper was one of the most important nationalist voices.

Lutfuzzaman Babul, the paper's editor and publisher, kept his small but dedicated team motivated by reminding them that the paper was not only being read in Dhaka but was also being smuggled to Muktibahini guerilla training camps in neighbouring India, where Bangladeshi volunteers were becoming armed freedom fighters. Everyone in that small office believed him. As they did in the impending freedom of Bangladesh, a nation where citizens would rise over religiosity and unite over their common Bengali language and culture.

As Bangladesh moved towards a bloody victory, *Freedom Fighter* grew from strength to strength, and on 16 December 1971, at the end of a nine-month war, a victory issue was published, with a picture of a smiling Sheikh Mujib and an article that praised him to the skies. To Biswas and others like him, Mujib was more popular than the Prophet himself, having won the support of people of all faiths. For their service to the cause of the freedom struggle, Mujib penned down a special note for the readers of *Freedom Fighter*.

Mujib got busy with building his new nation, and Khaleque Biswas travelled across the length and breadth of the country to report the ravages of war and the struggles of survivors. His excursions took him to Gangasagar to dig into the life of martyr Mostafa Kamal, who had saved his fellow fighters in the Muktibahini at the cost of his own life. In Gangasagar, Biswas met a man called Raihan Talukdar, whose house he stayed in as he researched the life and times of Kamal. Back in Dhaka, Biswas wrote about Mostafa Kamal's great sacrifice, posted a copy of the printed article to Raihan Talukdar with a thank-you note for his hospitality and went on more tours for new stories. Till a young man landed at his door with a letter from Raihan Talukdar, requesting Biswas to find a suitable job for this young man from his village. Remembering Raihan Talukdar's hospitality in Gangasagar, Biswas gave the young man, Nur Hussain, a place in the storeroom of his apartment.

In the days to come, Biswas would get to know that Nur Hussain had practically no skills to enter the job market, was a school dropout and had not even learnt to do manual jobs like welding, plumbing or digging. All he would do was sleep all day, and eat whatever was offered to him without complaint. When Biswas could find no job for Nur Hussain, he decided to keep him as his caretaker. Meanwhile, his own job came under strain.

Looking around him, Biswas saw Dhaka flooded by a sea of humanity descending from across the country. He saw poverty, hunger, looting and brutality. When he could take it no more, he went to his editor Lutfuzzaman Babul and said he wanted to write something different, a report that would demand accountability from the powers that be, including Sheikh Mujib, in failing to ensure food for everyone. Within a week, Khaleque Biswas was sacked and he became jobless like Nur Hussain. Attempts to get a job at other media houses proved futile, and Biswas worried if he would be able to keep the apartment with his savings dwindling fast.

One evening, after a stroll around the neighbourhood, Nur Hussain suddenly started reciting from Sheikh Mujib's historic 7 March 1971 speech, where the great leader had laid the seed for Bangladesh's independence and motivated Bangladeshis from all walks of life. It was a speech that Khaleque Biswas had been listening to on his cassette player regularly in the last few days.

Khaleque Biswas got irritated at first, then he noticed Hussain was speaking passionately and a crowd had started to gather around him. As he ended his speech with 'Joy Bangla', the crowd shouted back 'Joy Bangla' (a slogan meaning 'Victory to Bengal' that symbolized Bengali nationalism during the Bangladesh liberation war and is the official slogan of the Awami League). The people who had gathered, mostly those at the margins of society, started throwing whatever money they had at Nur Hussain.

The next morning, Khaleque Biswas noticed something: Nur Hussain had a certain resemblance to Sheikh Mujib. As he played Sheikh Mujib's speech again on the tape recorder, he found that even their voices were similar. Nur Hussain, Khaleque Biswas noticed, was a copy of Sheikh Mujib, something he had failed to see in the months that the two had stayed together in the same apartment.

Khaleque Biswas helped Nur Hussain memorize Mujib's full speech, took him to the barber for a haircut like Mujib's and got him a sleeveless black coat – which had become famous as the Mujib coat – and white *panjabi*, stitched. These, along with the Mujib moustache and a nine-inch, handcrafted walnut-wood tobacco pipe exactly like the one the great leader smoked, completed the transformation of Nur Hussain into Sheikh Mujib.

They made a winning team. Biswas became the de facto manager and decided on everything, from the choice of venue where Nur Hussain would speak, to what he would eat at home, while Nur Hussain perfected and delivered Mujib speeches and thralled crowds wherever they went.

Soon, they were contacted by Moina Mia, a senior leader of Sheikh Mujib's party, and offered big money to impersonate Mujib and give his speeches at venues chosen by the party. As Khaleque Biswas and Nur Hussain went from collecting coins thrown by cheering crowds to being on the payroll of the party in power, Bangladesh entered an abyss. The journalist in Khaleque Biswas could not help but notice the inadequacy of the government's developmental schemes, the mismanagement, the corruption all round by Sheikh Mujib's party leaders who wore the Mujib coat, hung his picture from office walls and looted in his name.

Public anger spilled over as angry graffiti on walls and the defacing of Mujib's face on currency notes with slogans like 'Death to the Dictator' written on them. Some notes had lines scribbled on them saying, 'Believing in freedom was not a crime; believing in Mujib was.' The government responded by declaring such notes invalid and threatening to arrest anyone in possession of them. The worst was yet to come.

By May 1974, the famine could no longer be hidden. Hundreds of unfed masses took refuge in school buildings, built tents in fields or any open spaces they could find, and dug holes in the ground to make ovens to cook and separate holes for toilets. Khaleque Biswas and Nur Hussain befriended one of them, the sixty-year-old singer Shah Abdul Karim who would sing songs of the terrible times that had come upon the country.

Biswas and Hussain invited Karim to stay with them, in the comfort of their apartment, away from the dust and grime of the neighbourhood school where he had taken shelter with other hapless villagers. The three weeks that Karim spent in their apartment had a big impact on Nur Hussain, who till now had blindly followed the path that Biswas had laid out for him. Gradually, Biswas saw a change in Hussain's behaviour as the latter started going out on his own, something he had not done before.

Even as Bangladesh suffered from terrible hunger pangs brought in by the famine, Moina Mia arranged a meeting of the duo with Sheikh Mujib himself. Mujib addressed Hussain as his brother, made him sit beside him and spoke to him about his life. Biswas was overwhelmed by Mujib's simplicity, while Nur Hussain answered his queries with broken sentences while cracking his knuckles. Hussain's callous behaviour before the prime minister frustrated Biswas. But the shockers were yet to come.

The Mujib coat vanished first, and then the shoes. Nur Hussain started giving away his belongings to the needy on the sly. Biswas tried hard to ignore it at first and decided to buy new clothes for Hussain's performance as Mujib. And then one day, Hussain walked out in rags like many of the villagers who had camped in the city and begged for a few morsels of food. Then came the disaster at Shaheed Minar where Hussain had delivered his first speech. Without informing Biswas, Hussain stood at the same venue and addressed the crowd as Nur Hussain and not as Sheikh Mujib for the first time in his life. He said that the words of Mujib that he had spoken before were devoid of hope, and that the prime minister had become a monster and was coming for them all.

As Bangladesh descended into madness, with the famine killing people like flies, Khaleque Biswas tried to reason with Nur Hussain one last time, but the latter was too far gone. Biswas assured Moina Mia that he could still salvage the situation. Biswas was aware of the power that the Awami League held over people through the likes of Moina Mia and their monopoly over violence. He knew he had to stop Nur Hussain from speaking out against Sheikh Mujib for the sake of their survival.

When nothing else worked, Biswas first imprisoned Hussain and then, in a fit of madness, killed him with a shovel after Hussain tauntingly called him 'little Sheikh Mujib'. To Biswas, it was the worst abuse Hussain could have hurled at him, as he would never be able to wash away Mujib's sins from his conscience. After killing Nur Hussain, Khaleque Biswas realized he had effectively destroyed himself.

Khaleque Biswas and Nur Hussain were figments of author Neamat Imam's imagination in the dark and dystopian portrayal of Bangladesh under Prime Minister Sheikh Mujib in his novel

The Black Coat. It was first published in India by Penguin Books in 2013. What was not a figment of the author's imagination was the Bangladesh he portrayed during the great famine of 1974, considered one of the worst famines of the twentieth century, caused largely by government mismanagement, food grain smuggling to neighbouring countries and flooding along the Brahmaputra. Why *The Black Coat* didn't receive the kind of fanfare it should have is thanks to the long shadow of Sheikh Mujib's legacy in Bangladesh. When the book came out in 2013, Sheikh Mujib's daughter, Sheikh Hasina, was the prime minister of Bangladesh, and Mujib, the founding father of the country, was untouchable, his statues dotting the Bangladeshi landscape, his face on currency notes, his portrait in every government office.

Such a novel would not have been possible if Neamat Imam had lived in Bangladesh. The fact that he was a Bangladeshi-Canadian living in Edmonton helped. Readers of Bangladeshi literature in English might have heard of *The Black Coat* when it came out; some might have even procured the book and read it on the sly, but open praise or publicity for an anti-Mujib book in the time of Hasina was unheard of.

Most books on the 1971 War of Independence published during the Hasina era sang paeans to Mujib, most of his biographies were hagiographies, there were graphic novels published on him to make him popular among children. And, just before the 2024 national elections, India and Bangladesh even got together to make a film on Mujib, directed by the legendary Indian film-maker Shyam Benegal, no less. *Mujib: The Making of a Nation* was released in Bangladesh on 13 October 2023, and in India and overseas on 27 October 2023. We watched the film and wrote critical reviews, calling it a 'hastily made election film' to help Sheikh Hasina win the next round of polls in Bangladesh.[1]

But it is not just Mujib – all founding fathers are holy cows in the Indian subcontinent. You build monuments, write hagiographies, institute peace awards and make movies in their memory. What chance of success does a critical historical work have when there is national sentiment at play? Be it Mohandas Karamchand Gandhi in India, Muhammad Ali Jinnah in Pakistan or Sheikh Mujibur Rahman in Bangladesh, is a hard look at their greys even possible?

It is.

But it would take the fall of the Sheikh Hasina regime on 5 August 2024 and the installation of an interim government under Muhammad Yunus for *The Black Coat* to find a new lease of life within Bangladesh.

On 7 March 2025, Shafiqul Alam, press secretary to the chief advisor of Bangladesh, Muhammad Yunus, wrote on Facebook: 'One day about a decade ago Penguin publishers sent a book to my office address. It was called *The Black Coat*. Its Canadian-Bangladeshi author, Neamat Imam, was unknown to me. I read parts of the book immediately and it was simply brilliant and breathtaking. Penguin wanted me to write a review of the book in the local press. The trouble was, it was 2015 or early 2016 and the book was a fictional take on Sheikh Mujib's era. Mujib's autocrat daughter was ruling the country, and there were chances you would be disappeared or incarcerated for blasphemy for writing a review.

'*The Black Coat* got a very good review. One reviewer said this book is considered the "gold standard for any book which seeks to engage with South Asian politics or history" and a "future classic". I became a friend of Imam on Facebook but never had the opportunity to interact with him. The student revolutionaries should invite him back to Dhaka and he should be given a much-deserved reception!'[2]

While Neamat Imam should indeed be feted for penning a hauntingly dark account of the Bangladesh that was, how much of what he wrote was actually true?

Again, it would take the fall of the Hasina regime for Naomi Hossain, professor of development studies, SOAS, University of London, to write in the Bangladeshi press about the famine in which 15 lakh people, about 2 per cent of the Bangladeshi people, died.

Hossain wrote that nothing since the 1974 famine has been even remotely as disastrous for Bangladeshis. 'Watch the video footage available on YouTube. Once you have seen them, the scenes of hundreds of thousands of people waiting listlessly, starving, for help from a government that had no cash, food, authority, or international goodwill, will never leave you,' she wrote. Hossain said it was horrific, yet it happened only three years after Bangladeshis of all classes had come together in a glorious struggle for freedom from neo-colonial rule.

For many years, Hossain said, people did not talk about the famine because it was deemed acutely politically 'sensitive', and the long and 'increasingly oppressive regime' of Sheikh Hasina did not look kindly on the inglorious topic, not that there was much chance to raise it. The public academic discussions that took place fifty years after Independence passed swiftly over the years following liberation, with the famine rarely receiving the mention it is due, according to Hossain, and publishers were also reluctant to take on the subject.

For Hossain, the sensitivities were both obvious and hidden. Sheikh Mujib's Awami League government was evidently to blame for the famine, she wrote, as governments are always culpable for disasters on their watch, even if, as was the case in 1974, they had very little choice about their response.

'Nothing absolves the failure, but it is notable that the 1974 famine stands out by virtue of being governed by a regime with powerful incentives to prevent it,' Hossain wrote. She gave the example of Haile Selassie, former Emperor of Ethiopia, who famously refused UNICEF assistance for his starving country in 1973 because famine reportage was too embarrassing. Hossain also spoke of Mao's government that pushed through with its Great Leap reforms even while tens of millions of peasants starved and the imperial powers that presided over the Late Victorian Holocausts of Mike Davis's famous work, which were unabashed in their genocidal projects of hunger across the global South.

'Sheikh Mujib, by contrast, went begging for assistance at the UN. He knew the famine was the end for his legitimacy. The famine was among the factors behind the Awami League's unpopularity – that among the anger about corruption, the brutality of the Rakkhi Bahini, the arrogance of the leadership and the loss of civil liberties,' Hossain wrote. The famine, she said, may help explain the lack of public mourning when the Mujib family was so brutally murdered.

Hossain went on to write that there was no doubt that the famine of 1974 contributed to the broader discontent and disillusion with the Awami League regime, and must be factored into the political violence and military takeovers that followed. 'If your people are hungry, your days in power are numbered,' Hossain ended her piece with the prophetic line.

Sheikh Mujibur Rahman's days were indeed numbered. The first president of Bangladesh was assassinated during a military coup on 15 August 1975. Along with him, most of his family members were killed at his residence in Dhaka, the historic Dhanmondi 32.

After the fall of the Sheikh Hasina government, Mujib was assassinated once more, as his statues were pulled down and defecated upon, his house attacked and a concerted effort was made to wipe him out from public spaces.[3]

How did Bangladesh go from worshipping its founding father to wanting to snub out his memory from collective consciousness? Was it just the unchecked rise of radicalism in the country after the fall of the Sheikh Hasina government that led to such attacks on Mujib's legacy, or were there gaps in a carefully constructed myth that had held Bangladesh together as a secular, democratic country till now? Apart from the devastating famine that took place under his watch, there are grey areas that Mujib's many hagiographies carefully sidestep.

Let us turn the pages of history and try to locate Sheikh Mujibur Rahman before the birth of Bangladesh, rather from a time when even the idea of Bangladesh was not born, a time when India was still undivided and Pakistan existed only in Jinnah's ambition and angry political speeches. The year is 1946, the month is August, and the belly of the great city of Calcutta is being ripped apart by the butcher's knife. It was the time of the Great Calcutta Killings. It was a time in the history of pre-Partition Calcutta that many post-Partition Indian history writers chose to downplay.

In his book *Shattered Lands: Five Partitions and the Making of Modern Asia*, historian Sam Dalrymple writes about those times. Dalrymple wrote that as the only province in which the Muslim League had an unequivocal majority, Bengal was the most tense before Direct Action Day (Direct Action Day, also known as the 1946 Calcutta Riots, was a day of widespread violence in Calcutta, initiated by the All-India Muslim League on August 16, 1946. The League had called for a general strike and 'direct action' to demand a separate Muslim homeland, Pakistan, following the British departure from India).[4]

Its new Muslim League premier, Huseyn Suhrawardy, had been minister of civil supply during the famine, and his appointment, Dalrymple wrote, 'horrified Hindus'. In his book, Dalrymple described Suhrawardy as a large aristocrat with pursed lips, silk pyjamas and a fondness for loud jazz. He said Suhrawardy was described by acquaintances as 'totally unscrupulous, but not communal or religious. He ate ham and drank Scotch and married a Russian actress. Long before he became a politician, Suhrawardy had been known as an expert lawyer who jumped at the opportunity to represent those who needed him, but he also did little to deny alleged links with the criminal underworld.'

'True to his nickname the "king of the goondas (thugs)", Suhrawardy had written ominously in the *Statesman* that "bloodshed and disorder are not necessarily evil in themselves, if resorted to for a noble cause".' Dalrymple said Suhrawardy subsequently formed an '"almost purely Muslim ministry … with an almost purely Hindu opposition", and when he announced that Direct Action Day would be celebrated as a public holiday across Bengal, Hindus everywhere felt their worst fears becoming reality.'

And where was the future Bangabandhu Sheikh Mujibur Rahman at that time when a 'dark cloud of death and destruction hovered over Calcutta' in Dalrymple's words?

Describing Mujib as Suhrawardy's acolyte, Dalrymple wrote that he was studying liberal arts at Calcutta's Islamia University. 'Mujib would one day fight feverishly to break up Pakistan and establish the nation of Bangladesh, but at the time he fiercely devoted to the Muslim League. He spent the day before Direct Action Day attaching loudspeakers to cars to blare out the League's demands across the streets,' he wrote.

Those bloody days in Calcutta come alive in Dalrymple's prose. He wrote that the air was thick and heavy, as if a storm were about to break, and Mujib and his friend Nuruddin rode their bicycles through Calcutta's streets at 7 a.m. to raise the Muslim League flag above Islamia University. Dalrymple then quotes Mujib himself, remembering that time.

'Nobody opposed us,' Mujib had recalled. 'But we came to know later that as soon as we had left, the flag was lowered and shredded to pieces.' Mujib had planned for unpleasant confrontations, but he wasn't ready for what greeted him back at his university hostel: a group of students covered in blood, suffering from stab wounds. When he learned that they had been attacked by a Hindu mob, he resolved to accompany some other boys and confront those responsible, Dalrymple wrote.

In no uncertain words, Sam Dalrymple wrote about Mujib's role in the mindless violence of the Direct Action Day. 'Student activists like Mujib would be instrumental in the start of Direct Action Day's violence. Mujib himself writes how he came across a maulvi 'chased by a group of people armed with sticks and swords ... A few of us immediately cried out "Pakistan Zindabad"... We picked up whatever bricks or stones we could find and started to attack them.'

A few hours after the scuffle outside his university, Mujib and his friends had joined a hundred thousand other Muslims at the Ochterlony Monument (now famous as Shaheed Minar) in

Calcutta's Maidan Park to witness Premier Suhrawardy's speech. Precisely what Suhrawardy said remains highly contested: many Muslims would claim he told them to go home and celebrate Ramadan, while many Hindus would assert he subtly hinted to the crowd that they were free to enact violence as they pleased. Whatever the case, Dalrymple wrote, Calcutta was a tinderbox waiting to blow ... Within hours of Suhrawardy's speech, scenes of looting and violence were widespread across Calcutta.

And what happened to Calcutta as the violence spread?

Dalrymple wrote that most chilling of all that happened was the way that everyday people simply turned on one another. He quoted an intelligence report that said men, women and children were slaughtered by both sides indiscriminately. When Mullick Bazar was burnt, three Hindu children were thrown into the flames. In north Calcutta, the report said, 'The severed heads of Muslims impaled on spikes were paraded through the streets.'

The events following Direct Action Day would soon become known as the 'Week of the Long Knives' or the 'Great Calcutta Killings'. Four thousand people were confirmed dead, but according to Dalrymple this is considered an underestimate because of just how many bodies had been burned or stuffed in sewage pipes.

Margaret Bourke-White, arriving in Calcutta after reporting on the Holocaust, described Calcutta the city as 'a scene that looked like Buchenwald'. The killings fractured the relationship of the Congress and the Muslim League beyond the point of repair, and a few days later, when Wavell (Field Marshal Archibald Percival Wavell served as the Viceroy of India from September 1943 to February 1947 and was succeeded by Lord Mountbatten) invited Jinnah's old friend Sarojini Naidu to dinner, she spoke of Jinnah 'rather as Lucifer ... a fallen angel, one who had once promised to be a great leader of Indian freedom, but who had cast himself out of the Congress heaven'. Later, when Wavell approached Nehru and Gandhi themselves to reconcile with Jinnah or face a potential civil war, Gandhi slammed his fist on the table and cried out, 'If India wants her bloodbath, she shall have it.'

The purpose of quoting these passages on Direct Action Day from Sam Dalrymple's book is not to pin the blame of the Great Calcutta Killings solely on Sheikh Mujib. Dalrymple quotes from official records and other historians to show that both sides participated in the madness that engulfed Calcutta during those bloody August days of 1946, exactly a year before India was partitioned. The purpose is simply to show that the beacon of secularism that Mujib became during and after the creation of Bangladesh was not the Mujib from 1946. In Shyam Benegal's biopic, Mujib is shown as a failed peacemaker during the bloody days of the Great Calcutta Killings. Dalrymple has quoted from historical accounts to show otherwise.

And what do people on the 'other side' think of Mujib during 1946? In his book, Dalrymple writes, 'As with many events to follow, Direct Action Day remains mired in controversy. Indian narratives tend to blame the Muslim League for staging the riots in order to demonstrate that Hindus and Muslims could no longer live together in harmony. Meanwhile, Pakistan and Bangladesh argue that Congress-sponsored thugs descended on peacefully demonstrating Muslims to teach them a lesson.'

If Suhrawardy and Mujib were on one side of the divide, who was on the other side? Who mounted the violent attacks on Muslim gangs during the Great Calcutta Killings?

Sitting in his office in Malanga Lane, opposite Ganesh Chandra Avenue in Central Kolkata, Santanu Mukherjee, a businessman and social worker in his late forties, pointed to the greying pictures on the wall. In most of them is a man, Gopal Mukherjee, infamously known as Gopal Patha, a key figure during the Great Calcutta Killings of August 1946, but who has since then been consigned to the dustbins of history. We had met Santanu Mukherjee before, done interviews with him and heard his frustration over the deliberate invisibilization of Gopal Mukherjee, his grandfather.

'My grandfather took up arms during the Great Calcutta Killings to save Hindus from marauding Muslim rioters that were killing men, raping women and burning down Hindu properties. But he bore no ill will towards Muslims,' he told us. At the time of the Great Calcutta Killings, his grandfather ran a butcher shop, which the family still owns, and bought goats from Muslim sellers before, during and after the mayhem. 'And he stopped the violence.'

Like Sam Dalrymple, other historians are divided on what happened between 16 and 21 August 1946. 'In Calcutta, although the violence was started by the (Muslim) League, the main sufferers were the Muslims of the city. Out-numbered and out-gunned, they lost more lives and had more homes burnt than their Hindu adversaries,' historian Ramachandra Guha wrote in a 2014 article for the *Telegraph* titled 'Divided or Destroyed – Remembering Direct Action Day'.[5]

Santanu Mukherjee does not disagree with Ramachandra Guha. 'My grandfather had given a clarion call: "If they kill one Hindu, I will kill ten Muslims". He had formed the Bharater Jatiya Bahini with Bengali, Odia, Bihari and Punjabi Hindus from the neighbourhood to take on the Muslim gangs that were unleashed by Suhrawardy. But he also laid down rules of engagement. Many do not know but my grandfather did not just own a butcher shop, he was part of the Anusilan Samiti, fitness clubs that supported secret societies of armed revolutionaries against British rule in India. And the Samiti made him a man of strong moral character. He told his men that they wouldn't attack innocent Muslims, nor would they touch their women, children and elderly. Only those who came to attack with arms would be dealt with,' Santanu Mukherjee tells us.

The Malanga Lane office room is tiny – a wooden table and a few red plastic chairs share space with faded memories trapped in black-and-white photo prints hanging from the wall. One of the photographs shows Gopal Mukherjee sculpting a statue of the great Indian revolutionary leader, Netaji Subhas Chandra Bose. 'My grandfather wanted to save Calcutta's Hindus from Jinnah and his henchmen. There was a militant outfit called the Muslim National Guard, associated with the Muslim League and tasked with killing and raping Hindus. Gopal Mukherjee did not spare them,' Santanu told us.

Was Sheikh Mujib complicit in the attack on Hindus during the Great Calcutta Killings? 'Where is the lie? He was a communal man,' Mukherjee says.

'This country does not belong to Hindus. This country does not belong to Muslims. Whoever thinks this country is theirs, this country will be theirs. Whoever feels happiness seeing this country prosper, this country will be theirs. Whoever will cry seeing this country sad, this country will be theirs. This country will also belong to those who have given away everything for this country's freedom and will do so in the future.' One of Sheikh Mujib's most famous quotes had laid down his idea of 'Sonar Bangla' or Golden Bangladesh as a secular, plural country where no one is inferior to anyone because of who they pray to. What changed between the Mujib of 1946 and the Mujib during the liberation war in 1971 and after?[6]

We dialled Syed Badrul Ahsan, Bangladeshi historian, author and the current editor-in-charge of the *Asian Age*, a publication based in Dhaka. Ahsan had extensively researched Mujib's political trajectory and written a book on him titled *From Rebel to Founding Father*. 'To Bangabandhu's credit, it has to be said that while he went into politics as a firm believer in Muslim League politics, by the late 1940s, once Pakistan had become a reality, he perceived that democracy was not the priority for the ruling classes. Besides, given his conviction that communal politics could only hold back democratic and social progress, he began to evolve into a secular political being,' Ahsan told us.

'This was remarkable, for the good reason that while many of the young men who like him had been involved with the Pakistan movement remained in a communal straitjacket, Bangabandhu veered away from such beliefs. His speeches in the Pakistan constituent assembly in the 1950s are reflective of his growing belief in the power of secularism to promote democracy in Pakistan. For

Bangabandhu, secularism by the early 1960s had become a creed, a powerful instance of which was the Six Points of 1966, a programme that was clearly aimed at promoting a secular polity in not only East Bengal but also in the entirety of Pakistan,' he said.

Not everyone was convinced of the efficacy of Mujib's secularism. Just as not all East Pakistanis were convinced of the need for the creation of Bangladesh by cutting the umbilical cord with Pakistan. There were many local collaborators, commonly called Razakars, who sided with the marauding West Pakistani officers and soldiers in trying to quash the armed revolution mounted by the Muktibahini.[7]

Ali Usman Qasmi, historian at the Lahore University of Management Sciences, said the Razakars were mostly Urdu-speaking migrants who moved to East Pakistan from India during Partition and were part of an auxiliary force created by the Pakistani military to support its operation to quell the rebellion in the East.

'The army needed local support,' Qasmi had said in an interview to Al Jazeera.[8] 'The student wing of the religio-political party Jamaat-e-Islami in East Pakistan provided them with men who believed that they must support the army.'

Qasmi said the men who volunteered to help the military were useful because they were well-versed in Bengali and familiar with the terrain. 'Initially, they were only called volunteers and were part of civil defence. But from May 1971 onwards, they were formally organised into two different groups, Al-Badr and Al Shams,' he said. 'They were trained by the military itself.'

Post independence from Pakistan, this venom that had wanted to kill the very idea of Bangladesh was allowed to remain in the country's bloodstream. In an interview, Abhijit Dasgupta, former director general, Doordarshan Kendra, Kolkata, who covered the war in Bangladesh, said that soon after the birth of Bangladesh in 1971, Sheikh Mujibur Rahman gave clemency to those who were pro-Pakistan.[9]

It was not just clemency to those who opposed the idea of Bangladesh, but Mujib's secularism, it has often been argued, had its limits. And though Bangladesh was formed in order to keep culture over religious identity, many policies of the Mujib government upheld Islamic cultural values in state affairs.

Bangladesh expert Mubashar Hasan wrote in the *Diplomat* that Mujib banned gambling and selling of alcohol in Bangladesh, and closed cinema halls on the Prophet's birthday. '[His government] established an organisation that was the forerunner of the Islamic Foundation, a state-funded Islamic missionary organisation, and reformed the Madrasah education board. In 1974, Bangladesh poet Daud Haider was forced out of the country for offending religious sentiments through one of his poems,' Hasan wrote.[10]

A rising star of the local poetry scene, in 1973 one of Daud Haider's works won the Best Poem of Asia award, handed out by the London Society of Poetry. Just a year later, a single poem criticizing religion, which led to allegations of offending religious sentiments, forever changed the life of the then twenty-two-year-old Haider.

He was arrested and a few months later put on a plane to Calcutta, India. He lived the rest of his life under the shadow of a fatwa. Haider became one of the earliest writers from South Asia to have faced the wrath of religious groups, long before his fellow writers Salman Rushdie and Taslima Nasreen.[11]

This happened under Sheikh Mujib's watch.

But it was his clemency towards fundamentalist forces, as Abhijit Dasgupta wrote, that worried even Fidel Castro. In his book *Mujib's Blunders*, Manash Ghosh writes about Castro's meeting with Sheikh Mujibur Rahman after he became the premier of Bangladesh.

'Fidel Castro was right in giving a prescient and timely warning to Bangabandhu that showing magnanimity to his political enemies, who had dourly opposed the Liberation War, would be considered as a sign of inherent weakness in his character and not as a moral virtue. His benevolence would only spur them on to conspire and act with greater gusto and vengeance against him and his government and, in the process, frustrate his dream of building a *Sonar* (golden) Bangladesh,' Ghosh wrote. 'Castro was among the few world leaders who had paid the most glowing tribute to Bangabandhu saying he had not seen the mighty Himalayas but had seen Mujib. And yet Bangabandhu paid no heed to Castro's advice as he thought that by accommodating the committed pro-Pak minded officers in the top echelons of his administration and uniformed services, he had been able to win their trust and confidence.'[12]

Perhaps nothing busts the myth of Mujib's secularism more than Ramna Kali Bari in Dhaka. The mandir dedicated to Goddess Kali was a grand structure with a 120-feet-high spire that was visible from most of Dhaka. It was more than 500 years old. In the wee hours of 27 March 1971, Pakistani soldiers surrounded Ramna Kali Bari and massacred between 100 and 250 men and women (different accounts give varying figures) – almost all of them Hindus – who had taken shelter in the mandir, bombarded the structure and took away a dozen Hindu girls who were never found.

When Sheikh Mujib returned to Bangladesh and took over the reins of the newly formed republic, Hindu Bangladeshis expected him to reconstruct the mandir. Instead, Mujib asked the public works department to bulldoze the remnants of the temple and clear the 2.22 acre expanse of land on which the mandir and the adjoining Anandamayee Maa Ashram stood. He converted the area into a park that was named after Suhrawardy, his political idol.

Every year since 1972, Hindus had been attempting to set up a makeshift structure to worship goddesses Durga and Kali during Durga and Kali Puja, but their efforts were always thwarted by the police. It was only in 1982, during the military rule of Lieutenant General H.M. Ershad, that permission was granted to Hindus to hold annual Durga and Kali pujas in a makeshift mandir. But, despite numerous petitions, permission was not granted for regular pujas at the makeshift mandir. In 2000, the Sheikh Hasina government finally granted permission for daily puja at the temple. However, the BNP government headed by Khaleda Zia tried to overturn this decision sometime in April–May 2006 and asked Hindus to shift the temple to another location.

The Bangladesh Puja Udjapan Parishad, a body comprising prominent Hindus, protested and the government junked the move just before the end of its tenure in October 2006. After Sheikh Hasina returned to power in January 2009, India offered to rebuild the temple and Hasina agreed in the face of stiff opposition from conservative Muslims and Islamists in her government and the country. The then Indian president, Ram Nath Kovind, inaugurated the new mandir in December 2021.[13]

If Sheikh Mujib was complicit in the communal violence that singed Calcutta during the Great Calcutta Killings, if his secularism was suspect even after the birth of Bangladesh whose citizens had pledged to rise above religiosity to come together as a nation built on common culture and language, why is Mujib venerated as a secular icon and a beacon of hope not just in Bangladesh but also India?

And then there is the troubling history of the BAKSAL, or the Bangladesh Krishak Sramik Awami League, a political front and the sole legal ruling party of Bangladesh from January to August 1975. It was formed by Mujib following the Fourth Amendment to the Constitution of Bangladesh, which effectively outlawed all other political parties. Since his tragic assassination happened soon after, on 15 August 1975, during a coup d'état, this attack on multiparty democracy is hardly spoken about.

It is only after the fall of Hasina that the devastating effects of BAKSAL on electoral democracy are being talked about. Author and researcher Mohiuddin Ahmad wrote that Sheikh Mujib wanted a one-party government and absolute power, and he believed that with absolute control he could manage everything.

'Awami League still believes that BAKSAL was a good initiative. After the 2008 election, Awami League followed a similar path. Although there was a facade of multi-party democracy, in reality, it was a one-person government under Sheikh Hasina's leadership. There are similarities between the two. I would say that this fascist tendency has been ingrained in Awami League's very essence,' Ahmad said in an interview to the *Daily Star*.[14]

Utpal Kumar, opinion editor of *Firstpost* and *News18* and author of the 2024 book *Eminent Distorians: Twists and Truths in Bharat's History*, had an interesting take on Mujib, the man behind the myth. 'Sheikh Mujibur Rahman, revered as Bangabandhu, is as much a product of myth as of history. Popularly hailed as the architect of Bangladesh's independence – a liberal, secular leader whose death supposedly paved the way for Islamism – Mujib's real story is far more complex, layered and often dubious. In his early years, as we know, Mujib was an ardent follower of Mohammad Ali Jinnah and the Pakistan movement. In his memoirs, written during his stay in jail as a state prisoner between 1967 and 1969, he called Mahatma Gandhi a "magician" who would bring Hindus and Muslims together, but when the Mahatma was alive his distrust for him was absolute. He was a trusted aide of Huseyn Suhrawardy during the 1946 Calcutta killings of Hindus. It was only post-Partition, after growing disillusioned with the dominance of Punjabi elites in West Pakistan, that Mujib pivoted to Bengali nationalism.

'Even after Bangladesh's liberation in 1971, thanks entirely to Mrs Indira Gandhi's intervention, Mujib's conduct revealed either deep-seated anti-India sentiment or calculated realpolitik,' Kumar told us. 'A striking example was the inauguration of the Ashuganj Bridge, rebuilt swiftly by Indian engineers. Mujib publicly lauded Britain's Sir Arthur Gold for securing UK funds, but pointedly ignored Subimal Dutt, India's high commissioner who made the project happen. He even offered Sir Arthur an exclusive helicopter ride to Dhaka, leaving Dutt to endure a long, uncomfortable train journey without food or water – an incident that quietly spoke volumes.

'Soon after, Mujib invited Pakistan's Zulfiqar Ali Bhutto to Dhaka, signalling where his loyalties lay once Bengali nationalism had served its purpose. His decision to release hundreds of pro-Pakistan Islamists and Razakars within years of Independence was equally telling. The immediate consequence was anti-Hindu violence during the 1972 Durga Puja in Old Dhaka's Sankhari

Bazar and Tanti Bazar areas, populated mostly by Hindus. The long-term consequence: Mujib's own assassination in 1975 – ironically at the hands of the very Islamist forces he sought to appease.'

But what explains India's role in sustaining the Mujib myth?

Kumar agreed that India played its own part in promoting and sustaining the Mujib myth, driven by two clear reasons. 'First, the TINA [There Is No Alternative] factor. In Delhi's strategic thinking, Mujib – and later his daughter, Sheikh Hasina – were always seen as the best options available. Their alternatives in Dhaka were often outright jihadi prototypes. It's not that minorities were particularly safe under Mujib or Hasina; it's just that the Islamists were kept on a tighter leash,' he told us.

'Second, the personal and political equations. The Mujib family has long enjoyed warm ties with the Gandhis, and by extension, Delhi's influential Lutyens' establishment. This cozy relationship helped cement the carefully curated image of Mujib as a secular, liberal icon – an image that suited both diplomatic narratives and Delhi's domestic ideological tastes.'

So, there is more to Sheikh Mujibur Rahman than the protagonist of Shyam Benegal's last film, *Mujib: The Making of a Nation*.

But as his daughter remains in exile in India at the time of writing his book, and as Mujib himself becomes persona non grata in the nation he helped birth, here is a take from a young Awami League politician, in hiding ever since his organization, the Bangladesh Chhatra League, was banned by the Yunus administration in October 2024.

From an undisclosed location in Kolkata, BCL president Saddam Hussain, twenty-eight, told us over the phone that whatever may be said against Sheikh Mujib, without him there would be no Bangladesh. 'Bangladesh needs to dream once more the dream that Sheikh Mujib had dreamt for it – the dream of a country free of corruption, communalism and discrimination of any kind. Bangladesh today stands at the brink of an abyss. If we have to come up as a nation again, we have to reimagine it through the vision of Bangabandhu Sheikh Mujibur Rahman.'

The BCL was banned by the interim government of Bangladesh on 23 October 2024 under the Anti-Terrorism Act, 2009. 'Many of my fellow activists were killed, maimed and jailed since the fall of the Sheikh Hasina government. What keeps us going is the impact Sheikh Mujib has had on our collective psyche through his words and actions, through his life's teachings and his martyrdom. And that is no small thing.'

6

Why Young Bangladeshis Hate India

On 27 September 2024, the second Test match between India and Bangladesh was being played at the International Green Park Stadium in Kanpur. The Bangladesh cricket team was touring India. In the first Test, Indian right-arm off spin bowler Ravichandran Ashwin had devastated Bangladesh as he took six wickets in the second innings and bowled India to a comprehensive 280-run victory on the fourth day in Chennai.[1] At Kanpur, though, the drama shifted from the cricket ground to the spectator stand.

A young man in garish body paint stood holding the Bangladesh flag in the stands. While it is not uncommon for cricket fans to carry flags of their countries or wear body paint in pre-celebratory excitement, this young man was clearly not one for subtlety. He had dressed himself in faux tiger skin and painted his face with black and yellow stripes like the dying breed of village theatre performers known in eastern India and Bangladesh's villages as 'Bohurupis' or quick-change village theatre artistes. The man suddenly fell to the ground as if in pain, and was promptly carried out of the stands by onlookers around him.

What looked like a minor disruption became big news soon after. News outlets identified the Bangladesh cricket fan as 'Tiger Roby' and said he had been rushed to the hospital after allegedly being assaulted. Roby claimed to have been struck on his back and lower abdomen by Indian fans sitting next to him.

Roby said the crowd had been hurling abuses at him since the start of the day's play and he had climbed to the balcony to keep himself safe. 'A cop told me not to stand at that block. I was there only because I was scared. They were hurling abuses since morning. I have watched enough Bollywood movies to understand the abuses,' he said.

This wasn't the first instance of tensions between Indian and Bangladesh cricket fans getting out of hand. During the 2023 ODI World Cup match in Pune between India and Bangladesh, another Bangladesh supporter, Shoaib Ali Bukhari, popularly known as 'Tiger Shoaib', was targeted by Indian fans and his tiger mascot ripped off.[2]

Tiger Roby's story soon took a U-turn. He retracted his statements and later the police denied the 'baseless reports' of the Bangladeshi fan being assaulted. It was said that Roby had fallen ill and was brought to a local hospital for treatment. Visiting Bangladeshi cricket journalists were quoted by Indian news outlets to paint Tiger Roby as 'an attention-seeker'. It was said his claims could very well be exaggerated. Reports also emerged of Tiger Roby abusing Indian cricketers during the first Test in Chennai, especially Indian fast-bowling sensation Mohammed Siraj.

Eleven months after the incident, Sheikh Iklas Audy, a leader of the Bangladesh Jatiotabadi Chhatradal, the student wing of the BNP, at the Aminur Rahman College, Magura district, told us over the phone that a majority of Indians had the tendency to look down upon Bangladeshis and that the Tiger Roby incident was irrefutable proof of that.

We told Audy that Tiger Roby had retracted his original statement of being assaulted at the cricket stadium and it was found later that he had fallen ill. 'Who found out? Your Godi media?' Audy asked with mild hostility in his voice. We were surprised to hear a term coined by a section of Indians to describe allegedly biased Indian news media being used by a Bangladeshi citizen.

We knew Audy. We had been to his village, Bashur Dhuljari, in Magura district as recently as January 2024 and several times before that in the last couple of years and enjoyed a warm reception from his family. We were connected with him through social media and would interact online every once in a while.

Thus, Audy's tone came as a surprise.

'And it is not an isolated incident. Indians do look down upon us.'

We told Audy that was not the case.

'Tell me then how are thousands of alleged Bangladeshi immigrants being deported without due process across India? And one hears they are being kept in camps in your border states like caged animals!'

While the number may not be 'thousands', Audy is referring to reports of Bangladeshi immigrants being deported by India and being handed over to the BGB.[3]

We did not debate with Audy, but let him bare his mind.

'And your home minister routinely abuses Bangladeshis in his election speeches. It has become a poll tactic for your ruling party, the BJP, to win elections in India by abusing Bangladeshis,' Audy said.

In September 2024, Indian Home Minister Amit Shah had said in a speech in the run-up to the Jharkhand assembly election that Bangladeshi infiltration was hurting the state.

'Our "Mati, Beti, Roti" [land, daughter and livelihood] are under attack. The BJP will not allow this to continue … We will bring in a stringent legislation to prevent the transfer of tribal land to infiltrators. We will also take back the land grabbed by them and drive them out,' Shah had thundered.[4] On 23 September 2024, Bangladesh had lodged a 'strong protest' against what it described as 'highly deplorable remarks' made by Shah during his visit to Jharkhand. In a protest note handed over to the High Commission of India in Dhaka, the Ministry of Foreign Affairs of Bangladesh said the comments caused a 'deep sense of hurt' in Bangladesh.[5]

'What is it about Bangladeshis that Indians hate so much? Is it xenophobia or plain Islamophobia?' Audy asked us.

We told him there were more Muslims in India than in Bangladesh but he was not convinced they were safe. 'You lynch

Muslims for eating beef, you harass Muslim girls for covering their heads, your news TV anchors spew anti-Muslim hate every evening on prime-time shows and then you lecture us on communal harmony in Bangladesh? How do you expect young Bangladeshis to embrace India?'

Snigdha Rezwana Karim, associate professor in the department of anthropology at Jahangirnagar University, Dhaka, told us over the phone that the 'words and actions of India's ruling party, the BJP, has turned a big chunk of Bangladeshi youth against India and Indians'.

'These utterances are not only xenophobic, they are downright communal in nature. Some of us who still hold on to the beautiful idea of a secular, progressive Bangladesh cannot help but point out the stark similarities between the rise of religious identity politics thanks to Islamist political parties like the Jamaat-e-Islami Bangladesh. But in the same breath one has to compare this to the gradual rise and political dominance of the BJP in neighbouring India,' she says.

Karim says she sees no differences between the Jamaat in Bangladesh and the BJP in India as both parties are trying to turn Bangladesh and India into an Islamist nation and a Hindu *rashtra*, respectively. She says the age of rage that has descended upon the youth of Bangladesh closely mirrors the age of rage in India.

'When the prime minister of a powerful neighbouring country wears his religiosity on his sleeve, proudly inaugurates a temple built on the ruins of an ancient mosque [the Ram Temple in Ayodhya], how do you expect the new generation of a Muslim-majority country like Bangladesh to remain immune to the lure of crude communalism?'

Karim is not the only Bangladeshi intellectual to have made this connection. As early as 1993, exiled Bangladeshi writer Taslima Nasrin's novel *Lajja* addressed the aftermath of the Babri Masjid demolition in India. The novel is about a Hindu family in Bangladesh facing persecution and violence after the demolition of the Babri Masjid. In Nasrin's work, even the youth in Bangladesh is snared by competitive religious fanaticism after the fall of the Babri Masjid.

Alongside the rise in what they see as 'Hindu fundamentalism', India's persistent support to Bangladesh's deposed prime minister Sheikh Hasina has over the years turned Bangladeshi youth against India.

Member of the central committee of the Communist Party of Bangladesh Lucky Akhtar told us how Sheikh Hasina betrayed the youth of Bangladesh for decades even as she got unstinted support from India. And that has made the youth of Bangladesh bitter.

'My comrades and I have given our lives to the cause of a secular, liberal Bangladesh. The streets have burned with our protests for over a decade. In 2013, millions erupted in outrage when war criminals escaped the highest punishment. We roared, "*Aposher ei ray manina!*" [We reject this verdict of collaboration!] – demanding justice for the Razakars. The left has never stayed silent. And who was lenient to war criminals? Sheikh Hasina! And then she rigged elections in 2014, and we marched again. When she did it again in 2018, we fought back, we boycotted. Year after year, we've exposed every injustice of her regime – corruption, repression and the farce of democracy,' Akhtar said.

'But who backed her? Who made sure Hasina stayed on in power even as she killed electoral democracy in Bangladesh? India! And today you ask me why the youth of Bangladesh is mad at India!'

Akhtar said not just the left in Bangladesh, but other political parties as well had demanded free and fair elections under a neutral interim government. 'In 2024, we called out the sham election – but the regime attacked us, ignored us. Yet we persisted, amplifying the people's voice at every level. The same struggle played out in the fight against the discriminatory quota system. For years, we demanded reform – but Hasina, enraged by mass protests, abolished quotas entirely. This wasn't justice – it was vengeance. And when the students rose again, the regime answered with bullets.'

Akhtar said her comrades paid the price of rising up in protest against Hasina. 'Mahmudul Hasan Rizvi, a leader of the left student union, was gunned down by police in Uttara, Dhaka city. Comrade Prodip Kumar Barman fell to state violence in Sirajganj on 4 August 2024, a day before Hasina fled Bangladesh. Their blood stains the hands of her regime,' she said.

So, was it anger against Hasina that had turned Bangladeshi youth away from India?

'To a large extent, it is. For ten years, the youth have been setting the stage for resistance – organizing, mobilizing, refusing to bow. Our presence isn't sudden; it's the constant heartbeat of this nation's struggle. While others compromise or retreat, we remain – unyielding, unbroken, the voice they cannot silence. We set the stage for this resistance for the last one decade. And now she is gone. To India!' Akhtar said.

Akhtar added that it was not only India's support to Hasina that alienated Bangladesh but also the sense that India was meddling in Bangladesh's internal affairs that made the youth of the country resentful.

Shortly after Hasina came back to power for the fourth straight term on 7 January 2024, the 'India Out' campaign began in Bangladesh, calling for a boycott of all Indian goods from Bangladeshi markets. India's position on the election went against people's expectations, which led Bangladeshis to launch the boycott campaign, BNP leader Zainul Abedin Farroque had said.[6]

Farroque, a member of BNP chairperson Khaleda Zia's advisory council, said Bangladesh remembered India's support during the 1971 liberation war from Pakistan, and the party still considered India a friend. 'But it can't be that there will be democracy in one country and no democracy in the other,' he had remarked. 'We're seeing on social media that the people of Bangladesh have boycotted Indian products because of the country's position against them.'[7]

And who was using social media to boycott Indian products? 'The youth of Bangladesh,' Sheikh Iklas Audy told us. 'I was one of those who did.'

Apart from India's support to keep Hasina in power by 'subverting democracy', both Audy and Akhtar said there was another issue which had pained Bangladesh, even as India refused to acknowledge it.

On 23 February 2024, soon after Sheikh Hasina came to power in Bangladesh, young journalist Saqlaine Rizve wrote a long news report to address a question that had haunted him for years: The two nations are friendly neighbours. Why, then, do Indian troops so frequently use lethal force along the border?

We had met Rizve in Dhaka in January 2024 after the polls, and he told us that with the BNP boycotting the polls and calling it a farce, and the Supreme Court of Bangladesh keeping the country's largest Islamist party, the Jamaat-e-Islami Bangladesh, out of the fray, it was a given that Hasina would stomp back to power. But why were the borders still bleeding, he asked.

Rizve said it was not safe to report on an issue as controversial as border killings, but he didn't care for his safety. The report came out on 23 February 2024, six months before Sheikh Hasina's fall.[8]

Rizve wrote of a typical day in April 2018, usually the hottest month of the year in Bangladesh. Rasel Miah, a fourteen-year-old boy from Phulbari Upazila in Kurigram, accompanied his father, Md Hanif Uddin, a farmer, to their field near the Bangladesh–India border, just beyond the 150-yard No Man's Land. As the sun began to set, Miah and his father were wrapping up their work to go home. Miah was holding on to the rope of their cow when out of nowhere two members of India's Border Security Force (BSF) rushed towards them.

'I was dressed in a lungi (a traditional garment worn by men in Bangladesh and various Asian countries) along with a T-shirt while holding our cow's rope. As they started to run to us, I ran with our cow. At one point, I jumped into a river, and suddenly, a BSF member fired *chita guli* [rubber bullets],' Miah, now twenty years old and studying philosophy at Uttar Bangla College in Lalmonirhat, another northern bordering district of Bangladesh, told Rizve.

'For a few minutes, I couldn't see anything, and to this day, I still don't see with my right eye,' Miah said.

'They claimed I was cutting the barbed wire fence. How could a fourteen-year-old boy cut the barbed fence of an international border? After returning home, the people who were working alongside us in the field mentioned that the BSF jawan appeared to be drunk at that time.'

Rizve wrote that there was extensive media coverage of the encounter and Miah's injury inflicted by the BSF officer. Following a diagnosis at a nearby hospital, Miah's family transferred him to Dhaka, where he underwent a month-long examination at a government hospital. Miah never got the vision back in his right eye.

Rizve wrote that Bangladesh and India share a 4,096 kilometre border, the fifth-longest in the world. The border separates the six divisions of Bangladesh and the Indian states of Assam, West Bengal, Mizoram, Meghalaya and Tripura. 'The border has been a source of various issues, such as smuggling, illegal immigration, cross-border terrorism, and human rights violations. Despite the friendly political relations, the border area is fraught with tension – and violence,' he wrote.

In his report, Rizve quoted Ain o Salish Kendra, a human rights organization in Bangladesh, to say that between 2013 and 2023 a total of 332 individuals were reported killed by the BSF near the Bangladesh–India border, an average of thirty people per year.

'And that estimate is on the low side. Another rights group reported that at least 1,236 Bangladeshis were killed and 1,145 injured in shootings by the BSF between 2000 and 2020. According to Dr Mohammad Abdur Rab's book *Bangladesh: Geography, Geopolitics, and Environment*, a total of 206 Bangladeshi civilians were reported killed by the BSF from 1990 to 1999,' he wrote.

The report said that smuggling activities were prevalent along the border, involving the illegal transportation of cows, drugs, arms and other goods. 'However, the use of lethal weapons against suspected smugglers raises serious concerns. There have been numerous cases where innocent individuals were shot by [the] BSF or abducted, actions that blatantly defy both legal and moral principles,' Rizve wrote.

'Accepting that smuggling is a crime, law enforcement agencies are required to apprehend the criminal, produce him before a court, and it would be for the judge to decide what punishment was to be administered.'

Rizve's report then quoted Md Touhid Hossain, former foreign secretary of Bangladesh, as saying the 'high leadership of India is on record saying that as long as "crimes" along the border continue, border shootings will also continue. Notably, the records indicate that the BSF intentionally shoots to kill. Non-lethal injury is comparatively rare. In my view, and I know many who also feel the same way, this is a phenomenon that is completely unacceptable. There is no reason why this should be a regular feature at the border between two countries who are supposedly role models for bilateral relations,' Hossain added.

Rizve then went on to narrate what his investigation on border killings threw up as perhaps the most notorious case that occurred on 7 January 2011 in the Anantapur border area in Kurigram. 'On that day, a 14-year-old girl's body was left hanging on the barbed wire fence that separates the two countries. The girl was Felani Khatun, a Bangladeshi who lived with her parents in Assam, a state of India bordering Bangladesh. She was supposed to don a red saree and jewels, traditional Bengali wedding attire, and sit in the wedding hall on January 8. To that end, she and her father, Md Nurul Islam Nuru, were illegally crossing the border with the help of brokers.

'Her father crossed the fence successfully. Then it was Felani's turn. When she climbed to the fence with a ladder, she was shot by a BSF soldier. Felani was left hanging on the fence for about four hours. During that time, she was still alive; villagers reported hearing her pleas for water and assistance, yet fear kept them from approaching. Gradually, Felani succumbed to her injuries and took her last breath.

'Thirty hours later her dead body was brought back, bound to a bamboo pole with her hands and feet restrained. She wore a white shroud instead of a red saree. The image of her body – first alive, then dead – hanging on the fence is enough to make many question the friendship between Bangladesh and India. And Felani was not the first or the last Bangladeshi civilian to be killed along a border that is among the world's deadliest, despite linking two friendly nations.

'Amidst public outcry in Bangladesh, Amiya Ghosh, a BSF soldier, faced charges. Despite a trial and retrial, he was finally acquitted on September 6, 2013, citing inconclusive evidence. Nuru, Felani's father, criticised the BSF court's decision as a mockery of justice.'

Rizve wrote that not only did the BSF kill Bangladeshi civilians, but there were also reports of civilians being abducted and tortured by the Indian border force every year. 'From 2013 to 2023 nearly 500 civilians were abducted. In 2013 alone, 175 were abducted; among them only 49 were brought back by the BGB. The other 126 are still missing.

'According to a research paper "Bangladesh–India Border Crisis: Nature and Remedy" by Dr Saleh Shahriar, an assistant professor of history at North South University, in addition to instances of fatal shootings, Bangladeshi citizens have reported enduring various forms of torture inflicted by the BSF. These include gunshot wounds, hacking wounds, restraining individuals by tying their hands and feet before submerging them in water, using pliers to pull out nails, bayonet stabbings, ear mutilation, physical beatings, burning the entire body or specific body parts with cigarettes. Even more severe actions include burning, maiming, genital mutilation, eye gouging, hanging bodies on barbed wire, and instances of rape,' he wrote.

Rizve's report shook Bangladesh and confirmed something the youth of the country already believed. 'The "friendship" between Bangladesh and India that Sheikh Hasina flaunted was a beautiful lie. If you care to check Bangladesh's borders with India, it wasn't even beautiful, it was just a lie. We won't live that lie any longer,' Sheikh Iklas Audy told us.

While the anger in Audy is palpable, a senior leader in his party, Amir Khasru Mahmud Chowdhury, a member of the BNP's International Affairs Committee, told us Bangladesh still wanted friendly ties with India. 'Irrespective of who comes to power and who loses it, India and Bangladesh cannot afford to not be friends. Mutual respect, bilateral peace and promotion of economy on both sides have to be our joint objectives. You can't change your neighbour, can you?' Chowdhury, seventy-four, says.

We called Audy again. Did the youth of Bangladesh see India as an enemy country? 'No! Most of us love Indians. Have you forgotten the boat ride we took along the Madhumati River the last time all of you were in my village? The walk inside the Kans grass forest, the early morning bike rides on unpaved streets to the local bazaar to haggle and buy the morning's fresh catch of river fish? We can so easily go back to being friends again, the youth of the two nations. Please do one thing for us to trust you again.'

And what is that?

'Send Sheikh Hasina back. She needs to face the law for her crimes against humanity,' Sheikh Iklas Audy said.

Bangladeshi political analyst Maruf Mullick has written that since Bangladesh's independence, India has wanted to control the country. 'It has continuously killed Bangladeshis along its border, it has withdrawn water from its rivers upstream to keep Bangladesh under pressure and ensure its own interests. It has interfered in one election after the other. But if India halts the border killings, shares river water on the basis of bilateral talks, refrains from interference in Bangladesh's internal affairs, then the anti-Indian sentiment will automatically dissipate and the security threats will drop,' he said.[9]

Mullick also pointed fingers at the Indian media for fermenting anti-India sentiments in Bangladesh. 'The attitude of a certain group of Indian media and politicians indicates that they are simmering in fury. Are they furious because Sheikh Hasina was toppled from power? Perhaps Sheikh Hasina had given all to India with open arms. Her fleeing has affected Indian interests. But India should control its behaviour concerning an independent, sovereign county's domestic affairs,' he wrote.[10]

Popular Bangladeshi political analyst and atheist blogger Asad Noor has a different view. Noor told us over a call from Canada that while all of these aspects may well be true in parts, they hid a deeper truth: the unmissable Islamization of a society built on secular values. '1971 was too long ago. The current generation has grown up on a potent diet of Islamism. The influence of Islamic preacher Zakir Naik on South Asian societies cannot be overlooked. Naik showed you that you can put on a sharp suit, speak clipped English and yet be Islamist. The angry Bangladeshi youth has discarded the values of a secular society for an Islamic one with sprinklings of modernity,' Khan says.

According to Noor, the Islamization of Bangladeshi youth is evident when young leaders of the 'freshly-minted political party NCP comfortably share space with the leaders of the Jamaat-e-Islami Bangladesh'.

'Not all but a big chunk of Bangladeshi youth has embraced the idea of Islamic nationalism. This makes it imperative for them to invent an enemy. And that enemy is Hindu-majority India, a country that stood behind Bangladesh during the 1971 War of Independence, trained its guerrilla army, the Muktibahini; it is today an enemy for all seasons. India hate has become a prerequisite for the neo-nationalist. Couched within it is Hindu hate, and that hate is visible to the world now by the silence of the Bangladeshi youth to the atrocities against the Hindu Bangladeshi. They cry for Palestine, take out processions in support of Gaza but do not shed a tear for their fellow citizen who prays to Hindu gods when she is raped or killed by Islamists. Thus, it is easy for them to hate India, a country bigger, stronger and overwhelmingly Hindu!'

Section II
Politics

7

Good Hasina, Bad Hasina

'Why "Inshallah Bangladesh"?'

We had not expected Sheikh Hasina to ponder over the title of the book we were writing.

It was on the day of Eid Al-Adha, popular as Bakrid, on Saturday, 7 June 2025, that our request to speak to her had been granted. The time was 6.13 p.m. IST. We dialled a private number at the exact time we had been asked to call, and after a few seconds, Hasina took the call herself.

It was hard to believe that on the other end of the line was Sheikh Hasina Wazed, Bangladesh's prime minister till 5 August 2024, who still signed off as Bangladesh's premier since she said she never resigned. The Mohammad Yunus administration was an unconstitutional, illegal one according to her.

A few hundred questions swarmed our minds, but 'no interview', we had been strictly told.

We exchanged Eid greetings with the woman who had ruled Bangladesh with an iron fist for fifteen straight years. She sounded like she was in good mood.

We told her we were writing a book on Bangladesh after the July Revolution. 'Don't call it a revolution!' Hasina's mood was suddenly stern. 'It was a terror attack on Bangladesh disguised as a students' revolt planned by America and executed by Pakistan. It was done to remove me from power. Whether it was Abu Sayed or other student leaders, the killings were not done by the police. They were killed by terrorists and the killings were passed off as police brutality to turn the public against my government,' she told us without pause.

This was the point where we could have posed a counter question to her or asked her to tell us more about the revolution that she believed was not one. Did she not see the large number of students on streets being attacked by her police?

But we had been warned that Hasina would not take any questions and this was to be only a courtesy call, not to be published in any news outlet.

Hasina had refused to speak to the press, local or global, ever since she had taken refuge in India. There had been speculative news about her whereabouts but no conformation.

Thus far, Hasina had only spoken to her party cadre over group phone calls and to Bangladeshi citizens through online addresses. After months of pursuing Awami League top leadership as well her personal aides, we had been granted a few minutes to greet her on Eid.

We did not interrupt her.

We told her we were writing a chapter on the July uprising and would try to explore all angles. She asked us again: 'Why is your book titled *Inshallah Bangladesh*? 'Bangladesh's fundamentalist Muslims do not read. They only hear what others say and come out on the streets to unleash violence. You may have used the word "Inshallah" figuratively, but they would interpret this as you criticizing Bangladesh using the name of Allah. These people do not read religious texts, they only hear things and react,' she told us.

We assured her the book would not take a reductionist view of Bangladesh or only look at the country after the events of July–August 2024 but attempt to go back in time and trace the origins of fundamentalism and social fissures. We would also put out the mistakes of her father Sheikh Mujibur Rahman and her government.

Hasina did not respond for a few seconds. Should we not have disclosed this bit about her father? Would the 'conversation' end abruptly now?

Then Sheikh Hasina spoke: 'Of course. You are free to criticize me, my party and my government. But do not criticize my country.'

That was not why we were writing the book, we assured Hasina. What we were trying to write about were the reasons behind the rise and spread of fundamentalism in Bangladesh before and after the upheavals of July–August 2024 and examination of the roles of major political forces, including hers, to abet or arrest such forces, we told her again.

'Write about these forces. Write how Pakistan's fundamentalist forces have not only supported such forces within Bangladesh even after 1971 but expanded their own terror networks inside my country. Make sure your book reaches not only Indian and Bangladeshi readers but readers across the world. Let the world see the true faces of the Bangladesh Jamaat-e-Islami and the BNP. Tell the world how these forces destroyed public property in the name of students' revolution, how they killed policemen, the meticulous design that went behind the killing of protesting students. Also let the world know how supporters, workers and leaders of the Awami League were targeted after 5 August, brutally killed, their houses set on fire, their business establishments snatched.' Hasina's voice was unwavering in cold anger.

We told her we were trying to research all of these facts and put them in the book.

'You know who is the main man behind all of this? It is Yunus. The Americans wanted St Martin's Island from me. If I had agreed they would not have removed me from power. But I did not agree to sell my country to remain premier. It was the Americans who used Yunus to plot against me and remove me. Yunus was behind the plotting, financing and execution of the terror attack on Bangladesh during July–August last year at the behest of the Americans. He is a cheat who has destroyed his country for his ambitions. Now he and his coterie are looting the country and running it to the ground. Write about this too so that the world knows,' she said.

We had been reporting on Bangladesh for our respective news outlets and would write on the current regime in our book, we told Hasina.

'Everybody is out to ruin my "Sonar Bangla". The student coordinators are involved in corruption, so also are the members of the new student's party, and the advisors of the Yunus administration. The media is not being allowed to report all this. I had tried to build a modern nation. They have destroyed everything,' she lamented over the phone.

We could have interjected at this juncture, asked her about the serious charges against her own administration. But we kept our promise to her top aides that this would not be an interview but a courtesy call. And getting to hear Sheikh Hasina's take on recent events in Bangladesh, even if it sounded like a rant against an adversary who had bested her, was priceless.

'My citizens are suffering. The media is not being allowed to report the truth. No one is in peace. Prices are skyrocketing, patients are not getting proper treatment at hospitals, public transport networks are shutting down because of unchecked corruption. It is now up to us to bring Bangladesh back from the brink. I have to save the country.'

Does she plan to return to Bangladesh? We managed to slip in a question. 'Inshallah, I shall return. I will deliver justice to my people and bring to book these people who have betrayed my nation. Listen, people now know they have been betrayed, they want to be set free from the clutches of these imposters. Soon they will be able to tackle these terror apologists and become free again. It is only a matter of time. I wish you luck with the book. Inshallah.'

We wished her good health in return as the line went cold.

We checked the time on our watch. It was 6.26 p.m. IST. We had spoken to Sheikh Hasina for thirteen minutes, mostly listening to her monologue which could be well be her next election speech if her party was allowed to participate in the polls. What would the Yunus administration say if they were to know of this conversation? Every time Sheikh Hasina had addressed her citizens there had been sharp reactions from the current government and from the vigilantes.

After a mob brought down the residence of her father, Sheikh Mujibur Rahman, in Dhaka on 6 February, 2025, the media reported that the violence was triggered by a speech that Hasina intended to deliver to her supporters from exile in India.[1]

How would the mob react if they knew Hasina had spoken her mind to one Bangladeshi and two Indian journalists? How would the peace-loving Bangladeshi react?

A thirteen-minute conversation with an out-of-power Hasina seemed woefully inadequate, even if it was a scoop of sorts.

Meeting Hasina at Gonobhaban

Seven years ago, as part of an international media delegation, Madhuparna Das had the chance to have a detailed face-to-face conversation with Sheikh Hasina at Gonobhaban, her official residence as prime minister of Bangladesh.

We met Das at the Starbucks outlet on the ground floor of the Skymark One business centre located at Noida's Sector 98 that houses, among other corporate outlets, the Network 18 office where she works as an associate editor covering policy.

'I remember the broad pebbled pathway – lined with mango trees, birdsong from a small private aviary, and a certain crispness in the Dhaka air that day. We were a small media delegation from India, privileged, perhaps unwittingly, to witness power at its peak. It was not that long ago, just seven years ago – Sheikh Hasina reigned not only as the prime minister but as an unchallenged and unflinching matriarch of modern Bangladesh,' Das told us over an Americano.

That day Gonobhaban had stood before Das not as the official residence of a prime minister, but a statement of permanence, stability and near invincibility. 'Today, I struggle to reconcile that memory with the jarring images that flooded social media and news TV channels on 5 August 2024: looted hallways, ransacked wardrobes, protestors holding up her sarees, her undergarments and accessories, imported bags and suitcases as trophies,' Das said, flinching.

The fall of Gonobhaban wasn't just about one big ransacked building to Das, who had the chance of seeing it from the inside. To her, it was the collapse of a crafted myth.

'Inside those red-brick-stone walls, everything seemed to be in order, manicured and secure. An organic garden bloomed with seasonal produce; the fish ponds shimmered in late morning light; her livestock and fields blended rural idealism with the trappings of executive neatness. Her residence was steps away from the prime minister's camp office and a short drive from the Parliament of Bangladesh. Yet, within the compound, I felt a little removed from the trappings of power. It was almost ... how do I say this ... domestic, there was a certain calm, away from the bustle.'

And then Hasina had stood before Das and other members of the media delegation.

'Sheikh Hasina walked in calmly, draped in her regular Dhakai saree with the ease of someone who had long lost the need to prove herself to the world. Her smile was disarming, almost familial. She greeted us like she knew all of us from before. When one of us addressed her as "Madam", she gently said, "*Apa bolo*" – call me Apa, elder sister. And just like that, the political veneer cracked to reveal the cordial warmth she was known to radiate in one-on-one meets.'

Hasina had sat with the team, not in a hurry, nor guarded. Initial pleasantries over, the journalists engaged her in myriad topics, flowing from geopolitics to cultural exchanges, to her hopes from India. 'And she was honest, did not mince her words – surprisingly so.'

On China, Das remembered, Hasina was measured but clear. 'They are reliable partners,' Hasina had said, 'but we do not belong to anyone's camp. We need to develop our country.'

That statement – curt, diplomatically balanced – had summed up much of Hasina's foreign policy postures to Das.

'Under her, Bangladesh walked a tightrope between historical intimacy with India and China's seductive infrastructure promises. The Chinese built bridges, roads, tunnels and power plants for Bangladesh. They gave loans on terms that raised eyebrows even among economists but got projects moving,' Das told us.

'And Hasina, always the shrewd strategist, kept them close – but not too close. She invited China to the Teesta negotiations but leaned towards Delhi. Her foreign policy was not non-aligned. It was self-aligned, designed to reinforce her authority first, and the nation's leverage second,' Das said.

And yet, as Das and the other visiting journalists walked through Gonobhaban's lush compound, through rooms decorated with portraits of Hasina's father, Sheikh Mujibur Rahman, and her family members and passed visitor lounges that had hosted global dignitaries, Das could not ignore the unspoken but conspicuous contradiction. How could a leader so keen on pushing narratives of sacrifice and a legacy of inherited pain become so synonymous with muzzling free speech and stifling dissent?

Das said that perhaps the answer lay in the very structure of Gonobhaban itself – a blend of rural nostalgia with hard concrete. The personal zoo, the mango, jackfruit and banyan trees, the lakes – all evoked a Bangladeshi countryside idyll. And the security arrangements, the private guest houses for officers and the air of elite exclusivity formed an architecture of control.

Over lunch, one of Hasina's aides told the media group that Hasina had hosted the weddings of three survivors of the 2010 Dhaka fire that killed at least 124 people at Gonobhaban. 'Apa always cares,' he had told the journalists.

'She probably did care – there was no denying it. Her warmth did not seem like an act. She remembered names. She listened to us carefully. She often responded emotionally, even impulsively. But care, in Sheikh Hasina's world, was not divorced from command. Today, I really wonder how that world of "care" came undone so quickly, like a house of cards,' Das told us.

Seven years after that day, as Das watched and read about the rampage after Hasina flew out of Dhaka, it looked to her like decades of rage – against economic inequalities, elite impunity, a system where leaders appeared unaccountable and unreachable – had spilled out on to the streets. The protestors did not just loot, they bared what was most private. Her undergarments, suitcases, linens – clicked and broadcasted with obscenity, theatricality. 'It was less rebellion, more reckoning,' Das said. And it punctured the myth Hasina had built around herself and the Awami League so carefully.

Das, who had kept reporting on Bangladesh even after that visit, told us that for a large section of Bangladeshis, the opulence of Gonobhaban, the sprawling fields, the private zoo and the organic enclosures, represented everything the average citizen could not even aspire for. 'While inflation ballooned and opportunities shrank, the palace stood out like a middle finger to Bangladesh. The healer who had once hosted the grieving now appeared to have ruined their days,' she said.

To her question of banning the BNP just before the elections, Hasina had said she would respond, but off the record, which meant Das would not be able to report it.

'I cannot take a chance. If something goes haywire, the BNP will finish me, my legacy and ruin the nation,' Hasina had said to Das somewhat nonchalantly.

'And now, Gonobhaban is empty and in ruins,' Das smiled as she looked out of the glass window next to the corner table at Starbucks. Our coffee had gone cold; we had barely taken a few sips as she narrated her day with Hasina at Gonobhaban.

We were meeting Das in the week after our phone conversation with Hasina on Eid Al-Adha. 'Have you guys seen any pictures of Gonobhaban after she left?' Das asked us. 'Only on the day of her departure when the mob ransacked it,' we told her.

'Those manicured lawns, organic gardens, lakes, the fish breeding zones, mango orchards and that private zoo – all must be ransacked and abandoned. The birds that once fluttered in private aviaries must have flown away. The big trees, I hear, were cut, stripped not just of flowers and fruits, but of meaning,' Das told us wistfully.

'And I, as a foreign Bengali journalist in Dhaka – who once sat inside Hasina's plush drawing room, who addressed her as "Apa", who walked the Gonobhaban compound with quiet admiration – am now left with a sense of disquiet. Was I witnessing a leader at the height of her conviction that day or at the beginning of her alienation? Maybe both.'

To Madhuparna Das, Gonobhaban now stands not as a fortress, but a cautionary tale of the vagaries of unchecked power. 'But her warmth, you know …' Das looked out of the glass window again.

Make Bangladesh Great Again

How was Hasina out of power? Perhaps that old adage 'power corrupts, absolute power corrupts absolutely', worn out by overuse for so many world leaders played on Das's mind after meeting Hasina, even as she was disarmed by her warmth. We had a thirteen-minute conversation with a powerless Hasina, but it was a monologue, a rumination of what was and what should be.

And then there was the memory of Purnima Rani Shil.

Madhuparna Das may have walked away from Gonobhaban with doubts, but in 2001 Purnima Rani Shil had walked up to Hasina in despair. We had met Shil at the conference room of a Dhaka media office in the summer of 2023. Purnima avoided the press like the plague after the story of her gangrape became fodder for clickbait headlines. But she had agreed to speak to us.

'I never became whole again,' Purnima had told us. 'But whatever was left of me, whatever I could pick up of myself after they did what they did to me, I took to Dhaka. Because the Bangladesh countryside from where I come is full of horrors, and being a woman in Bangladesh is a curse and being a Hindu woman can become a double curse at the whim of a *huzoor* [a Muslim religious preacher] or the poisonous whisper of a neighbour.'

We knew what had happened to Purnima Rani Shil before we met her. But we were not prepared to sit in front of her as she told us the story of her ordeal. It was a story that took her down a very dark tunnel at the end of which Sheikh Hasina had emerged as a ray of light.

In the 2001 Bangladesh national election, Sheikh Hasina had lost power. The BNP and Bangladesh Jamaat-e-Islami led coalition won the election.

In the post-election violence that followed, Awami League workers, supporters and religious minorities became the targets.

Shil was a twelve-year-old polling agent of the Awami League in Perba Delua in Ullahpara Upazila, Sirajganj district. She had protested against electoral malpractices by the BNP workers during the election. For this, her home was attacked by around thirty to forty men on 8 October 2001. Shil, a minor, was not spared.

'They tore my clothes and tied my face with a gamcha. I knew their voices; I could see their faces in the light of their torches. They took me to a nearby field and raped me one after another until I lost consciousness,' Shil had said without a tremor in her voice.

In the attack, Purnima's sister lost her eyesight and her father's saloon was robbed. Her family was forced to flee. Shil came to Dhaka and members of the Awami League arranged for her treatment. She would never go back to her village again.

The trial against her rapists started after the Awami League returned to power in 2009 under Sheikh Hasina. On 4 May 2011, eleven men were sentenced to life for their involvement in her gangrape. They were also fined 1 lakh Bangladeshi taka each. Six of her rapists were sent to jail, five remained on the run. Purnima was not happy when the verdict came as she believed at least two of the accused, who were from her village, should have gotten death.

But while the court could not give her the justice she deserved, an out-of-power Hasina had compensated by treating this simple village girl as her very own.

After she came to Dhaka, Purnima had met Hasina, the Opposition leader, and the latter asked Purnima to stay with her for her safety. Hasina also gave her money for education. 'I call her Mamoni. She did for me what even my relatives didn't. She cared for me as if I was her own. She was who she was then, the former prime minister of Bangladesh, but she helped me without knowing me from before,' Purnima had told us.

Hasina's support and encouragement and her own grit had helped Purnima become an electronics and telecommunications engineer and landed her a job that paid well. But after some time, her colleagues got to know her story and she had to quit. 'Why should I blame strangers for judging me when my own family had disowned me? You know who had not judged me? Sheikh Hasina Wazed. Whatever peace and sanity I have in my life is because of her,' Shil had told us that afternoon.

Like with Shil, Hasina had sought to bring succour to the lives of the indigenous people of the Chittagong Hill Tracks, like the Chakmas, the Marmas and the Tripuris, by ending decades-long racial discrimination and attacks, by signing the historic Chittagong Hill Tracks Peace Accord on 2 December 1997. The treaty was signed between the Hasina government and the Parbatya Chattogram Jana Sanghati Samiti, a left-wing political party formed to represent minority communities and indigenous tribes of the hill tracts.

A year after, for bringing peace to the hill tracts, the United Nations honoured Hasina with its UNESCO Houphouet-Boigny Peace Prize in 1998.[2] Handing over the award on 24 September 1999, then UNESCO director general Federico Mayor would tell her:

> Following the footsteps of your father, who dedicated his life to founding a nation, you in turn have taken that nation along the road of peace and reconciliation . . . Your peace-making efforts within your country's borders have been matched by your dedication to the cause of a global culture of peace.[3]

Hasina would go on to win many more international accolades like the Pearl S. Buck Award 1999; FAO's CERES Medal; Indira Gandhi Peace Award 2009; and the Visionary Award by the Global South South Development Expo 2014.[4]

Listing her achievements in the World Leaders Forum page on their website, Columbia University would describe the positives of Hasina's first term in office thus:

> In the 1996–2001 term, Sheikh Hasina's government achieved laudable successes in many fields, the most significant being the 30-year Ganges Water Sharing Treaty with India; the Peace Accord on Chittagong Hill Tracts; the Bangabandhu Bridge; and food security. She also introduced beneficial programs for farmers, and social safety nets for the distressed, landless and deprived. These included allowances for distressed women, widows, the disabled and freedom fighters; Shanti Nibas for elders; Ashrayan for the homeless and 'One house-One farm' scheme.

When she returned to power in 2009, the Columbia website again summed up her achievements:

> In the 2009–13 term, Sheikh Hasina's government's achievements included power production capacity reaching 11,000 MW; GDP growth over 6%; 5 crore people raised to middle class; ICT services centres in all union parisads; forex reserve over US$ 20 billion; distribution of agri-cards and scope to open bank accounts with Tk 10 only for farmers, poverty level reduced to 26 percent in 2013 from 31.5 in 2010 and adoption of her Peace Model by an UN resolution.[5]

But Sheikh Hasina wasn't just clocking years in office and collecting awards – she was rewriting the playbook for leadership in Bangladesh. She became the driving force behind Bangladesh's comeback story, blasting it onto the world stage with a mix of grit and vision.

Under Hasina's leadership, Bangladesh witnessed remarkable economic growth and development due to her stringent policies. 'Over the past 15 years, Bangladesh has enjoyed a steady gross domestic product (GDP) growth rate averaging 6.29% annually. Moreover, the per capita income has surged from $698 in 2009 to over $2,500 in 2023, making it one of the highest in the region, surpassing India for the first time. Additionally, the current account balance has seen a steady increase from $3.56 billion to $4.39 billion, while foreign direct investment rose from $900 million in 2009 to $1.63 billion in 2022. Exports of goods and services have more than doubled, growing from $1.87 billion in 2009 to $4.22 billion in 2023. These impressive figures highlight the effectiveness of her economic policies and governance strategies,' the Turkish newspaper *Daily Sabah* summed up on 22 August 2024, weeks after Hasina's fall.[6]

'Significant strides have also been made in primary infrastructure development. The provision of electricity has expanded from 57% in 2009 to over 99% in 2023. Access to clean fuels and technologies for cooking increased from 12% in 2009 to 28% in 2023, while the percentage of the population using the internet has increased substantially from 3% in 2009 to 39% in 2023, demonstrating the effectiveness of her welfare policies,' the report went on to say.

But …

Why were angry students and citizens out on the streets screaming for her removal from power? Who backed the student-led July Revolution, and who infiltrated the movement is another story, but large swathes of her country were indeed crying for change, so fed up with Hasina that they didn't even fear the police bullet.

What gives?

Hasina's Hard Power

For Rezwana Karim Snigdha, it was a classic Freudian paradox as Sheikh Hasina gradually became her own nemesis. Over a Zoom call from Dhaka, the associate professor at the department of anthropology in Jahangirnagar University, a leading voice on gender justice in Bangladesh, told us she had cheered for Hasina when she returned to power in 2009. But as she held on to power with election after rigged election, Snigdha saw Hasina become what she had fought against.

As the longest-serving female head of government in Bangladesh, Hasina's rule was marked by the misuse of her country's security forces, most notably the paramilitary force Rapid Action Battalion (RAB). Her opponents, like Nitai Roy Chowdhury, vice chairman of the central committee of the BNP, whom we spoke to, accused her of using forces like the RAB to abduct and kill opposition members and rig the elections.

Bangladesh's leading English-language news publication the *Daily Star* reported on 7 May 2023 that Bangladesh has been struggling to uphold democratic values and human rights since 2014 – a challenge that has only intensified in recent times. 'The two most recent elections, which were held under the Awami League government in 2014 and 2018, were heavily criticised by the international community, with widespread human rights violations occurring during this period. The regime has employed various means to suppress dissent, including the Digital Security Act,' the *Daily Star* report read.[7]

And then there were reports saying that even the judiciary became compromised during her tenure, forcing a chief justice to flee the country after he opposed her in a ruling.[8]

And what happened to those that didn't flee or fit into her scheme of things?

In April 2019, Michael Chakma was picked up by unknown men off the streets of Dhaka, bundled into a car, blindfolded and thrown into a dark cell. Chakma was a passionate campaigner for the rights of his people at the Chittagong Hill Tract, the same region where, to bring peace, Hasina had signed the Peace Accord on 2 December 1997 and won the UNESCO Houphouet-Boigny Peace Prize in 1998. But the abuses by the military on the people of the Hill Tracts had not stopped and Chakma had come to the Hasina administration's attention after years of campaigning.

The tiny cell he was kept in had no windows and no sunlight, and only two exhaust fans. Gradually, Chakma lost sense of time.

'I used to hear the cries of other prisoners; though I could not see them, their howling was terrifying,' Chakma would tell the BBC after his release once Hasina was out of power. He would come to know those cries were a result of hard interrogations which he would face himself.

'They would tie me to a chair and rotate it very fast. Often, they threatened to electrocute me. They asked why I was criticising Ms Hasina,' Chakma told the BBC.[9]

Chakma would come to know later that he was held inside the dreaded Aynaghar or House of Mirrors, a building deep inside the compound of the DGFI.

A Netra News investigation published on 14 August 2022 would find that since 2009, after Hasina returned to power, enforced disappearances into Aynaghars became common practice for the government. The report quoted a tally maintained by the rights group Odhikar that said that at least 605 citizens became victims of enforced disappearance in Bangladesh between 2009 and September 2021. The list included terror suspects, alleged criminals, Hasina's political opponents and vocal as well as ordinary people.[10]

On 12 February 2025, the world got to see the horrors that were Aynaghars when the chief advisor to Bangladesh's interim government, Muhammad Yunus, visited three secret detention centres and his press wing released photos and videos. 'That a thing such as humanity exists, [Aynaghar] has taken it too far from that (and) erased it entirely … It all appears so atrocious and we are in disbelief,' he told reporters after visiting the sites in the Agargaon, Kachukhet and Uttara areas of Dhaka.[11]

Hasina is facing over a hundred cases, including that of mass murder and corruption, since her ouster. Most of her party's minister and leaders have been arrested or have escaped from Bangladesh. On 12 May 2025, the Yunus government officially banned all activities of the Awami League and its allies over allegations of crimes against humanity and attempts to destabilize the state. Hasina and several of her senior ministers and aides have been indicted by Bangladesh's International Crimes Tribunal for committing crimes against humanity during the SAD-led protest.[12]

Bangladesh press has reported extensively on a documentary by the *Financial Times* that alleges that around $234 billion was illicitly siphoned off from Bangladesh during Hasina's fifteen-year regime.[13]

The documentary, titled "Bangladesh's Missing Billions, Stolen in Plain Sight", was published on 11 September 2025 by the UK-based Financial Times.[14]

The *Financial Times* talked to protesters, politicians, business people and experts about how money was taken out of the country and what, if anything, could be done to get it back.

According to the documentary, the stolen wealth was channelled abroad through over- and under-invoicing of trade, informal transfer systems such as hundi and hawala, and property deals in the UK. The documentary said that London, in particular, emerged as a favoured destination as a lot of money allegedly stolen from Bangladesh has ended up in the UK.

Chief Adviser Muhammad Yunus was also featured in the film.

'People say you can't get all of them. I said, whatever amount we can get. We have to find concrete evidence, follow the track and get the support of relevant governments,' he added.

He also stated that one estimate indicated $234 billion was looted from the banking and business sectors through various means.

'This is probably the biggest money plundering from any country in the world,' he added.

But for Rezwana Karim Snigdha, Hasina's biggest crime was the betrayal of Bangladeshi women. 'One of the things Hasina had promised us were laws for the empowerment of the women of Bangladesh. Instead, she negotiated with the radical Hefazat-e-Islam Bangladesh, and pushed the country back into the hands of the very fundamentalists she had vowed to fight against,' Snigdha told us.

Comprising mainly Sunni clerics heading a network of 19,199 Quami madrassas and its students in Bangladesh, Hefazat, with Hasina's backing, tore apart bit by bit not just the secular fabric of Bangladesh, but also choked the voices of independent women like Snigdha. 'Before 2008, there were not so many madrasas in Dhaka. It was a modern, cosmopolitan city. Now every lane has a madrasa and all credit goes to Hasina,' she told us.

'I am a Muslim but I love wearing the *teep* (bindi). My students get them from India. But today Islamists are dictating what women should and shouldn't wear. It is Hasina who had emboldened them. And India kept believing the well-constructed lie that Sheikh Hasina runs a secular government!' Snigdha said.

Could there be a chance of Sheikh Hasina being back in Bangladesh politics? 'If the Awami League says sorry for all the misdeeds of the Sheikh Hasina government and comes up with a new leadership, maybe the party will have a space here. But it is over for Sheikh Hasina. Bangladesh won't give her another chance.'

If only we could ask Sheikh Hasina for a reaction.

8

A New Messiah?

10 December 2006 should have been a day of ecstatic public celebration in Bangladesh. A day of pride and joy. It was the day Muhammad Yunus, a son of the soil, was to receive the Nobel Peace Prize at a ceremony in the Norwegian capital of Oslo. The first, and so far the only Bangladeshi to get the coveted award, Yunus was, of course, already famous in the country.

Bangladesh's leading English-language daily, the *Daily Star*, proudly proclaimed[1] in a special edition brought out that day that the award ceremony would mark the 'beginning of a new chapter' in the country's 'eventful history'.

But the people of Bangladesh chose to largely ignore the event in Oslo. In fact, the expat Bangladeshi community in London was more enthusiastic than their fellow countrymen back home – they organized a decent reception for Yunus during his visit to that city on 15 December 2006.

Even after Yunus landed in Dhaka on 19 December with the Nobel medal and citation, there were no public ceremonies to honour him or celebrate the achievement. It seemed that Yunus was celebrated more in distant shores than in his own country. At that time, everyone in Bangladesh had heard of him and his pioneering work in microcredit, and were justifiably proud of the laurels he brought to the country.

But somehow that did not seem enough for them to come out on the streets and celebrate him after he was awarded the Nobel Peace

Prize. In fact, Habibul Bashar, the then captain of the Bangladesh cricket team, received far more adulation a year prior to Yunus's Nobel when Bangladesh registered its maiden win in international Test cricket against Zimbabwe under his captaincy.[2] This is evident from a comparison of the public engagements of the two in late 2006 and early 2007: Bashar received many more invitations to public events and was more feted than Yunus at the time.

To be fair, domestic events had, to some extent, clouded the glittering award ceremony in Oslo on 10 December. Prime Minister Begum Khaleda Zia had stepped down at the end of her five-year tenure on 29 October 2006. But instead of a neutral caretaker government headed by the immediate past chief justice of the country's Supreme Court taking charge from her as had been the norm, controversies arising out of Zia's alleged attempt to install a favoured retired chief justice as the chief advisor (the head of the caretaker government) led to the incumbent president, Iajuddin Ahmed, taking charge as head of the caretaker government. That led to considerable disquiet and doubts over the fairness of the next parliamentary elections because the president himself was perceived to be close to the BNP headed by Zia.

A quick dive into Yunus's early career graph would be relevant here.

After his return to Bangladesh on 19 December 2006, Yunus concentrated on expanding the humbly named Grameen conglomerate which included Grameen Motsho (a network of fisheries all over the country), Grameen Krishi (farmers' cooperatives), Grameen Green Capital Management Limited, Grameen Cybernet Limited, Grameen Bitek Ltd, Grameen Solutions, Grameen IT Park, Grameen Star Education Ltd, Grameen Knitwear, Grameen Mutual Fund, Rafiq Autovan Manufacturing Industries Limited, Grameen Shamogree, Grameen Bank, the flagship Grameen Telecom which runs the mobile phone monopoly Grameenphone, and quite a few other mid-sized and mega enterprises.

Yunus, a native of Chittagong in southeastern Bangladesh, had completed his graduation and postgraduation in economics from Dhaka University and his PhD from Vanderbilt University, USA. While he was teaching (1969–72) at the Middle Tennessee State University at Nashville, the 1971 liberation war broke out and he got involved in publishing a newsletter to build up support for the independence of his country. Significantly, he wrote glowingly about Sheikh Mujibur Rahman and hailed Bangabandhu as a stalwart and a revolutionary. He continued his praise for Mujib for many decades after that, even though under his tenure as the caretaker to the interim government in Bangladesh, many would argue Mujib's legacy is being systematically erased.

Yunus returned to the newly created Bangladesh in 1972, and his loyalty to Mujib was promptly rewarded with a membership of the country's Planning Commission. But, as renowned author Alan Jolis writes in his book *Banker to the Poor: Micro-Lending and Battle against World Poverty*,[3] Yunus found the job mundane and joined Chittagong University as head of its economics department.

The devastating Bangladesh famine of 1974 prompted Yunus to start working on poverty reduction and rural livelihood enhancement models. Over the next two years, he worked closely with poor households in rural areas and in 1976 he founded Grameen Bank and came up with the microcredit model. As Alan Jolis documented in his book, Yunus saw that the womenfolk of Jobra village in Chittagong district who used to weave cane furniture had to take loans at extortionist rates from moneylenders because banks refused to give them unsecured loans.

Yunus lent those women a few hundred Bangladeshi taka from his own savings to buy cane, and all the women not only repaid the loan but, for the first time, made a tiny profit after meeting all expenses. That was the birth of the microcredit model that Yunus pioneered, a model that has been introduced and implemented successfully across the world, including India.

Observing the success of the first microcredit experiment by Yunus at Jobra, Bangladesh's state-owned Janata Bank agreed to support Grameen Bank in giving out microloans at concessional rates to the poor at Jobra village. Grameen Bank helped the women form small cooperatives. The loans were given to these cooperatives, which then distributed the money to their individual members who needed it the most. The women supported each other, and that ensured timely repayment of the loans. To further ensure financial discipline, the members of the cooperatives which took loans formed 'solidarity groups' whose members acted as co-guarantors for each other. This entire model proved highly successful, and the Janata Bank expanded this microfinance project to other parts of the country. In six years' time, by 1982, loans were being regularly given out to 28,000 cooperatives of women, small fish farmers, weavers, artisans, etc., all over the country. Grameen Bank grew by leaps and bounds, and in the one-year period between June 2006 and May 2007, the bank had disbursed loans worth 50.42 billion Bangladeshi taka ($729.44 million at the rates prevailing that time). The bank posted a loan recovery rate of an impressive 98.28 per cent.[4]

By the time Yunus returned to Dhaka on 15 December 2006, he was already well-known in international academia and other influential circles. One of his most ardent supporters was former US President Bill Clinton. Clinton had got to know about Yunus when he was the governor of Arkansas in 1985. Inspired by Yunus's work, Clinton created a microfinance programme in his home state. Clinton hosted Yunus at the White House a number of times during his presidential years between January 1993 and January 2001. The two have remained good friends till date. The Clinton Foundation has been one of Yunus's strongest supporters. Clinton, by his own admission, had been lobbying for the Nobel Peace Prize for Yunus since his first term (1993–97) at the White House.

But it wasn't just Clinton who Yunus counted amongst his friends. Yunus, said Professor Abbas Asif, a former associate, possessed good networking skills and 'took particular care' to impress Westerners. 'He [Yunus] is soft-spoken, dresses humbly and comes across as very sincere. In the initial years, he actually did some very good work on alleviating rural poverty through microfinance which he is rightly credited with. While his work in microfinance and his contribution in helping tens of thousands come out of acute poverty impresses westerners, the whole "Yunus package", as I call it – his down-to-earth and humble image, his ordinary and plain attire, his self-effacing and even timid demeanour – makes him a darling to Westerners who like non-Westerners to be deferential towards them,' said Asif. Asif, who taught at Chittagong University and now lives in Malaysia, has observed Yunus for a number of years from very close quarters.

A former associate of his at Grameen Bank, who had a bitter fallout with him and does not want to be identified because he lives in Bangladesh, told us: 'Yunus knows very well how to impress people who matter in the West. He has always been very submissive in the company of fair-skinned people, especially ones who are in positions of power or influence. He would be very ingratiating towards Westerners who used to visit the [Grameen] bank, but he was often very harsh towards his fellow citizens. He has a dual personality, one for Westerners or people he wants to impress and the other for people who do not matter. He's not abusive to the latter, but his sarcasm and castigation, delivered with sarcasm, can cut through one's heart like a knife. He has a very sharp tongue and can deliver humiliating put-downs,' said this former executive at Grameen Bank.

Apart from those in Bangladesh who have known him closely and have turned against him, there are quite a number of his fellow countrymen who are not enamoured of him at all. One of them is a retired professor of economics who taught at Dhaka University. This academic, a septuagenarian, also studied economics at Dhaka University like Yunus, though about a decade after Yunus passed out of the varsity.

'Yunus is celebrated as a Nobel laureate. But why was he not considered worthy of the Nobel Prize in economics? The Nobel Peace Prize makes no sense. Yunus is an economist, so he ought to have been judged in his area of expertise and given the relevant award if deemed fit for it. Recipients of the Nobel Peace Prize, as we all know, are chosen on political and many other considerations. Tremendous lobbying takes place and the selection process is hardly objective. It is well known that Bill Clinton and other powerful and influential people and organizations lobbied very hard for Yunus and so he got the Nobel Peace Prize. But he did not get the Nobel Prize in economics. Two other Bengalis got it: Amartya Sen and Abhijit Banerjee. This means that Yunus's work in his own area of expertise, economics, has not been good enough to warrant a Nobel Prize. The selection process for a Nobel Prize in economics is much more objective, rigorous and peer-driven,' said this former Dhaka University economics professor.

Be that as it may, Yunus started courting controversy very soon after he received the Nobel. By that time, the army was actively conspiring to take over power. 'The army, by mid-December 2006, had already put in place its plans to wrest power from President Iajuddin Ahmed and appoint someone else the chief advisor of the caretaker government while exercising power from behind the scenes. We learnt later that the then army chief, General Moeen Uddin Ahmed, got in touch with Yunus within two days of his return to Bangladesh (after receiving the Nobel Prize) and discussed the uncertain political situation in the country,' former Awami League leader Mohammad Rofiquzzaman told us.

Rofiquzzaman, seventy-six, now lives in the UK where his son is a physician. 'Yunus agreed with the army chief that the situation in the country was not good and a spell of army rule would set things right. He expressed support for the army chief's plans to stage a coup,' Rofiquzzaman said. When General Ahmed finally intervened (on 11 January 2007) and asked President Iajuddin Ahmed to step down as chief advisor of the caretaker government, Yunus expressed his full support. He told AFP in an interview then that 'politicians in Bangladesh are corrupt'[5] and expressed complete support for the army chief's plans to crack down on corruption.

It is believed that Yunus supported the army chief's plans to install Fakhruddin Ahmed, a fellow economist and his contemporary from Dhaka University, as the head of the caretaker government in place of President Iajuddin Ahmed. Fakhruddin, a former governor of Bangladesh Bank (the country's central bank), was known to be an acolyte of Yunus at that time. Immediately after being installed as the chief advisor of the caretaker government on 12 January 2007, Fakhruddin Ahmed proclaimed a state of emergency throughout the country, imposed night curfew, banned political activities and launched a massive operation against 'corrupt' politicians, bureaucrats, businessmen and others. More than 160 top politicians, bureaucrats and others were arrested and put behind bars.

'This witch-hunt against leaders of the two major political parties [the Awami League and the BNP] and top bureaucrats had the full support of Muhammad Yunus,' said Awami League leader Mohammad Rofiquzzaman. He pointed out that Yunus had been campaigning against alleged corruption in politics for quite some time and had, in March 2006, unveiled a twelve-point formula to ensure that 'honest and competent' candidates were fielded in the elections scheduled for early 2007.[6] That triggered rumours that Yunus had started harbouring political ambitions. Yunus had denied those rumours and asserted that his only intention was to ensure clean governance so that the country could develop. But the rumours persisted and grew stronger with his hobnobbing with the military brass in December 2006 and January 2009.

Yunus's long-concealed political ambitions were revealed when he wrote an open letter, which was published in the *Daily Star*, asking the people of Bangladesh for their opinions on his plans to float a new political party.[7] In his letter,[8] Yunus claimed that 'many people' had requested him to join politics and he had taken their request 'with utmost importance'.

'I, like you, witnessed where our political culture has brought the country and how it attempted to destroy the country's future possibilities. The way the present caretaker government is trying to

Sahidul Hasan Khokon with President of Bangladesh Md Shahabuddin Chuppu on 13 February 2023, a day after Bangladesh press reported he would be the next president

Deep Halder with former Bangladesh Home Minister Asaduzzaman Khan in Delhi

Bangladeshi model Asma Ul Husna Bristy posing with a fellow model in Dhaka

Bangladeshi artiste Ashna Habib Bhabna shared her portrait of Bangabondhu Sheikh Mujibur Rahman on Facebook on his death anniversary on 15 August 2020.

Actress–activist Deepanwita Martin shared a morphed pic of a slipper on a picture of convicted 1971 war criminal Delwar Hossain Sayeedi on her Facebook page.

Pinaki Bhattacharya is one of the most influential Bangladeshi YouTubers and social media influencers. Picture from his Facebook page.

The stairs where Sheikh Mujib was shot and killed on 15 August 1975. This picture was taken after a mob attacked the house on 5 February 2025.

Deep Halder outside a deserted haveli in Kolakopa village near Dhaka city in July 2023. The village lies deserted today after decades of Hindu exodus.

On 2 September 2025, Bangladesh press reported that in Gaibandha district in Rangpur zilla, Durga idols were set on fire. The picture of the incident and snapshot of the news item in Bangladeshi local press.

Student protestors on Dhaka streets during the July Revolution of 2024 that ousted Sheikh Hasina. Picture by Saqlaine Rizve.

Why has Bangladesh Nationalist Party's acting chairman Tarique Rahman not returned to Bangladesh from exile in UK? Picture shared by him on his Facebook page.

create an acceptable atmosphere by carrying out necessary reforms has made me optimistic along with all citizens of the country. In this situation, I feel it with my heart that I should, showing due respect to the people's expectation of me, participate in the mission of taking the nation to the height it deserves. It is now clear to all that it is not possible to reach the goal [by] maintaining the existing political culture; it is only possible by bringing a comprehensive change to the culture. Through my work and experience, I feel with all my heart that the people with their innate sense of endeavour and creativity can achieve the impossible if political goodwill, competent leadership and good governance can be established. If I have to form a political party in response to the people's desire, it will be dedicated to this very objective,' Yunus wrote in the open letter. Asking for people's 'active participation and assistance' in his political endeavour, Yunus asked people to communicate directly with him.

Yunus penned a second open letter[9] on 23 February 2007, which was published in the front page of the *Daily Star*,[10] announcing that he had decided to go ahead and launch a new political party named Nagorik Shakti (Strength of the People). In his letter, he said he was overwhelmed by the huge response of people asking him to go ahead with his plans to enter politics.

Outlining the ideology of his party, Yunus wrote, 'Our politics would be the politics to materialise the dream of the liberation war. This politics would be a politics of unity, a politics of peace, a politics to establish honesty, a politics of labour, a politics to change the fate of the people as quickly as possible by reviving a new work ethic, a politics to send poverty to the museum. This politics will be non-communal, secular, democratic, good governance, free from corruption and against politicisation. It will be the politics of equity for women in all spheres, building the future of the young generation and not to bow down to foreign powers and to stand in the world holding the head high'.

Yunus also called upon his supporters to form twenty-member 'primary preparatory teams' in each village and locality across the country.

But on 3 May 2007, Yunus did a U-turn. He wrote a third open letter[11] that was published on the front page of the *Daily Star* the next morning, announcing that he had abandoned his plans to set up the new political party. Yunus attributed this decision to his failure to create a 'strong organising team' that 'can boost my confidence'. Yunus explained in his letter: 'It became increasingly clear to me that the people who I needed with me to present a strong and bright alternative to the people will not be with me. Some of them are involved with political parties, some of them who are not in politics but are enthusiastic about it. They all want a new political path to be established and they are enthusiastic about changing the country's political culture. But I could not bring them with me. Those who initially showed encouragement, I saw that they are becoming less and less encouraging.'

Why the U-turn? Significantly, Yunus had met Fakhruddin Ahmed, the chief advisor to the interim government, on the morning of 3 May 2007. He penned the letter withdrawing his plans to launch a new political party the same evening. It was thus apparent that the meeting with Fakhruddin Ahmed held the key to his decision to abandon his political plans. But what transpired at the meeting?

According to multiple sources in the Awami League, the BNP and other political parties, as well as those who were with Yunus at that time, the Nobel laureate had wanted a guarantee from the army that the ban on political activities that was in force at that time would not apply to his new party. Yunus, say these sources, also wanted a moratorium on fresh elections for at least three years in order to enable his new party to gain enough strength so that it would be able to compete with the established political parties when elections were eventually held. Yunus also wanted various sorts of institutional and state support for his party.

'Yunus argued that when parliamentary elections are held, his party should have a level playing field with other established parties. It takes time for a new party to gain strength and critical mass. So he wanted a three-year moratorium on elections and other favours that would strengthen his party. But the army brass refused to play ball. Fakhruddin conveyed this to Yunus when the two met on 3 May morning. Yunus then realized that he would never achieve his political ambitions through the electoral route and junked his plans to float the political party,' said Jakir Hossain, a retired bureaucrat who was an aide to one of the advisors of the interim government at that time.

Interestingly, Yunus is now being accused of favouring his favoured party, the Jatiyo Nagorik Party or the NCP formed by leaders of the July 2024 uprising against Sheikh Hasina, and protecting it from political adversaries.

Yunus's aborted plans to form a political party brought him into the crosshairs of Sheikh Hasina, who launched multiple probes against him after coming to power in January 2009. Soon after, Yunus announced his plans to float a new political party, Sheikh Hasina, without naming Yunus, strongly criticized him.[12] Hasina told a group of cultural personas that 'usurers' (meaning Yunus) have been exploiting the poor of the country and carrying out a tirade against 'corrupt politicians' while wanting to join politics themselves. 'The usurers have not only failed to eradicate poverty but have also nurtured poverty,' she said. That was the first time that Sheikh Hasina criticized Yunus; the two had had cordial ties till then.

The Sheikh Hasina government formally announced a probe into the activities of Grameen Bank on 11 January 2011. Whistleblowers came up with revelations of various wrongdoings – like siphoning off funds and fudging accounts – against Yunus and other top executives of Grameen Bank and its associated enterprises.

Within a month of the government launching a formal probe, a newly formed organization by the name of 'Friends of Grameen' started drumming up support for Yunus. Former Irish president

Mary Robinson, another ardent supporter of Yunus, was the prime mover behind this initiative to save Yunus. Many other prominent figures from across the world, including former World Bank president James Wolfensohn, former chief justice of India Jagdish Sharan Verma and French American actress Yeardley Smith, voiced support for Yunus.[13]

But the Bangladesh government remained undeterred.[14] The country's finance minister, Abul Maal Abdul Muhith, told the media that Yunus should stay away from Grameen Bank while the bank was being investigated.[15] While launching the probe against Grameen Bank, the government had appointed a former employee of the Bank, Muzammel Huq, as its chairman. Huq announced on 2 March 2011 that Yunus had been sacked as managing director of Grameen Bank.[16] Yunus filed a petition before the Bangladesh High Court challenging his dismissal.[17] More international support poured in for Yunus; prominent US Senator John Kerry became one of the strongest voices against what he termed was the persecution of Yunus on trumped-up charges. Thousands of employees and customers as well as beneficiaries of Grameen Bank also staged massive demonstrations in Dhaka in support of Yunus.[18] But on 8 March 2011, Bangladesh High Court Judge Muhammad Mamtaj Uddin Ahmed upheld Yunus's sacking.[19]

The Sheikh Hasina government initiated more moves to wrest control of Grameen Bank from Yunus and his coterie. In August 2012, it passed an ordinance increasing government control over the bank, a move that evoked US concerns.[20] In September 2013, another probe was ordered by the government into Yunus's financial transactions in his later years as Grameen Bank's managing director.[21] Sheikh Hasina accused Yunus of evading taxes on his Nobel Peace Prize money and book royalties, and of receiving them without due permission from the government.[22]

In October 2013, the cabinet approved a new law that would grant Bangladesh Bank complete control over Grameen Bank. The Parliament enacted it into a law on 7 November 2013.[23] The government filed a number of lawsuits against Yunus. Between 2011 and 2024, Yunus faced 174 lawsuits related to financial misappropriations, labour law violations, money laundering, corruption and even food adulteration. On 1 January 2024, Yunus and three other executives of Grameen Bank were sentenced to six months' imprisonment for labour law violations, but the sentences were kept in abeyance pending appeals by the convicted.[24] Amnesty International termed the convictions as a 'blatant abuse of the judicial system'.[25] Not surprisingly, after the fall of the Sheikh Hasina government and a day before Muhammad Yunus returned to the country to become the chief advisor of the interim government, a labour court quashed the convictions and dismissed the case against Yunus and his co-convicted.[26] Four days later, on 11 August 2024, Yunus was acquitted by the Anti-Corruption Commission in graft cases pending against him.[27]

Despite the popular perception that Yunus had been hounded by a vindictive Sheikh Hasina regime for many years, there are those who believe Yunus is guilty of most, if not all, the charges levelled against him.

One of them is independent London-based Bangladeshi-British journalist Sushanta Das Gupta. In an email interview, Das Gupta, founder of AmarMP.com, a civic-tech initiative to hold politicians accountable, said that he had exposed Yunus's corruption by investigating multiple areas where his name repeatedly appeared in court proceedings, audit findings and whistleblower testimonies.

'The most serious and legally proven case involved the embezzlement of over 25.22 crore taka (approximately $2.3 million) from the Grameen Telecom Workers' Profit Participation Fund, which was supposed to benefit employees but was allegedly misappropriated for other purposes,' he said.

Das Gupta said he was first alerted to these activities through confidential communications from former Grameen Telecom insiders. 'I then cross-checked this information with documentation from the Anti-Corruption Commission (ACC) of Bangladesh, and

I released my findings through my networks including ATeam, AmarMP.com and Dainik Amar Habiganj, of which I was the editor,' he said.

'In June 2024, a Dhaka court formally accepted the ACC's charge sheet and indicted Yunus and thirteen others, legally confirming what I had been reporting independently. That indictment was a landmark moment – it proved that the truth about globally celebrated figures can and must be confronted,' he said.

Das Gupta said his investigations and findings are based on whistleblowers from Grameen Telecom who exposed irregularities in profit distributions, internal financial records showing misrouted employee funds, court documents and government charge sheets, including the June 2024 embezzlement and January 2024 labour law conviction and suppressed reports from Bangladeshi journalists who were either pressured or bribed into silence.

Asked about Yunus's work as a pioneer of microfinance, Das Gupta said: 'Yes, Dr Yunus pioneered microcredit at a time when rural communities had no access to banking, and he brought Bangladesh positive global recognition through the Nobel Peace Prize. However, that legacy has been severely compromised. Microloans under Grameen Bank often charged interest rates higher than commercial banks, pushing many poor borrowers into perpetual debt cycles. His other ventures, like Grameen Telecom, have now become subjects of criminal trials for embezzlement and labour exploitation.'

'So while I credit his early innovation, his later career reflects a troubling descent into opaque governance, unchecked power and ethical failures,' he added.

Das Gupta asserts that 'every major allegation I've presented has passed through formal judicial scrutiny'. 'For example, on 2 June 2024, Dr Yunus was indicted by a special court in Dhaka under the Anti-Corruption Commission Act for embezzling workers' welfare funds. In January 2024, a labour court convicted him for violating Bangladesh's Labour Act by not regularizing sixty-seven employees and denying them statutory benefits. These aren't opinions, they're legal facts reflected in official judgments, case files and charges recognised by the courts. Anyone doubting the story can review the public records,' he says.

Lately, fresh controversies arose over special privileges and permissions granted to Grameen Bank by the interim government headed by Yunus. The interim government fast-tracked approval for Grameen University and granted it special privileges, gave Grameen enterprises special tax waivers, granted special licences for manpower export to the Grameen conglomerate and allowed Grameen Bank to launch a digital wallet. Critics have flagged these and alleged conflict of interest since the interim government granted special privileges to Grameen Bank and Grameen enterprises in which Yunus has deep personal interests.[28,29]

But Yunus faces far graver criticism from other quarters. After being sworn in as the chief advisor to the interim government, one of his primary tasks was to get a grip on the law and order situation in Bangladesh. His administration failed to rein in murderous and rioting mobs from attacking leaders, activists and supporters of the Awami League, policemen, Hindus and other minorities.

On 13 July 2025, *Dhaka Tribune* put out a report saying the interm government had said that improving law and order would be their first priority. 'Instead, analysts say violence and "mob justice" have surged under the new administration. According to an analysis of police data from August 2024 to June 2025, a total of 108,695 criminal incidents were reported across the country over the last 11 months. Among them, 3,504 were murders, averaging over 10 killings per day. Crimes against women and children remain deeply concerning, with 17,900 reported cases,' the report read.[30]

The Yunus government has also been accused of giving a free rein to Islamists. Whose support he requires, and has obtained, his critics within the Bangladesh press have told us on the condition of anonymity because of his testy ties with the BNP as well as the army, the two powerful institutions in the country that are not in his control.

One of his first acts was to order the release of the chief of the Ansarullah Bangla Team (ABT), Jashimuddin Rahmani. The ABT is a proscribed terror outfit. His government lifted the ban on the Jamaat-e-Islami Bangladesh and has allowed radical Islamists take control of many institutions. Yunus has been accused of whitewashing crimes against Hindus by passing off attacks on the community as political in nature. Yunus, and his team of advisors who include leaders of the uprising against Sheikh Hasina, stand accused of installing pliant judges in the Bangladesh High Court and Supreme Court, appointing their favourites in the Election Commission and other bodies, shunting off independent bureaucrats and compromising all institutions of governance. Ironically, Yunus has been accusing the Sheikh Hasina government of the same misdeeds.

But what has drawn international attention towards the workings of the Yunus-led interim government and the state of democracy in Bangladesh after the fall of Hasina, is the state of the media. *The Hindu* quoted a New Delhi-based rights group to report that Bangladesh, after the fall of the Hasina government, recorded a 230 per cent increase in attacks on journalists.

The Rights and Risks Analysis Group, that *The Hindu* quoted, said press freedom in Bangladesh deteriorated under Yunus, with attacks on 878 journalists between August 2024 and July 2025, almost 230 per cent more than the 383 journalists attacked from August 2023 to July 2024, when Hasina was the prime minister.

The rights group said the number of criminal cases against journalists increased by 558 per cent from 35 cases during 2023–24 to 195 cases during the first year of Dr Yunus as the Chief Advisor. 'While the Hasina regime was not known to have denied any accreditation to journalists, Dr Yunus used accreditation as an instrument to punish the journalists allegedly associated with the previous regime and denied accreditation to 167 of them,' the group's director Suhas Chakma was quoted as saying.[31]

Suppression of the voice of the free press apart, many term the interim government 'illegitimate' since questions have been raised about the manner in which it was installed after the Sheikh Hasina regime fell. Career diplomat and former Bangladesh ambassador to Morocco, Mohammad Harun Al Rashid, told us in an email interview from Canada where he has taken refuge, that the Yunus regime is 'not a legitimate government'.

'It seized power through a violent uprising that was one of the most effective terrorist offensives in the history of Islamist extremism. Since Prime Minister Sheikh Hasina stepped aside, the rule of law in Bangladesh has effectively collapsed. The July–August 2024 insurrection, led by Jamaat-affiliated militants – some of whom later formed the NCP – was coordinated with other Islamist groups, foreign backers and supported logistically by the BNP,' the 2001 batch foreign service cadre diplomat wrote to us. 'This was not a political transition. It was a calculated, forceful hijacking of the state,' he added.

'The conspiracy was meticulously planned and was far-reaching. Foreign money was funnelled into nearly every sector – artists, singers, university teachers and public intellectuals, all co-opted under a design later revealed by Yunus himself during an event in New York attended by former US President Bill Clinton,' said Rashid, who has served in his country's missions in Egypt, Mexico, Italy and Spain.

While Yunus has announced that the next round of national elections will be held before Ramadan in February 2026, Rashid remains doubtful. The former diplomat says it is unlikely that Yunus would hold elections on time, since he has been delaying the dates till now.

On 1 June 2025, Bangladeshi press had reported that the BNP and Yunus administration were not on the same page over poll dates.

Bangladesh Nationalist Party Standing Committee Member Dr Khandaker Mosharraf Hossain had used strong words to make his disagreement with the interim government known on this matter and demanded elections by December 2025.

'We believe that the longer the election is delayed, the more the illegitimate government will engage in conspiracies. We are already witnessing some of those conspiracies. Therefore, holding elections by December would be best. The interim government will eventually have to step down. We believe that if they do so by December, they can step down with dignity,' Hossain had said.[32]

'Any attempt on his part to influence or delay elections using non-governmental leverage or foreign backers will only fuel further instability. I believe he may try to stall democratic processes under the guise of "reforms" or "national dialogue". It is more likely that he and his backers will extend or derail election plans than facilitate a legitimate vote. This is not about reform, it's about power without accountability,' Dasgupta told us. Das Gupta, a member of the National Union of Journalists (NUJ), UK, and the International Federation of Journalists (IFJ), also hosts the GenocideBangladesh.org project that's aimed at fighting historical denialism and political misinformation.

Dasgupta said given Yunus's global connections, adverse news about him never used to get published in the Bangladeshi media even when Sheikh Hasina was in power. 'This is something I've personally monitored. Several national-level news outlets published coverage of the embezzlement charges and the labour law conviction, only to remove the articles within hours. Why? Because of the immense global and domestic influence Yunus wields through his NGO and donor connections. In some cases, editors told me they were advised to "avoid unnecessary controversy". Others feared defamation suits. This kind of censorship through intimidation or influence is part of what I seek to expose. Not just the corruption, but the system that enables it,' he said.

Harun Al-Rashid sounds the dire warning that Yunus's continuation in office would adversely affect India's interests.

'Since Yunus's takeover, the regime has consistently tried to provoke India while concealing its long-term aims. Although India has so far taken a cautious, observant stance, it is critical to recognise that the very parties which enabled this regime's rise are built on platforms of India-bashing, Hindu-hating and religious extremism. Should any of these factions consolidate power further, they will almost certainly attempt to destabilize India through direct or proxy terrorist activity. In the long run, I believe India will inevitably be affected by the consequences of what is unfolding in Bangladesh,' Harun Al-Rashid told us.

But all these allegations apart, what perhaps should rankle a career economist most is the health of the Bangladesh economy. On 25 August 2025, the *Daily Star* put out a report quoting the Dhaka Chamber of Commerce and Industry (DCCI) to say Bangladesh's economy is grappling with multiple challenges, including slowing growth, stubborn inflation and a sharp fall in private investment.

'Private investment dropped to 22.48 percent of the GDP in FY25, the lowest in the last 5 years. Both the opening of LCs and the import of capital machinery have declined,' DCCI President Taskeen Ahmed was quoted as saying. 'Strengthen law and order and ensure uninterrupted and reliable energy supply to improve the business environment,' he added.

The report noted that in trying to curb inflation, the Yunus government has squeezed private sector credit and dampened economic activity, creating a medium-term crisis. A multimodal approach was needed to tackle both issues simultaneously.

To restore investor confidence, it recommended stabilizing the banking sector, ensuring political stability and removing bureaucratic bottlenecks to improve the ease of doing business.

A globally feted economist, a Nobel Peace Prize winner and now the premier of Bangladesh at eighty-five, Muhammad Yunus has led a glorious life till now. One year and a few months is too less a time to mop up the mess created by his predecessors. But leaving behind a failed state and a collapsed economy should not mar his CV. For those who died for a better Bangladesh and those who still believe he would do the right thing, that would be a grave betrayal.

9

Boys and Girls in King's Party

'Like Saturn, the Revolution devours its children.'

—JACQUES MALLET DU PAN,
eighteenth-century Genevan political journalist

On 3 September 2024, almost a month after Sheikh Hasina fled to India, the Indian online news platform *ThePrint* published a long interview with the information and communications tech adviser to the interim government of Bangladesh, Nahid Islam. The interim government had taken over the reins of Bangladesh from 8 August 2024 under Professor Muhammad Yunus, and by then, the twenty-seven-year-old Islam had become famous not just within Bangladesh but for anyone following Bangladesh's tumultuous period of sociopolitical changes.

Islam was known not just as a member of the new government, but as the face of SAD, a platform of student activists formed in 2024 during the nationwide student-led quota reform movement which led the July Revolution that toppled Hasina.

Nahid Islam was the revolution's own victorious child.

Islam told *ThePrint*'s Ananya Bhardwaj that the July Revolution was an 'organic protest' as people felt for the cause and the idea gained popularity across the country very soon.[1]

'We organised these protests under the banner of the Students Against Discrimination (SAD) from 1 July (2024). These protests started against the quota movement and grew organically. That is when we coordinated with the leaders of these movements across universities to make it bigger.'

Islam said that SAD soon became an open platform where any student or student organization could raise their concerns. It was not based on anyone's politics or political identity, he said. 'This became an open platform for students. In Bangla, it is called Boishommo Birodhi Chhatro Andolon. Since it was open and accessible to all, it was able to engage everyone quickly and became something people could put their faith on.'

When Bhardwaj asked how the protests became violent, Islam said that the Sheikh Hasina government gave orders to 'shoot students' and that is when the protests resorted to violence 'to end oppression'.

Islam said that it was a very peaceful protest in the beginning and that it was the government that added 'fuel to the fire'. 'They attacked women, children, and university campuses were shut down. It was actually the government that made this movement turn violent. When the police started firing indiscriminately at unarmed civilians, they had no option but to retaliate,' he said. 'Had the government not used violent tactics, a peaceful transition would have been possible, but that did not happen.'

In the interview, Islam alleged that till her last day in Bangladesh, Hasina tried 'using brute force to remain in power', despite being given time to resign and leave.

'We have seen that until the last day, until the morning of 5 August, civilians have been shot at. Till her last day, Sheikh Hasina tried to remain in power using brute force. When the government is applying brute force, state machinery is being used against civilians and students, people will revolt. This turned into a violent situation, and Sheikh Hasina created a civil war-like situation,' he said.

'Had she wanted, Sheikh Hasina could have made a peaceful transition; she could have calmly resigned. We repeatedly gave her time. She, however, even during the movement and afterward, when we gave her time to resign, became more violent – arrests were made – so the people were left with no choice but to protest.'

Islam said that although they expected an impact, they never thought it would lead to the fall of the government. He added that the end of the 'autocratic rule was inevitable'. 'We did not expect that it would happen like this, but it is part of Bangladesh's history that every autocratic ruler has seen their fall through student movements,' he said.

'Bangladesh has been under fascism for the past 15 years. The people were expecting an uprising. So when the students rebelled for their rights and the people came out in support, it grew big. The pent-up anger of the citizens and the economic crisis all played a role in the beginning of this movement and the eventual fall of Hasina and her government.'

Islam said that across universities, 'torture of students by the Awami League's student wing had become a norm'. He alleged there was no freedom for dissent or freedom of speech in campuses, and students would lead inhuman lives.

'They (students) have wanted to revolt at times in the past. At the national level, there was massive corruption, and protestors were crushed. There were three unfair elections where citizens did not have voting rights. There was no governance and power was concentrated in the hands of a few people,' an impassioned Islam told Bhardwaj.

'The Hasina family, which had turned into a dynasty, harboured all the money, power, and privilege. Citizens were unhappy, abused and tortured, and that is what motivated the people to join this movement and lay down their lives for the fall of Sheikh Hasina.'

So, what after Hasina?

Islam said in the interview that reforms would be brought about, but would be done with the consensus of the people and all political parties.

'This is a huge chance for Bangladesh, where we will rebuild it. So this government will look at that reformation project, and these decisions will not be made individually but based on a national consensus. All the political parties will have a say in it.'

He said that, going ahead, old politics would not work and that political parties would have to undergo a transformation and present a new face to the students who were part of this uprising.

'An uprising took place and certain aspirations, spirits, and commitments have been created. Going ahead, Bangladesh will have to place faith in this spirit and govern according to those commitments,' he said. 'Consequently, reforms might be needed even within the parties. The old politics will not work in Bangladesh. It is not attractive to the new crowd.'

When asked if the student body planned to make a political party of its own, Islam said that what Bangladesh needed at the moment was 'national unity'.

'We are not thinking of a separate political party at this moment. We are part of the interim government. A huge chunk of the students are directing the government so that the spirit of the uprising remains, and the government works accordingly. We want national unity, so we don't want to get into any conflicts or get tangled in the power games at this moment,' he said. 'When elections take place, we will decide according to the situation and the will of the people.'

Within five months of the interview, with the young politician categorically stating that he was not thinking of a separate political party but of national unity, the NCP was formed on 28 February 2025, with Nahid Islam as its convener.

On 7 March 2025, Islam declared at a press briefing: 'The Anti-discrimination Student Movement is no longer where it was. A student organisation has emerged from it. A political party has emerged. The label "coordinator or anti-discrimination" no longer applies.'[2]

The press and the people welcomed the NCP with open arms and predicted the birth of a 'Second Republic' replacing what they said was the rot that had become Bangladesh.

Shafi Md Mostofa, associate professor of world religions and culture at the University of Dhaka and a post-doctoral research fellow of the Democracy Institute at the Central European University, Hungary, said the NCP represents a bold attempt to redefine Bangladeshi politics with its vision of a 'Second Republic' and a discrimination-free Bangladesh. He recounted how the NCP's origins are deeply rooted in the July 2024 uprising, a watershed moment in Bangladesh's history, and the uprising, led by students and supported by the masses, was a response to years of authoritarian rule, systemic corruption and the erosion of democratic institutions under Sheikh Hasina's government.

The movement, which began as an anti-quota protest demanding equal opportunities for all, quickly evolved into a broader call for systemic change after Hasina ordered a brutal crackdown on the students, he wrote. The students' success in toppling Hasina's regime and forcing her to flee the country marked the beginning of a new political era, according to him.

'The NCP's formation is a direct outcome of this revolution. The absence of Hasina and her Awami League created a power vacuum, which the new party seeks to fill. The NCP's founders, many of whom were at the forefront of the July uprising, have positioned themselves as the torchbearers of a new political order. Their vision is encapsulated in the concept of a "Second Republic", which seeks to fundamentally reimagine the state and its institutions,' he said.

Mostafa believed that drawing inspiration from historical examples, such as the United States' transformation after the Civil War and France's multiple republics, the NCP aimed to draft a new democratic constitution through an elected constituent assembly. 'This new constitution would prioritise democracy, equality, and social justice, addressing the systemic failures that have plagued Bangladesh since its independence in 1971,' he wrote.

Within less than six months, the Bangladeshi press began singing a slightly different tune. On 6 July 2025, Bangladesh's leading English-language daily, the *Daily Star*, wrote that the past, it seemed, was catching up with the present.

'There is something painfully ironic when those providing leadership to a movement, built on the premise of justice and reform, become the subject of criminal investigations. That irony is now manifesting in the public sphere as multiple individuals associated with Bangladesh's recent anti-government student platforms – particularly the Anti-Discrimination Student Movement (SAD), Bangladesh Ganatantrik Chhatra Sangsad (BGCS), and the political camp National Citizen Party (NCP) – face serious allegations of extortion, impersonation, and criminal misuse of power. The accusations are not just isolated headlines; they speak to a deeper, structural pattern that has historically tainted Bangladesh's student and political activism,' it said.[3]

Things have come to such a pass that even NCP leaders cannot distance themselves from the *Daily Star* opinion column or the other reports that have come out in the press against party members.

Hasnat Abdullah, chief organizer (southern region) of the NCP, has condemned party members who, he alleged, are engaging in extortion by misusing the party's name and banner.

'It is very unfortunate that many are getting involved in extortion using our name and identity, using the NCP's banner. Our activists say we want a new political arrangement, but then go and commit extortion – these things we will not tolerate,' Abdullah said at the NCP's 'July March to Build the Nation' and street rally in Mymensingh.[4] 'We do not need millions of activists. We do not need millions of leaders. The NCP will not be a safe haven for extortionists,' he said.

A month later, on 10 August 2025, *Prothom Alo English* reported that NCP has issued show-cause notices to ten of its central leaders over various incidents, including breaches of discipline, moral turpitude and involvement in controversies in the last six months. Five of these ten leaders are members of the party's key decision-making body, the Political Council.

The *Prothom Alo English* report put out a long list of complaints against NCP leaders. On 9 June 2025, the report said that NCP

Executive Member Zobairul Alam was issued a notice. During an Eid reunion programme in Chattogram's Anwara, Zobairul Alam had reportedly said, 'There's no bigger mafia than us.'

In May 2025, NCP Joint Member Secretary Zainal Abedin (Shishir) was accused of involvement in unrest at the *Daily Janakantha* newspaper office.[5]

The *Daily Star* wrote that for movements that claim to champion equality and accountability, these developments are not just reputational blows – they are existential threats. 'As various leaders scramble to issue statements, suspend local committees, and distance themselves from the accused, the public is left wondering: how did we get here? More importantly, what does it say about the nature of political transitions and grassroots mobilisations in Bangladesh?

'What we are witnessing now is the familiar pattern of transformation: a moral crusade turning into a power mechanism, and then eventually into a money-making enterprise. In many ways, it mirrors the lifecycle of movements globally, where momentum and mass mobilisation attract not only the idealists but also opportunists.'[6]

End of a Dream?

A year and a month after the fall of the Hasina government after a students' protest against quotas in government jobs, demonstrations rocked Nepal in September 2025. Predominantly organised by students and young Nepalis, it came to be known as 'the Gen Z protests', following a nationwide ban on numerous social media platforms. But the protests also reflected the public's frustration with corruption and display of wealth by Nepal government officials and their families, as well as allegations of mismanagement of public funds.

Even as the protests escalated with wide-spread violence against government officials and vandalism of government and private property across the country, parallels were drawn with the protests in Bangladesh and its aftermath.

On 12 September 2025, M. Niaz Asadullah, Head of the Southeast Asia cluster of the Global Labor Organisation and a visiting professor of economics at the University of Reading, wrote an opinion piece on the Bangladesh protests for the *Nepali Times*, an English language weekly newspaper in Nepal.

Asadullah wrote that the past year has shown tech-savvy, cross-class youth coalitions can outmaneuver entrenched patron-client politics, but the initial optimism may prove short-lived. He said major fault lines could cause the Bangladesh revolution to end like the short-lived Arab Spring of the early 2010s. 'The NCP's growing credibility issues are a warning sign. With two members in government, it is considered a king's party... The party is already facing corruption allegations, including accusations of institutionalising mob justice and exploiting privileged access to public institutions for political gain. Violent clashes with political opponents have further damaged its reputation,' he wrote.[7]

Young Dhaka-based journalist Saqlain Rizve who works as the Bangladesh correspondent for the *Diplomat* tells us in an email interview that many Bangladeshis had hoped for the emergence of a new political force in post–Sheikh Hasina Bangladesh that could break the monopoly of traditionally dominant parties like the Awami League and the BNP. The NCP represented that hope.

Rizve covered both, the violent July Revolution, risking life and limb, as well as the formal launch event of the NCP on 28 February 2025 at the Manik Mia Avenue near the Jatiya Sangsad (Bangladesh Parliament) in Dhaka. So popular was this new political idea that in online opinion polls, several names were proposed for the party, like 'Revolutionary Popular Struggle Party', 'National Revolutionary Power', 'People Against Discrimination', 'Bangladesh Citizen Party', 'National Citizen Committee, Student–People's Party', 'National People Power Party' and 'National Citizen Power'. Finally, the NCP was chosen with the water lily as the party symbol.

'I was present on the ground to cover the event. Attendees came from across the country, including people versed in both leftwing and rightwing politics, illustrating a broad spectrum of political interest. At the launch event Nahid Islam introduced the concept of a "Second Republic". The party pledged to hold a Constituent Assembly election to draft a new democratic constitution – what they describe as necessary to dismantle entrenched systems of "constitutional autocracy" and replace them with a rights-based and inclusive republic,' Rizve said.

Today, Rizve finds the allegations against the NCP deeply disappointing. 'People were genuinely hopeful about the rise of a new political force. But these early allegations – especially involving senior leaders – risk derailing that momentum. While it's encouraging that the party has formed a disciplinary committee and issued internal warnings, the real test will be whether it upholds transparency and accountability in practice. Without that, the NCP may lose the public trust it so urgently needs.'

Rizve has not lost hope, though. He believes the NCP can improve and succeed in fulfilling the aspiration of a young nation. 'Their key goal, establishing a "Second Republic", remains compelling and could resonate with many if pursued sincerely and effectively. However, it is noticeable that the NCP has been associating somewhat more closely with right-wing parties. For example, sharing the stage with groups like Jamaat-e-Islami Bangladesh and Hefazat-e-Islam at rallies. Currently, all parties seem to regard the BNP as their main rival,' he says.

'Since the NCP claims to be a centrist political force, such close ties with the right wing could gradually push them more in a right-leaning direction, which might be in conflict with their stated ideals. Moreover, the NCP currently receives some positive support from the interim government, but this support may not continue once a new elected government takes office. How well the party can withstand that and sustain itself politically remains uncertain and will be crucial for their future. 'That said, some of their initiatives are promising. For instance, in July 2025 "Desh Gorte July Padojatra" (Foot March to Build the Nation), they organized programmes in all sixty-four districts of Bangladesh. This grassroots outreach can help the party connect with ordinary people beyond urban centres and build broader support.'

Rizve did not think much of the NCP's electoral prospects and said that it was unlikely to form the next government. 'Although it may secure a modest position, achieving substantial electoral success is doubtful. Bangladesh's political landscape is deeply complex. For example, the Jamaat-e-Islami Bangladesh – the country's third-largest party after the Awami League and the BNP – has never even won one-third of the seats in a single election, let alone form a government on its own. The NCP's lack of popularity is evident outside Dhaka. Its rallies often require visible law enforcement protection, underlining its weak grassroots strength. The party is also facing scrutiny and criticism on talk shows and public forums for relying heavily on security assistance during its events.'

While Rizve still hoped the NCP would course correct, Mohammad A. Arafat, minister of state for information and broadcasting in Sheikh Hasina's cabinet, asked how could a party whose inception was in hatred, not hope, and which had continued to show little regard for Bangladesh's history and its hard-fought freedom be a true builder of the 'Second Republic'.

In exile, Arafat did not shy away from talking about Bangladesh after Hasina. In interviews with us, he rued Bangladesh's 'descent into darkness'. When asked about the NCP's role in shaping Bangladesh's future political narrative, Arafat was extremely critical. 'In less than six months, several key members of the party have been exposed for engaging in extortion, corruption and for inciting mob violence against dissenting voices, or anyone who does not align with their political beliefs. This is the behaviour of an authoritarian outfit designed to serve the interests of an undemocratic leader and not to ensure the welfare of its people, nor the democratic values of its country. Within the party, internal dissent speaks to deeper corruption. Many key members of the party have resigned, alleging that the party has been reduced to little more than a money-making machine. Similarly, female activists have highlighted deep-seated gender-based discrimination. These transgressions have not been lost on the public, and support for the NCP has already begun to wane as it fails to deliver on its promises. Last-ditch attempts to blame Awami League members for its own shortcomings will not save the party,' he told us.

'The NCP has also chosen to align itself closely with the Jamaat-e-Islami, an extremist Islamist outfit intent on erasing the legacy of Bangladesh's liberation war against Pakistan. Like Jamaat, the NCP's leaders have publicly campaigned for the dismantling of Bangladesh's constitution – a constitution that was foundational when it was drafted for introducing secularism. The Jamaat-e-Islami has always opposed the country's independence and its constitution and was responsible for carrying out acts of genocide alongside the Pakistan Army in 1971.

'Those who support the liberation movement and the upholding of secular values will be unlikely to vote for any party that seeks to dismantle these foundational tenets. What's more, any party that supports the banning of one of the longest standing and most-supported political parties in Bangladesh, the Awami League, can never claim to represent the true will of the people,' Arafat told us.

Arafat also drew our attention to the close ties that NCP leaders enjoyed with the interim government, especially Muhammad Yunus, that had led to the party being called the 'king's party'.

'With the King's Support'

On 4 August 2025, Transparency International Bangladesh (TIB), the Bangladeshi branch of the Berlin-based Transparency International, a civil society organization dedicated to fighting corruption, described the NCP as the 'king's party'. The statement came at a media conference organised by the TIB to publish a research report titled 'One Year After the Fall of an Authoritarian Regime: Expectations and Reality'.

Transparency International Bangladesh executive director Iftekharuzzaman said that a king's party had been formed under the patronage of the government. Painting a grim picture of the corruption and lawlessness that had become Bangladesh's reality after the fall of the Sheikh Hasina government, the TIB report said that extortion amounting to 22.1 million taka per day was taking place at fifty-three transport terminals and stands in Dhaka that were previously under the control of the Awami League.

Additionally, TIB said that some NCP members have allegedly been guilty of looting of boulders from rivers and quarries in Sylhet, as well as taking control of leases for bridges, markets, ferry terminals, balumahals (sandbanks) and waterbodies. Politically motivated lawsuits have also been filed.

The report also observed that mobs have been formed, roads blocked, police stations surrounded and protests staged, all of which contributed to the deterioration of law and order. And in all these activities, along with older political parties, the NCP had entered the fray.[8]

London-based Bangladeshi journalist Sushanta Dasgupta told us over the phone that the NCP was nothing more than a puppet outfit serving the ambitions of Muhammad Yunus, who had become the civilian face of a pro-Pakistani, anti-sovereign agenda. Dasgupta said that under the guise of democracy and civility, Yunus was working with international lobbies and the Jamaat influence to destabilize Bangladesh from within. 'The NCP's very existence is proof of that unholy alliance between external geopolitical interests and domestic anti-liberation forces. From day one, I saw the NCP not as a new hope but as a dangerous political project designed to bring back what the people of Bangladesh had decisively rejected after 1971. It was clear this was a top-down creation, not born out of any people's movement. The language of "consensus" was simply a façade to reintroduce the forces that historically stood against our independence and liberation. As a young journalist, it was deeply disturbing to see these elements rebranded and given legitimacy,' Dasgupta told us.

The BNP had also been critical of the NCP and referred to it as the king's party from the beginning. The party's vice chairman, Barkat Ullah Bulu, had also slammed its leaders for their questionable financial dealings.

'A student who used to live in the dormitory before 5 August, who used to tutor, suddenly became the owner of so much money … They ride in cars worth three, four, or five crore taka … this is a bad omen for the nation,' Bulu had said.[9]

'1,400 people were killed, and thousands more suffered severe, life-altering injuries during the July–August anti-Hasina stir in Bangladesh. For what? For democracy? Or to have a so-called students' party hijack the political narrative in Bangladesh with the blessings of Muhammad Yunus?' Dasgupta asked.

Dasgupta pointed to the massacre in Gopalganj district in Bangladesh on 16 July 2025 where NCP leaders clashed with Awami League political activists after the former delivered allegedly inflammatory political speeches against Sheikh Mujibur Rahman.

'The incident left five dead and over a hundred injured. But you know who opened fire on Awami League activists and escorted NCP leaders in armoured vehicles to safety? The Bangladesh army! If there is a law-and-order issue inside the country, who is responsible for the safety of citizens? The police. Imagine, the army was instructed to open fire on those who clashed with NCP leaders! Who in Bangladesh can give such an instruction except Yunus, tell me?' Dasgupta said.

Can the NCP course correct?

Bangladeshi atheist blogger Asad Noor, who had taken asylum in Canada after death threats from Islamic fundamentalists for his views on Islam and religious extremism, told us that broadly two groups of young women and men came out to protest during those tumultuous days of July–August 2024.

'One group wanted an end to Hasina's authoritarian rule and the stolen elections. The other wanted a return to the pre-1971 values in Bangladesh. And what was Bangladesh before 1971? East Pakistan! This second group hid behind the first group and said they wanted a "Second Republic", a new Bangladesh free of authoritarianism. Yet, the second group, now in the form of the NCP, is pushing for a return to authoritarianism and is constantly attacking Sheikh Mujibur Rahman. It is one thing to be anti-Hasina, quite another to target the founding father of Bangladesh and what he stood for,' says Noor.

Nahid Islam said on 19 March 2025, 'On 5 August 2024, the people of Bangladesh defeated the force and actually ousted Mujibbad [Mujib's philosophy] and the fascist Awami League. So, there should be no place for Mujibbadi politics in the future politics and Bangladesh elections.'[10] He was addressing an iftar party at Dhaka Ladies Club, which was hosted by the BNP in honour of the leaders of different political parties.

Asad Noor said pointedly, 'The revolution has indeed eaten its children and created a monster that is the NCP.'

10

India's New Headache?

Undoubtedly, Sheikh Hasina brought Dhaka closer to Delhi. After her fall, in the political map being redrawn by Dhaka, Islamabad was closer than Delhi.

In earlier chapters we have written how, soon after Sheikh Hasina's government collapsed, celebrations broke out. There was jubilation on the streets of Dhaka and in cities and towns all over the country. In earlier chapters we have also written how there was a lot of gore as well – murderous mobs killing policemen, Awami League functionaries and supporters, and Hindus, in a brutal fashion.

Students of the country's oldest and most prestigious university, Dhaka University, who had been at the forefront of the protests against reservations in government jobs (which had quickly turned into a mass uprising against the Awami League regime), led the celebratory marches down the streets of Dhaka and within the university's expansive campus.

While the slogans they raised mostly hailed the 'July Revolution' and derided Hasina's 'fascist regime', many slogans were directed against India which was widely perceived as the puppeteer which controlled Hasina and was thus complicit in her alleged crimes by association. But it wasn't only anti-India slogans that were raised; these included rhymes about making India's northeast a part of Bangladesh.

A video that went viral at that time featured a woman research scholar of the university mouthing a limerick that spoke of

Bangladeshis visiting Arunachal Pradesh and Nagaland that would soon become part of their country even as her colleagues cheered her on. This was not just the youthful exuberance of a young woman celebrating the downfall of a tyrannical regime; it revealed the extent of anti-Indian sentiment latent in Bangladesh.

Delhi's strategic circles read this as an expression of a pro-Islamist, anti-Hindu mindset that had afflicted many Bangladeshi Muslims. In Bangladesh, India is viewed as a 'Hindu country'. Many Bangladeshis have bought into the Islamist narrative that because large parts of the Indian subcontinent were under Muslim rule before the British, they should rightfully be ruled by Muslims once again. A 'Hindu India' is anathema to them, a 'Dar-al Harb' that awaits subjugation by Islam.

Veteran Bangladesh watcher Jayanta Roy Chowdhury, editor-in-chief of the Secretariat, a politics and public policy website, said that Bangladesh was standing at a dangerous ideological crossroads. Roy Chowdhury said that a radical map floated by a group called Sultanat e Bangla – calling for a Greater Bangladesh – had triggered alarm in Indian diplomatic circles. 'Meanwhile, Bangladesh is witnessing the rapid rise of Islamist forces. Jamaat-e-Islami, Hefazat-e-Islam and the new National Citizen Party have emerged as street power, openly backed by sections of the interim government. Minority communities, secular voices and liberal thinkers are facing arrests, disappearances and brutal repression. Entire regions like Gopalganj have been subjected to military lockdowns and mass detentions,' Roy Chowdhury said.

What he found even more worrying was the systematic effort to erase the secular foundations of the country. 'Attacks on Hindus, Christians, Buddhists, Ahmadiyyas, and Sufi shrines are becoming frequent. Calls for Sharia law and blasphemy legislation are drawing massive crowds. Meanwhile, the Awami League remains in disarray. While Sheikh Hasina has issued messages from exile, her party continues to operate in fear, scattered under different banners,' he said.

Roy Chowdhury warned that a dangerous transformation was underway and Bangladesh could soon become unrecognizable – not just to its own people, but to the entire region.

Since the fall of the Sheikh Hasina government, anti-Indian sentiments have intensified in Bangladesh and been, to no small extent, encouraged by those perceived to be close to the Yunus administration, including leaders of the July uprising, army veterans, former bureaucrats and diplomats and civil society members.

The Hasina Factor

The fact that India offered refuge to Sheikh Hasina angered the new dispensation in Bangladesh, which would have preferred to throw her in prison and try her in their court. They were angered that India had denied them an opportunity to make Hasina pay for her 'crimes', and this fury found expression in rallies and statements against India. The day after Sheikh Hasina fled to India, the Indian Cultural Centre in Dhaka that was named after Indira Gandhi, who played a key role in liberating Bangladesh from Pakistan, was reduced to ashes.[1]

As has already been elaborated in earlier chapters, the uprising against Sheikh Hasina is being perceived in many quarters to have been orchestrated by external forces, prominent amongst them being Pakistan,[2,3] and according to Sheikh Hasina herself, the United States of America. Pakistan, which already had deep ties with Islamists in Bangladesh, has reportedly used them to mobilize the masses and trigger the uprising against Sheikh Hasina.

The Islamists, it is now widely being believed, played a key role in the July uprising and, naturally, have been wielding influence since then. They were also at the forefront of the hate campaign against India. For instance, when flash floods devastated large parts of Bangladesh in late August 2024, the Jamaat-e-Islami Bangladesh accused India of releasing water from its dams. They incited Bangladesh's gullible masses to stage angry protests all over the country.

Interestingly, it was not only the masses who bought into the false propaganda that the floods were caused due to India releasing water from its reservoirs, when they were actually caused by heavy and incessant showers in the catchment areas of some of Bangladesh's rivers in Tripura, Assam and Meghalaya. Even teachers and students of various universities like Dhaka University, Jahangirnagar University, Rajshahi University, Islamic University, Barisal University, Shahjalal University of Science and Technology, Begum Rokeya University, Jessore University of Science and Technology and Dhaka University of Engineering and Technology – staged angry demonstrations and raised vitriolic anti-Indian slogans. Their common refrain was that India was exploiting Bangladesh.[4] Calls for Bangladesh to send its armed forces to occupy northeast India rang out from these rallies.

That the interim government headed by Muhammad Yunus also stoked this anti-India campaign was evident when the then information and broadcasting advisor, Nahid Islam, told reporters in Dhaka: 'Without any prior warning and without giving us time for preparation, the dam was opened. Through this, India showed an inhuman approach and is demonstrating non-cooperation with Bangladesh.'[5] Islam was flanked by two senior advisors when he spoke to reporters and his false accusations against India came after a meeting convened by Yunus to discuss the floods in the country. It is highly unlikely that the act of levelling these false allegations did not have Yunus's sanction. Islam also played a key role in organizing anti-Indian protests.

One of the major accusations against India levelled by the Yunus administration – these accusations have been repeated so often by Yunus and his advisors as well as Bangladesh's Islamists that they find wide resonance among the people of Bangladesh – is that Sheikh Hasina bartered away Bangladesh's interests by signing many trade, transit and investment agreements with India that were beneficial only to India.

The hawkish foreign advisor (the de facto foreign minister) Mohammad Touhid Hossain announced in end-August 2024[6] that the interim government would review all MoUs and agreements signed with India by the Sheikh Hasina government and scrap those which were not beneficial to Bangladesh. These included ten MoUs on blue economy and maritime cooperation, railway links through Bangladesh, capacity building, health, academic cooperation, fisheries and disaster management that were signed during Hasina's visit to New Delhi in June 2024.[7] That no MoU or agreement with India signed during Sheikh Hasina's rule has been scrapped, even after more than a year has passed since Yunus took over despite intense and often critical scrutiny by his administration is proof of the fact that none of these were weighed against Bangladesh or compromised the country's interests.

Yunus lent his voice to the allegations that Sheikh Hasina bartered away Bangladesh's interests to India and also intensified the anti-India pitch by raising the Teesta water-sharing issue. This had been a sore point in Bangladesh since 2011 when West Bengal Chief Minister Mamata Banerjee turned away from the Teesta Agreement. Delhi believes Mamata Banerjee's reluctance over signing a water-sharing agreement with Bangladesh pushed Bangladesh into China's arms.[8]

Yunus said that the improvement of ties with India would hinge on a water-sharing deal that would give Bangladesh its fair share of the waters of the Teesta river as a lower riparian state.[9] That this deal has not been signed – and there are no chances of one being reached because the flow of the river has come down drastically and there is little water to share with Bangladesh during the lean season – is often used by Islamists and anti-India elements in Bangladesh to bash India.

The anti-India environment in Bangladesh instigated by Yunus and his compatriots in the interim government as well as their Islamist supporters encouraged many in the country to adopt extreme postures. Army veterans, civil society members, academics and intellectuals got into the game of outdoing each other in India-bashing and this led to a situation where India was blamed for everything that had gone wrong with Bangladesh. This also provided an opportunity to the pro-Pakistan Islamists, who had always been present in Bangladesh since its creation, to steer the country towards Pakistan.

One of the most aggressive anti-India demonstrations witnessed in Dhaka in the post 5 August 2024 phase was staged by retired armed forces officers. On 7 December 2024, a large number of Bangladesh army, navy and air force veterans gathered in Dhaka under the banner of a newly formed National Unity and Solidarity Council to protest 'Indian hegemony' and India's 'Hindu supremacism'. A number of armed forces veterans railed and ranted against India and accused New Delhi of pursuing a 'policy of dominance and aggression'.[10]

That India was being equated with 'Hindu', and anti-India sentiments were actually a camouflage for anti-Hindu feelings, was evident from the rally of veterans and also many other demonstrations, marches and speeches by a wide cross-section of Bangladeshis. The latent animosity towards Hindus, derogatorily referred to as 'malauns' (derived from the Arabic term 'maleun' meaning 'accursed' or 'one who is undeserving of Allah's mercy'), has led to continuing attacks on Hindus; killings of Hindus, rapes and forcible conversion of Hindu women to Islam, desecration and destruction of temples, takeover of Hindu-owned properties, acute discrimination against Hindus in education, employment and even healthcare, and largescale displacement of Hindus. That is why Dhaka University professor Abu Barkat said in 2016 that there would be no Hindus left in Bangladesh by 2045.[11] Barkat, a renowned economist, said at that time that about 2.3 lakh Hindus flee Bangladesh every year due to religious persecution.

'The surge in anti-India sentiments since the July 2024 uprising emanates from a deep animosity towards Hindus. The Islamists equate India with Hindus and their hostility towards Hindus segues easily to antagonism towards India. Sheikh Hasina used to keep these Islamists firmly under control. But now that she is in exile and

Yunus is in power, these Islamists have become very powerful,' said a senior functionary of the Bangladesh Hindu Bouddha Christian Oikya Parishad,[12] who did not want to be named due to fear of reprisals. This functionary of the Parishad, a lawyer who practices in the Supreme Court of Bangladesh, said that Bangladesh had become more Islamist in recent years and that had automatically led to a rise in pro-Pakistan sentiments. That is why, he pointed out, Pakistan was widely cheered by many Bangladeshis during India–Pakistan cricket matches.

During Operation Sindoor in May 2025, when India launched strikes on terror camps and military infrastructure in Pakistan, a large number of Bangladeshis rooted for Pakistan and expressed their outrage against India. Once again, not just the Islamists in Bangladesh, but also students and teachers of universities, professionals, lawyers, retired bureaucrats and judges and many others aligned themselves with Pakistan, a country that had tormented and massacred lakhs of East Pakistanis a little over five decades ago.

Bangladesh's Islamists and Islamist parties like the Jamaat-e-Islami Bangladesh, Hefazat-e-Islam, Hizb-ut-Tahrir and Islami Oikya Jote were, of course, the most vocal in expressing support for Pakistan. One such anti-India voice which stood out was that of retired Major General A.L.M. Fazlur Rahman, who wrote on his Facebook account that 'if India attacks Pakistan, Bangladesh should occupy the seven states of Northeast India'.[13]

Rahman, who was appointed chairman of the National Independent Commission to probe the February 2009 revolt by jawans of the Bangladesh Rifles (the predecessor of the present BGB) in which fifty-six army officers – nearly the entire top rank of the paramilitary force – were massacred,[14] is considered to be close to Yunus.

A deep dive into Rahman's profile is revealing. He was the director general of the Bangladesh Rifles (BDR) for a seventeen-month period from February 2000 to July 2001. During this short period, the BDR got involved in bloody clashes with the border guards of both Myanmar and India. The BDR is said to have provoked the clash with their Myanmarese counterparts. In April 2001, the BDR under Rahman's command laid claim to the Khasi-inhabited Pyrdiwah village in Meghalaya and tried to occupy it with the help of hundreds of armed Muslim civilians from Bangladesh. Sixteen BSF jawans stationed at a BSF post in the village, caught unawares, were taken hostage and brutally massacred. The incident caused outrage in India, more so since the bodies of the BSF jawans were mutilated by BDR troops.[15] Sheikh Hasina, who was prime minister at the time, had to do a lot of tightrope walking to assuage India's indignation.[16]

After retirement, Rahman floated a platform that he named Nirdolio Jono Andolon (Non-Party Peoples' Movement) whose manifesto spoke of raising a 'national army' to invade India and 'liberate' northeast India and Sikkim, and annex Assam, West Bengal, Bihar and Odisha and incorporate these Indian states into Bangladesh.[17] Rahman believes that crores of Bangladeshi-origin Muslims living in Assam, West Bengal, Bihar and Odisha can become the 'fifth column', rise in revolt against the Indian state and help the Bangladesh armed forces during an attack on India. Rahman said this to a Pakistani journalist, Sultan M. Hali, during the latter's visit to Dhaka in early 2005. Hali's account of his conversation with Rahman in Dhaka was published in the *Pakistan Observer* in its edition dated 2 March 2005.[18]

The point here is that it is not only young impressionable men and women, or the uneducated and radicalized masses in Bangladesh who harbour ambitions of severing northeast India and incorporating eastern Indian states in Bangladesh. Many senior army officers, bureaucrats, diplomats and intellectuals of Bangladesh also feel the same. Delhi's strategic circles believe that the already large tribe of anti-India Bangladeshis is only growing by the day, thanks to the encouraging environment created by Muhammad Yunus's interim government.

Though Yunus, foreign advisor Mohammad Touhid Hossain and others in the interim government have denied links with Islamists and with anti-Indian forces, actions actually speak louder than words. Like the release of Jashimuddin Rahmani soon after Yunus came to power, which we have mentioned before.

Rahmani is a rabid anti-Indian and the ABT calls for the extermination of Hindus and Ghazwa-e-Hind (conquest of India to establish an Islamic republic there). Soon after his release from prison, he called on West Bengal chief minister Mamata Banerjee to 'declare independence' from India.[19] Far from gagging him, the Yunus dispensation is said to be egging Rahmani on and has given him a free rein to expand the ABT's network.

Rahmani was not the only Islamist radical to be released. Bangladesh Nationalist Party leader and former deputy education minister Abdus Salam Pintu, a prime accused in a grenade attack on an Awami League rally in Dhaka in August 2004 that killed twenty-four people and injured Sheikh Hasina, was also released from prison and the charges against him dropped.[20]

Abdus Salam, who was sentenced to death in the grenade attack case, had aided the Pakistan-based terrorist outfit Harkat-ul-Jihad-al-Islami (HuJI) in carrying out terror attacks against India. According to investigations carried out by Bangladesh earlier, he had helped HuJI in weapons procurement, recruitment and training programmes in camps in Pakistan-Occupied Kashmir (POK).[21] Incidentally, HuJI leader Maulana Tajuddin is Abdus Salam's brother.

Yunus also freed BNP leader and former minister of state for home Lutfozzaman Babar, a co-accused in the grenade attack case.[22] Babar was the person behind the foiled bid to supply arms and ammunition to the United Liberation Front of Asom (ULFA) in April 2004 when the BNP was in power. Bangladesh police and the Coast Guard intercepted ten trucks carrying sophisticated arms and ammunition that had been unloaded from a ship docked at Chittagong Port.[23] Babar was acquitted by the Bangladesh High Court bench in the arms haul case.

The interim government has forced many independent judges, including the Chief Justice of the Supreme Court, Obaidul Hasan, and five top judges of the country's apex court to step down following demonstrations by students on 10 August 2024.[24,25] Those protests were believed to have the blessings of Yunus and others in the interim government. Since then, many more judges have been forced to step down. Hence, the judiciary in Bangladesh is widely perceived to be pliant and do the government's bidding.

It thus came as no surprise when the same court that acquitted Babar in the Chittagong arms haul case also reduced the death sentence on ULFA chief Paresh Barua to life imprisonment.[26] Barua had fled Bangladesh after Sheikh Hasina, who returned to power in January 2009, launched a crackdown on the leaders and cadres of militant outfits of northeast India who had been granted shelter as well as training and arms by the BNP regime.

There are no takers in Delhi's strategic circles for Bangladesh's argument that the executive (that is, the interim government under Yunus) has no control over the judiciary when it is evident that the judiciary has been rendered completely subservient. The manner in which judges are routinely threatened and made to reject or accept cases and bail applications purely on political considerations by leaders of the July uprising, the Islamists and those in the interim government itself makes it clear that the judiciary granted bail and dismissed cases against Rahmani, Abdus Salam, Babar and many others on the directives of the government.

Along with giving Islamists a free rein in the country and acquiescing to their sectarian and anti-India agenda, the Yunus administration has effected a deep reset in Bangladesh's foreign policy by forging very close links, especially military and strategic links, with Pakistan and Turkey. Yunus has very eagerly made Bangladesh a strategic ally of Turkiye and Pakistan and a part of the Turkiye-led league of Islamic nations. Turkish president Recep Tayyip Erdogan dreams of establishing a global Islamic caliphate headed by his country. Sheikh Hasina had warded off Turkiye's overtures and steered Bangladesh clear of plans to establish a modern Islamic caliphate. That policy has been completely overturned by Yunus.

Top army officers from Pakistan, and its intelligence agency the ISI made multiple trips to Bangladesh and even visited areas near the Indo-Bangladesh border at Rangpur in northwestern Bangladesh and the Chittagong hill tracts in southeastern Bangladesh[27] in January 2025. This particular Pakistani delegation was headed by ISI chief Lieutenant General Asim Malik. This visit by the Pakistanis was preceded by the visit of principal staff officer of the Bangladesh army, Lieutenant General S.M. Kamrul Hassan, to Pakistan to hold secret meetings with the top brass of Pakistan's armed forces, including Pakistan army chief General Asim Munir.[28]

Yunus met Pakistani Prime Minister Shehbaz Sharif twice, the first on the sidelines of the UN General Assembly session in New York on 25 September 2024[29] where the two decided to forge closer ties in various fields, and then again on the sidelines of the D-8 summit in Cairo in December 2024.[30]

At the Cairo meeting, Yunus requested Sharif to 'settle issues from the 1971 war', saying the non-resolution of those 'issues' were bedevilling harmonious ties between Bangladesh and Pakistan. Pakistan has never apologized for the 1971 genocide and has not paid Bangladesh the huge sums of money it owed to the new nation.

The 1971 genocide and non-repatriation of huge sums of money – Bangladesh claims $4.52 billion – that rightfully belonged to East Pakistan and its people is still a sore point with many in Bangladesh, and Yunus knows that these issues can be leveraged any time by the Awami League or others to sabotage his efforts to foster close ties with Pakistan. If he does not raise these issues with Pakistan, Yunus runs the risk of being accused of 'selling out' to Islamabad, just as Sheikh Hasina was accused of selling out (Bangladesh's interests) to Delhi. However, Yunus does not seem keen on pushing Pakistan too hard to resolve these issues because Pakistan is adamant on not issuing any apology for the horrific genocide of Bengalis in 1971 or repatriating the money that Bangladesh seeks. Cash-starved Pakistan, which is in a deep financial crisis, is in no position to give Bangladesh even a fraction of that money. Pakistan insists that all issues between Pakistan, the newly created Bangladesh and India were resolved through the 1974 tripartite agreement.[31]

Yunus's tactic will be to raise these issues with Pakistan periodically to demonstrate to the people of his country that he wants them resolved, but he won't allow them to come in the way of stronger economic, military, social and political ties between Bangladesh and Pakistan.

This was evident from the removal of the then foreign secretary, Mohammad Jashim Uddin, from his post soon after he forcefully raised these issues at the Foreign Office consultations with Pakistan during the visit of his Pakistani counterpart, Amna Baloch, to Dhaka in April 2025.[32] Yunus and all those within and outside his government who are rooting for intimate ties with Pakistan were also unhappy over the foreign secretary's strong objection to a Pakistan-backed proposal to establish a 'humanitarian corridor' to channel humanitarian aid to residents of the war-ravaged Rakhine state, including the Rohingyas there.

Analysts said that the true intent of Pakistan, suspected to be backed by the US in this, was to provide military aid to the Arakan army that was waging a battle to wrest control of the entire Rakhine state from Myanmar's military rulers and also to establish a strong base in the Chittagong region where it would provide refuge, training and arms to northeast India's militant groups. Jashim Uddin opposed this, as did the army chief, General Waker-uz-Zaman,[33,34] and the plan had to be junked. Bangladesh's national security advisor, Khalilur Rahman, who is known to be close to Pakistan, was pitching for this plan along with Lt Gen Kamrul Hasan, who had met the Pakistan army chief earlier.

Yunus has also taken Bangladesh into Turkey's orbit. There have been high-level visits between diplomats, military brass and others between the two countries. The most significant of these was the visit by Professor Haluk Gorgun, the head of Turkiye's Defence Industry agency (SSB), to Dhaka in early July 2025. He met Yunus and the three service chiefs and discussed deepening military ties between the two countries. The two sides 'reiterated their commitment to advancing strategic projects, technology transfers and joint development platforms' as well as the 'integration of Bangladeshi industries into Turkey's expansive supply chain network with a view to developing an inter-dependent, resilient and NATO-standard eco-system'.[35] Earlier, in May 2025, Ashik Chowdhury, the executive chairman of the Bangladesh Investment Development Authority, led a high-powered delegation to Turkiye.

What is worrying and holds adverse security implications for India is Turkey's financial and logistical support to Bangladesh's Islamists, especially the Jamaat-e-Islami Bangladesh. The 'foreign operations directorate' of Turkiye's notorious spy agency, Milli İstihbarat Teşkilatı (MIT),[36] has established close ties with the Jamaat and other anti-India and pro-Pakistan Islamist outfits in Bangladesh and is financing them. The MIT recently financed the renovation of Jamaat's office in Dhaka and organized visits by Jamaat and other Islamists as well as some leaders of the July uprising to Turkish arms manufacturing units. The MIT, Indian intelligence agencies strongly suspect, is planning to provide technical know-how and also military hardware to these Islamist groups in Bangladesh.[37,38]

Yunus himself seems to harbour delusions of Bangladesh playing an outsized role in South Asia at the expense of India's interests and positioning his country as an important player in the Turkey–Pakistan Islamist axis. Also, by cosying up to China. That is why he made the controversial statement during his four-day visit to China in end-March 2025 that Bangladesh can be China's gateway to northeast India. 'The seven states of India, eastern part of India, called seven sisters … they are a landlocked country, a landlocked region of India. They have no way to reach out to the ocean. We are the only guardian of the ocean for all this region. So this opens up a huge possibility. This can become an extension of the Chinese economy,' Yunus had said during his visit.[39]

Such posturing, which stokes anti-Indian sentiments in Bangladesh, has led to an intensification of such sentiments in recent times. The growing radicalization of Bangladesh's youth, and the country's pivot towards Turkiye and Pakistan, are causes for deep worry in Delhi. Growing belligerence displayed by the BGB along the Indo-Bangladesh border,[40] the deepening of ties with China, Pakistan and Turkiye,[41] and the free rein given by Yunus to the country's Islamists and Islamic terror groups is dangerous not only for Bangladesh, but also for India. Bangladesh risks becoming the playground of foreign players – China, Pakistan, Turkiye and also the US – with their conflicting agendas and interests.

A researcher at the Bangladesh Institute of Peace and Security Studies told us recently: 'The current leadership of Bangladesh, especially the leaders of the Anti-Discrimination Students' Movement which led the uprising that unseated Sheikh Hasina from power, is not mature and sagacious enough to deftly handle and fend off pressures from external powers. The country is in the grip of Islamists. In this scenario, allowing these foreign powers to deepen their interests in Bangladesh is suicidal.'

'Due to the wide-ranging purges carried out by the new dispensation, our foreign policy and strategic affairs establishments have considerably weakened. A lot of talent has left and so we lack the expertise now to balance the interests of external powers while protecting our own interests. That requires a lot of dexterity and expertise, and we are lacking in that now,' said the researcher, who did not want to be named for obvious reasons.[42] What this means is that Bangladesh runs the risk of plunging into internal turmoil and destabilization. That translates into a deep headache for India.

Top Indian strategic thinkers feel a deeply hostile Bangladesh is, undoubtedly, a security challenge for India. New Delhi has to tackle this challenge head-on.⁴³ New Delhi must draw clear red lines for the new regime in Bangladesh. Lines like encouraging anti-India Islamists, border transgressions and allowing Pakistan to use Bangladesh for anti-Indian activities that should not be crossed.⁴⁴

And repeat it to whoever comes after Yunus.

Section III

People

11

A Hindu Homeland

On 22 December 2001, the BBC put out a report saying that Altaf Hossain Chowdhury, then home minister of Bangladesh, had said that some members of the country's minority Hindu community were engaged in a plot to promote separatism in the country. 'Mr Chowdhury told the mass-circulation Bengali language newspaper Ittefaq that a movement was being revived to create an independent country comprising several south-western districts of Bangladesh. He was quoted as saying that the movement aimed to establish what he called "Bangabhumi" and that personnel were being recruited and camps established inside India near the border with Bangladesh,' the BBC report said.

The report went on to add that 'the comments came in the wake of reported violence against Hindus in Bangladesh after the October general election won by the BNP'. 'Hundreds of families fled to the Indian state of West Bengal, saying they had suffered violence and rape,' the report said.[1]

On 30 May 2025, the BBC put out another report on its website with a warning that the article contained details some readers might find distressing. The report was about the video of a woman being sexually assaulted that had caused nationwide uproar in Bangladesh. The clip had been shared widely online. 'The woman, who has been interviewed by local media, says she was raped at her father's house last Thursday. The clip shows several people at the scene. Police have arrested five people, including the alleged rapist, and authorities have said they will investigate the case "with utmost seriousness",' the BBC said.

The article went on to add that protests had broken out across the country over the weekend after the clip was circulated, and several human rights groups had demanded severe punishment for those involved. 'The survivor was visiting her father's home in central Bangladesh's Cumilla district when a neighbour broke in and assaulted her, according to police. The woman, who is from a Hindu minority community, gave interviews to several local outlets saying the accused "entered the house with bad intentions and tortured her",' the report said.[2]

What is common between these two BBC reports twenty-four years apart? They both talk about atrocities against members of the Hindu community in Bangladesh. The 22 December 2001 BBC report also talks about 'some members of the country's minority Hindu community' who were 'engaged in a plot to promote separatism in the country'. We will come to that shortly.

For now, let's return to the BBC report published on 30 May 2025.

We had seen the video on X, formerly Twitter, and were aghast at how a rape video could be shared on a social media platform in severe violation of all ethical and legal norms. Ostensibly, it was shared by several Indian accounts to draw attention towards the increasingly disturbing level of violence against minority Hindus in Bangladesh. But why it was shared by Bangladeshi social media users and made to go viral?

Mohammad Harun Al Rashid does not know the answer to that question, nor has he seen that video. But the former ambassador of Bangladesh to Morocco tells us over an email interview from Canada that incidents like these have become common since August 2024. 'The rise in targeted persecution has been reckless and horrifying. Friends send me evidence of such atrocities almost daily – photos, videos, testimonies. The pattern is clear and deeply disturbing,' said Rashid.

He told us that many crimes that were communal in nature were not reported by Bangladesh's mainstream media. He believed that like every other sector in Bangladesh, the media has been deeply traumatized under the 'brutal rule of Yunus and his jihadist regime'. 'Almost all major media houses, which once operated with a degree of freedom, have either been taken over or silenced by fundamentalist forces. What we see now is widespread self-censorship – journalists working under fear, surveillance and threat. This has given Yunus and his usurper government ample room to hide the crimes against humanity being committed against secular Muslims and Hindu minorities. The silence of the press is not just complicity; it's the result of systematic repression,' he said.

A distinguished career diplomat, Rashid joined the twentieth batch of the Bangladesh Civil Service in 2001 as a foreign service cadre. He has served in the embassies of Bangladesh in Cairo, Mexico City, Madrid and Rome and was the director-general of the public diplomacy wing at Bangladesh's Ministry of Foreign Affairs. He was the former deputy high commissioner of Bangladesh to Canada.

In October 2023, Rashid was appointed the ambassador of Bangladesh to Morocco. After the fall of the Sheikh Hasina government, Rashid was ordered to return home in December 2024. He did not. Instead, he posted on Facebook against the Muhammad Yunus–led interim government. He titled his post, 'A Plea for Bangladesh – and for Myself. Subject: Bangladesh's Descent into Anarchy under Yunus: The World's Silence Is Painful'. The interim government cancelled his and his family's passports.

Why did he resign?

Rashid said he was compelled to leave because the 'jihadist regime that took over Bangladesh last year was fully aware of my progressive and secular stance'. 'As a published novelist, my political beliefs are no secret. At the time, I was serving as Bangladesh's ambassador to Morocco when Yunus's regime abruptly summoned me to headquarters without offering any explanation. I knew exactly what that meant. Many other secular intellectuals have faced the same fate – forced to flee the country or go into hiding simply to stay alive. Secularism is a crime in Bangladesh now,' he said.

In reply to our question on what could be a possible solution to the targeted violence against Hindus in Bangladesh, Rashid wrote that the only real solution was to dismantle the political and economic power of jihadist forces and to rebuild Bangladesh according to the ideals of 1971: a secular, pluralistic democracy where no citizen is judged, threatened or brutalized because of their religious identity.

We had sent Rashid a question we thought he would skip. We asked him if he was aware of a demand for a Hindu homeland within a large section of Bangladeshi Hindus.

Rashid did not skip the question.

'Bangladeshi Hindus have long endured persecution – if not always physical, then certainly psychological – since the partition of colonial India. Many were forced out of their homes, their land and belongings seized by grafters, creating conditions that drove large numbers to migrate to India. This is not anecdotal; it is demographic fact. In the early years after Independence, Hindus made up about 15 per cent of Bangladesh's population. Today, they account for less than 8 per cent. While this decline is partly due to migration, it also reflects a lower birth rate among Hindus compared to the rapid population growth in radicalized Muslim families.

'It is deeply disheartening to witness such marginalization in a country founded on the ideals of secularism and progressive democracy. Sadly, only the Awami League has consistently upheld secularism as a political principle. Other major parties, such as the BNP and the Jatiya Party, have either ignored or dismissed it. Groups like Jamaat-e-Islami openly call for a theocratic state.'

Rashid admitted that even under Awami League rule, the situation was far from ideal. 'Still, Hindus retained some protection and dignity due to the party's stated secular policies and its inclination to shield minorities. Under the BNP or Jatiya Party governments – both of which lean towards Islamic majoritarianism – Hindus were often relegated to second-class status, whether explicitly or in effect,' he wrote.

'The situation deteriorated sharply in August 2024 when jihadist forces led by Yunus took control. Since then, persecution has become intolerable – not only for Hindus, but also for secular Muslims. Under such humiliating conditions, it is not surprising that some Bangladeshi Hindus are contemplating a separate homeland.

'Given Bangladesh's size and the vision on which it was founded, partition is neither practical nor desirable. The real solution lies in dismantling the political and economic power of jihadist forces and rebuilding the state according to the aspirations of 1971: a secular, pluralistic democracy where no citizen is judged or threatened because of their religious beliefs.'

'Time and Patience Running Out'

Founder and general secretary of the Bangladesh Sanatan Party (BSP), Sumon Kumar Roy told us over the phone that Hindus had little patience left to help rebuild Bangladesh according to the aspirations of 1971. 'The BSP has not been registered yet. It came into being on 26 August 2022, but the Hasina government did not register it as a political outfit because of opposition from radical elements. The Election Commission that is tasked with ensuring free and fair polls is not an independent body, and has never been. It works according to the wishes of either the government or the army. Tell me, how will I tell my people to keep patience? Be patient for what? Are you aware what is happening to Hindus in Bangladesh? It is not about one rape video that has gone viral!' Roy told us.

On 10 July 2025, *Prothom Alo* published a report titled 'Bangladesh Sees 2,500 Incidents of Communal Violence in 330 Days'. Quoting the Bangladesh Hindu Buddhist Christian Oikya Parishad, a nonprofit established to protect rights of minorities in the country, the report said the acts of violence against minorities include 'murders, violence against women, rape and gang rape, attacks on places of worship, arrests over allegations of blasphemy, forced occupation of homes and businesses, assaults on indigenous communities, forced resignations (from official positions)'.

'The organisation highlighted that the highest number of incidents of violence against minorities occurred between 4 August and 20 August last year, with a staggering 2,010 cases reported during this short period. Apart from that, there have been 132 incidents of violence against minorities between 21 August and 31 December last year, with a further 258 incidents between 1 January and 30 June this year. Victims included men, women, and adolescents from minority communities. The organisation criticised the government for allegedly politicising communal violence by assigning political tags to it and failing to prosecute the real offenders, thereby allowing criminals to go unpunished,' the report said.

The *Prothom Alo* report quoted the acting general secretary of the Bangladesh Buddhist Christian Unity Council, Monindra Kumar Nath, as saying: 'In reality, the government is ignoring incidents of oppression against religious minorities. We demand a fair and proper investigation into the incidents.'[3]

About two weeks after the publication of the report, on 25 July, we met Prafulla Ketkar, editor of the *Organiser Weekly*, the mouthpiece of India's Hindu nationalist and voluntary organization Rashtriya Swayamsevak Sangh, at Delhi's Constitution Club where a photo exhibition-cum-discussion was being held on the communal violence in West Bengal's Murshidabad district between 8 and 13 April 2025. While most of the discussants pointed to illegal Muslim immigration from Bangladesh as one of the primary reasons for what they termed as 'anti-Hindu violence' in Murshidabad and elsewhere in West Bengal, we asked Ketkar about his view on Hindus from the other side of the border who might legally want to migrate to India.

Ketkar said that when Bangladesh was created in 1971 by the separation of East Pakistan from West Pakistan, language was the binding force, and not religion. He lamented how Bangladesh in 2025 was moving towards Islamism like Pakistan had done in 1947. 'So it is natural for Hindus in Bangladesh to look for other political options to survive. Look at Pakistan. The Hindu population has almost vanished in the last seventy-eight years. So the demand for a Hindu homeland from Bangladeshi Hindus is natural.'

Ketkar admitted that if the incidents of targeted attacks on Hindus did not come down, India would eventually have to confront the problem.

On the issue of a separate homeland for Hindus being carved out from Bangladesh, Ketkar said it was up to Bangladeshi Hindus to internationalize their plight by speaking up about atrocities on them at various global forums. 'India can give refugee status to some Hindus who are escaping persecution. But if there is an existential crisis like in 1971 and the world wakes up to it, then it is another matter,' he said.

The Bangladeshi Hindu community leaders we spoke to on condition of anonymity told us that Hindus across Bangladesh were getting organized under the leadership of Chinmoy Krishna Das Brahmachari and he had plans of taking the Hindu cause to the world. But the Brahmachari is now in jail and the movement he started has all but collapsed.

The Jailed Monk

'If anyone wants to evict us from this country and live in peace, it will become Afghanistan or Syria. There will be no democratic force. Bangladesh will become a sanctuary of communalism,' Chinmoy Krishna Das Brahmachari had said at a huge gathering of Hindus in Chittagong on 25 October 2024.

Brahmachari, a former ISKCON monk and a leader of the Bangladesh Sanatan Jagaran Mancha, a platform in Bangladesh advocating for the rights and security of Hindus and other minority communities, had been at the forefront of protests by Hindus against targeted attacks on them since the fall of the Sheikh Hasina government.

During the Sanatan Jagaran Mancha's 25 October protest in Chittagong, Brahmachari and others had allegedly placed a saffron flag over the Bangladesh flag. The image of the flags went viral on social media. Subsequently, the saffron flag was removed.[4]

A sedition case was filed against Brahmachari, and on 25 November 2024, the monk was arrested at Dhaka's Hazrat Shahjalal International Airport for allegedly disrespecting Bangladesh's national flag.[5] On 24 July 2025, Bangladesh press reported that the monk was denied bail in five cases, including one over the murder of lawyer Saiful Islam Alif in Chittagong. Brahmachari has been in jail ever since.[6]

India has urged Bangladesh to hold a fair trial for the jailed monk. India's response came on 3 January 2025, more than a month after the Brahmachari's arrest. Meanwhile, two other Bangladeshi Hindu monks who had gone to meet Brahmachari in jail were also put behind bars on 29 November 2024.[7]

'Tell me how will Hindus unite in Bangladesh and come under one umbrella and let the world see what's happening to us? Anyone daring to do so will meet with the same fate as Chinmoy Krishna Das Brahmachari,' Ranjit Roy told us. We were at Roy's one-bedroom rented apartment in New Town, the swanky satellite city on the northeastern periphery of Kolkata. Roy (named changed to protect identity), fifty-seven, a Bangladeshi Hindu rights activist and writer, has been here on an extended medical visa since December 2024.

'I lost faith in the Hindu cause after the arrest of Brahmachari. The cases against him are fabricated. Bangladesh knows this, but the courts functioning under the *farman* [diktat] of the Yunus administration won't give him bail. India's appeal for a fair trial has fallen on deaf ears. Even his lawyer has been attacked,' Roy said.

ISKCON Kolkata spokesperson Radharamn Das had said that advocate Ramen Roy, who defended Brahmachari in court in a legal case there was brutally attacked by 'Islamists'. 'Please pray for Advocate Ramen Roy. His only "fault" was defending Chinmoy Krishna Prabhu in court. Islamists ransacked his home and brutally attacked him, leaving him in the ICU, fighting for his life,' Radharamn Das said.[8]

'They won't let Brahmachari out of jail. They will stub out the last remaining hope for Hindu consolidation in Bangladesh. Do you know what else is happening to Hindus that the papers won't tell you?' Ranjit Roy asked. He alleged that the rape video the BBC reported was spread with the intention of causing fear among Hindu families in Bangladesh's hinterland.

'There are many instances now of Islamists raping Hindu women with impunity across Bangladesh's small towns and villages. But no one will dare report those rapes because there is fear that if they do so, the rape videos will be made public, bringing shame to families,' Roy shakes his head in disgust.

Hindu Homeland Inevitable?

At the 25 July 2025 event on the Murshidabad violence at the Constitution Club in Delhi, India's information and broadcasting ministry's senior advisor Kanchan Gupta made a powerful statement. He called for further amendments to the Citizenship Amendment Act (CAA) and said the legislation, by itself, solves nothing. Passed by the Indian Parliament on 11 December 2019, and becoming a law the next day with presidential assent, the CAA amended the Citizenship Act 1955, by providing an accelerated pathway to Indian citizenship to refugees of persecuted religious minorities from Islamic countries Afghanistan, Bangladesh and Pakistan who arrived in India by 2014.

Addressing the plight of Bangladeshi Hindus, Gupta proposed a law that would enable any Hindu to legally return to India as its citizen, with some checks and balances, reminiscent of how Israel treats every Jew who can naturally call Israel their homeland. Gupta said the checks could vary. 'So long as he or she [a Hindu] is not an accused in a criminal offence or has a criminal background, they will have the right to return to India and get full citizenship and rights associated with it,' he said.⁹

New laws apart, there has been some chatter in India on the issue of carving out parts of Bangladesh, even if they have come as reactions to statements made by Dhaka. Pradyot Kishore Debbarma, founder of the TIPRA Motha party, the BJP's coalition partner in Tripura, has said that India needs to 'break up Bangladesh' to gain access to the Chittagong sea port. Debbarma's remarks came after Yunus said that Bangladesh is the 'only guardian of the ocean' in the region due to the landlocked nature of India's northeast.¹⁰

Yunus's remarks had raised Delhi's security concerns over the strategically important 'Chicken's Neck' or the Siliguri Corridor, a stretch of land around Siliguri city in West Bengal. It is not more than 20–22 kilometres at the narrowest section, and is a geopolitical and geo-economical corridor that connects the seven states of northeast India to the rest of India. Nepal and Bangladesh lie on each side of the corridor and Bhutan lies at its northern end.

Debbarma also maintained that India's 'biggest mistake' was to let go of the Chittagong port in 1947 despite the people in the hills dotting the region wishing to be a part of India. 'Rather than spending billions on innovative and challenging engineering ideas we might as well break up Bangladesh and have our own access to the sea. The Chittagong hill tracts were always inhabited by indigenous tribes which wanted to be part of India since 1947. There are lakhs and lakhs of Tripuri, Garo, Khasi and Chakma people who reside in Bangladesh in terrible conditions in their traditional lands,' he said.¹¹

Debbarma was not the only Indian politician to react to Yunus's statement in strong words that threatened to break up Bangladesh.

On 26 May 2024, Assam chief minister Himanta Biswa Sarma said that those who 'habitually threaten' India on the 'Chicken Neck' corridor should note that Bangladesh has two such narrow strips of land which are 'far more vulnerable'. Bangladesh's first

'Chicken Neck', he said, is the 80-kilometre-long North Bangladesh Corridor between Dakhin Dinajpur and South West Garo Hills. 'Any disruption here can completely isolate the entire Rangpur division from the rest of Bangladesh,' he said. The second one is the 28-kilometre-long Chittagong Corridor, from South Tripura to the Bay of Bengal. 'This corridor, smaller than India's Chicken Neck, is the only link between Bangladesh's economic capital and political capital,' he said.[12]

Are these just angry political reactions to Yunus's statement? The answer is 'no'.

For some time now, especially after the fall of the Hasina government in Bangladesh, there have been top-level discussions in Delhi's strategic circles on the redrawing of Bangladesh's map, given the security threat to India's northeast and the treatment of Hindus in the country. Geopolitical analyst Pathikrit Payne told us that the call for a separate homeland for Hindus in Bangladesh may or may not gain much traction in India, 'but if push comes to shove, and India decides to go for the choke points of Bangladesh, then even the die-hard opponents of the Modi government in India would find it difficult to oppose it for fear of complete political isolation and electoral rout. Such is the level of sentiments running now in India'.

'If the chief advisor of Bangladesh has any illusion that he has his back covered by both the US and China, even as he continues with his agenda of pricking India, then Operation Sindoor is a glaring example for him to learn lessons from,' Payne says.

Ranjit Roy told us that the Hindu community leaders he was in close touch with wanted the six districts of Jessore, Khulna, Faridpur, Kushtia, Barishal and Patuakhali to be freed by India to carve out a Hindu homeland. 'There is a group that is working towards this goal,' he claimed.

We ask Roy what group is this. 'Banga Sena. They have a West Bengal chapter also and they have made their goal public,' Roy told us.

How come no one knew about this?

'Well, you haven't dug deep enough,' he said.

Chittaranjan Sutar and a Hindu Homeland

Let us return to the BBC report from twenty-four years ago—the one published on 22 December 2001 that spoke of then Bangladesh home minister Altaf Hossain Chowdhury alleging a plot by members of the Hindu community in Bangladesh to create an independent country comprising several southwestern districts of Bangladesh. He had said that the movement aimed to establish what he called 'Bangabhumi' or a Hindu homeland carved out of Bangladesh.

The BBC report went on to say that Chowdhury had named two people, Kalidas Baidya and Chittaranjan Sutar, as leaders of the alleged separatist movement. 'However, Mr Sutar has strenuously denied the allegations against him. He told the BBC's Bengali service that he did not believe in a two-nation solution to the question of the Hindu minority in Bangladesh,' the report said.

'Bangabhumi,' the BBC report added, 'the movement for a separate Hindu homeland, was reportedly first launched after the 1975 military coup in Bangladesh, when many Hindu leaders fled to India. Most of them belonged to the Awami League party, which was forced from power in the coup and whose leader, Sheikh Mujibur Rahman, was killed. The BBC's Waliur Rahman in Dhaka says that although the movement itself was much talked about for a decade or so, there was never any concrete evidence that it existed.'[13]

Ranjit Roy said, 'Let me tell you what the BBC report did not. This Chittaranjan Sutar did not have to wait for the assassination of Sheikh Mujib to know Hindus will not be able to stay in Bangladesh. He was in fact a close aide of Mujib who got totally disillusioned with the founding father of Bangladesh soon after the country's Independence in 1971 and founded the Bangabhumi movement.'

But didn't the BBC report say Chittaranjan Sutar denied any role in the movement?

'He would, wouldn't he? Who would accept such an allegation from the then home minister of Bangladesh before the movement had been properly launched or seen some degree of traction?' Roy said.

Ranjit Roy told us that Sutar had become an MP in Pakistan's National Parliament in 1970 from East Pakistan (now Bangladesh) and soon after was sent to Calcutta (now Kolkata) by Sheikh Mujib to prepare for Bangladesh's war of independence.

'Chittaranjan Sutar was the main liaison person between Congress leader Pranab Mukherjee (later President of India), then Indian Prime Minister Indira Gandhi and Sheikh Mujib. But soon after the birth of Bangladesh Sutar understood that Mujib was not as secular as he appeared to be and that Hindus had no future in Bangladesh. He launched the Bangabhumi movement, permanently shifted to India in 1975 and continued to spearhead the movement among Bangladeshi Hindus through his contacts in Bangladesh. There were reportedly a secret army of Bangladeshi Hindu volunteers known as the Banga Sena who I have told you about,' Roy says.

What happened to Chittaranjan Sutar?

'Nothing much is known about him. Except he was in close touch with Pranab Mukherjee till his death.'

And the movement died with him?

'Read this.' Roy sent us the link to an online report from *Uttarbanga Sambad*, a Bengali-language media outlet headquartered in Siliguri, West Bengal. The report is titled: 'Let 6 Districts of Bangladesh Be Broken Away for a New Nation: Bangla Sena's Demand for Bangladeshi Hindus'.

'Banga Sena has demanded that Jessore, Khulna, Faridpur, Kushtia, Barishal and Patuakhali districts be cut off from Bangladesh to form a Hindu homeland for the persecuted minorities of the country. They have said they need no land from India, but has appealed to India to protect Hindus. The Sena has said the persecution of

Hindus in Bangladesh leave them with no option but to call for a separate Hindu homeland,' the report said.[14]

So, the Banga Sena is still active?

'When were they not!'

We mailed Mohammad Harun Al Rashid again. We told him about the Banga Sena and their Bangabhumi movement. What does he think about this? Rashid does not want his country carved up. But he says a lot will depend on the proposed July Proclamation. The Anti-Discrimination Students Movement of Bangladesh and other constituents of the July–August 2024 uprising in Bangladesh against the Sheikh Hasina government wanted a 'July Proclamation' or a new constitution for Bangladesh that would bury the 1972 constitution.[15]

'If the very constitution of Bangladesh as a secular, democratic nation is buried, I guess the call for a Hindu homeland will become a war cry loud enough for the world to hear. What else can the Hindus do?'

12

No Country for Other Muslims

On 13 September 2024, at around 3 p.m., around 100 angry men gathered outside the Shah Sufi Fasih Paglar Mazar, a Sufi shrine in Gazipur district's Porabari area in Bangladesh. Within the district, not more than 25 kilometres north of Dhaka, is a major textile hub. The district is also home to mazars and shrines that draw people of all faiths in their thousands every year.

Like the St Anthony of Padua shrine in Ghazipur's Panjora village. It is a major Catholic pilgrimage site that attracts tens of thousands of Christians, Muslims and Hindus who come to seek blessings from St Anthony, believed to have miraculous powers. St Anthony's religion has never mattered to his devotees, nor has the sect of Sufi saints mattered to their devotees. Till 13 September 2024.

The 100 angry men stormed the mazar and vandalized it for over an hour. They stopped local believers and journalists from taking pictures and videos. Their justification to those who had come to stop them was that the devotees of Fasih Pagla would sing and dance inside the mazar, conduct musical programmes and smuggle drugs. The attackers complained that the devotees collected a large amount of toll from people who drove along the highway next to the shrine in the name of the mazar. And what did they want? That the shrine be completely demolished and a mosque built in its place.

Langta Kabir, head of the Shah Sufi Fasih Paglar Mazar, told reporters that he was leaving the shrine as it had been vandalized.

And did so with three other devotees. Zakir Hossain, a Gazipur local involved in the mazar's management, said the attackers were lying. Drugs were banned inside the mazar as there was an orphanage within the shrine's premises, he said. Hossain complained to whoever would listen to him that the needy were helped with the money that the mazar collected. But who could have stopped 100 angry men.

Later, Mustafizur Rahman, officer-in-charge of Gazipur Sadar Police Station, told the press that he had heard about the mazar being vandalized. The army and paramilitary forces reached the crime scene around 4.30 p.m. It was too late by then.[1]

Shah Sufi Fasih Paglar Mazar was not the only mazar that became a target of Islamist ire after the fall of the Sheikh Hasina government. The Babe Jannat Dewanbag Sharif shrine in Madanpur area of Narayanganj's Bandar upazila and the shrine of Hazrat Shah Poran in Sylhet were also vandalized, among other mazars.[2]

On 23 January 2025, the Bangladesh chapter of the Global Sufi Organization, an apex body that represents Sufi shrines, darbar sharifs and their followers in the country, held a meeting at the Jatiya Press Club in Dhaka and announced that as many as eighty mazars and dargah sharifs had been vandalized since the fall of the Hasina government.

One of the main speakers at the event, associate professor of Persian language and literature in Dhaka University, Md Ahsanul Hadi, spoke to us over the phone on the extent of damage to the Sufi shrines. 'Between 5 August 2024 and the end of January 2025, not three or four, but as many as eighty mazars and dargah sharifs were attacked, looted and set on fire by Islamists,' Hadi told us, his voice seething with anger over the phone.

'Eighty! But the local press did not mention this number.'

'The local press has failed to cover the extent of damage to the most sacred religious sites of Sufis. They are making a mistake of treating these attacks as isolated incidents. These are pre-planned, coordinated attacks on Sufi traditions that transcend narrow religiosity and embrace a larger humanity. But Islamists do not think of us as the right kind of Muslims. To them, we are the bad Muslims who should be given no space in Bangladesh,' Hadi said. 'Which is ironical. As it was the Sufi saints who brought Islam to this part of the world.'

History supports Md Ahsanul Hadi's claim that Sufis have a long tradition in the region that is known as Bangladesh today. It was the Sufis who had brought Bengal into contact with Islamic thought and practice before its conquest by the founder of the Khilji dynasty, Ikhtiyār al-Dīn Muḥammad Bin Bakhtiyār Khaljī's, in 1203. Around the twelfth century, a substantial number of Turkish speakers from Central Asia were driven into the Iranian plateau and from there towards India by the ferocious Mongols. These fleeing Turkish speakers gathered around Sufi leaders who amassed many followers as they arrived in Bengal.

Since then, Sufism has played its part in Bengal's syncretic, more multicultural Islamic tradition, and influenced the sociocultural life of Bangladesh, trying to push back the increasing spread of Islamic orthodoxy in the country. While the tradition exists primarily in Bangladesh's villages, Dhaka is not immune to Sufism, and many mazars dot the city with pirs or saints who exert social and political influence.[3]

Laleh-Naz, a student of Middle Eastern studies at Cambridge University, wrote in the *Daily Star* an interesting story about a friend whose great-grandfather was the first in the family to become a Sufi. 'His [the friend's] family descended from Pathans in Afghanistan, and are based in Kushtia [a city on the banks of the Gorai river in Bangladesh]. My friend said that one day, under the guidance of Pir Hazrat Abu Zaheer, his great-grandfather decided to give up all his material possessions and follow the spiritual path of God.

'His (the friend's) family's beliefs descend from this. After his great-grandfather's death, his younger son, a student of zoology at Dhaka University at the time, said that he had been called, and immediately left his education to become a pir in Kushtia – where he continues to guide his *murids* [disciples]. My friend stressed the importance of this encounter with a pir, saying, "In a spiritual line, you have to have a pir. You won't be able to do without this."'⁴

Laleh-Naz goes on to write that the father of prominent Bangladeshi journalist Shafiqul Alam (Alam is currently the press secretary to Mohammad Yunus) was also drawn to Sufism through his relationship with a pir from India. Laleh-Naz claimed Alam's father used to stress that he and his own pir were like brothers, and that his pir emphasized the values of education to his *murid*s, encouraging them to be educated, go abroad and earn PhDs.

'Every year, his father saved up to get a bus to Kolkata and join his pir's gathering, held annually in February or March. Shafiq Bhai stressed that Sufism is not about practice; you go to a pir and he gives you some prayers to study … some people need some guidance and having a pir also provides a strong brotherhood,' Laleh-Naz wrote.⁵

Was this one of the reasons why the interim government strongly condemned the attacks on mazars? Condemning the attacks on religious, cultural sites and shrines of Sufi, the interim government said in September 2024 that it was acting to bring the 'unscrupulous forces involved in the attacks to book'.

'We are stating in unambiguous terms that we will remain a country of harmony and any attempts to disturb religious or cultural tolerance and harmony will be strongly dealt with without discrimination,' the government said after seven people were injured during the attack on the shrine of Hazrat Shah Poran in Sylhet.⁶

But it is not just about the Sufis. The Ahmadiyyas also feel unsafe in the new Bangladesh. Ahmadiyya is a branch of Islam founded in 1889 by Mirza Ghulam Ahmad (who claimed to have been divinely appointed as the promised Messiah) in British India. The movement was a messianic one that believes Ahmad was the promised Mahdi and Messiah expected to appear towards the end of times. While Ahmadiyyas consider themselves to be part of Islam, they are often not recognized as such by more conservative Islamic groups.

On 6 August 2024, the day after Sheikh Hasina fled to India, Bangladeshi local media reported that masjids and houses belonging to Ahmadiyyas were attacked with at least twenty injured. Ahmad Tabsir Chowdhury, media cell coordinator of the Ahmadiyya Muslim Jamaat Bangladesh, told the press his organization was not part of any political party, and it was those who had always campaigned against Ahmadiyyas and wanted to deny them the right to exist as equal citizens in Bangladesh who were responsible for the attack.

'We as a community are scared that the attacks won't stop. We are appealing to the administration to take immediate steps to contain the attacks on us,' Chowdhury had said in August 2024.[7]

On 7 October 2024, Islamists formed a human chain in the Panchagarh district in Rangpur division in northern Bangladesh demanding the withdrawal of twenty-three cases that Ahmadiyyas had filed following two incidences of mob violence. They called Ahmadiyyas heretics and demanded that the interim government amend the constitution to declare the community 'non-Muslims', as Pakistan has done. They also accused the Ahmadiyyas of targeting innocent Muslims with false cases.[8]

A year down the line, at the end of July 2025, we dialled Ahmad Tabsir Chowdhury.

'Are Ahmadiyyas feeling any safer in Bangladesh now?'

Chowdhury laughed. 'We were never safe in Bangladesh. We were the "other Muslims". But now we are not even considered Muslims. Let me give you an account of what we are going through here which media reports won't tell you,' he said.

'On 5 August 2024, the Ahmadiyya mosque in Taraganj, Rangpur district, was targeted; on 6 August, the Ahmadiyya mosque in Bamnail village, Rajshahi district, and the one in Choraikhola, Nilphamari district, were attacked. The same day, the Ahmadiyya mosque in Madartek, Dhaka city, faced two incidents of assaults by religious extremists. Also on 6 August, religious fanatics vandalized an Ahmadiyya mosque and houses in Rangtia in Sherpur district. On 9 August, another attack on the Ahmadiyya was orchestrated by fanatics,' Chowdhury told us.

Chowdhury said outfits like Bangladesh Jamaat-e-Islami, Hefazat-e-Islam Bangladesh and Islami Andolan Bangladesh which have a reductionist view of religion and society were behind these attacks. 'Their demand is to officially declare Ahmadiyyas non-Muslims and push us to the margins of society. Over the years repeated attacks on members of our community have forced us to stay away from Sunni-majority areas in cities and towns,' he said.

Chowdhury said that in 2023 Islamists attacked the Ahmadiyya Annual Convention in Ahmadnagar, Panchagarh, where a member of the community was killed, and over 100 were injured. The attackers looted, vandalized and burnt over 200 Ahmadiyya houses.

'It was not always safe for us before also. But now we fear we will be hunted down wherever we go and whenever they wish,' he said.

Chowdhury alleged that no steps had been taken to prevent attacks on Ahmadiyyas, and no action initiated against the perpetrators of the attacks. Instead, he said, legal cases had been filed against members of the Ahmadiyya community. 'Many of the Islamist groups I mentioned are in close touch with the current political dispensation. Who do we turn to?'

Desperately Seeking Lalon

Fakir Lalon Shah died on 17 October 1890, eighty-one years before Bangladesh was born on the values of Bengali nationalism, secularism, democracy and social justice. No one knows for sure when Lalon was born, but till today in Bangladesh and beyond, they sing his songs of life, love and liberation. The mystery surrounding the birth of the composer of thousands of songs in Bengali is an abiding one. Many believe the fakir lived for 116 years in Chheuriya village, near Kushtia (a town in Bangladesh), during British colonial rule.[9]

But it was not how long he lived but what he taught through his songs that informed the sociocultural choices of a modern Bangladesh more than a century after his death.

'It is possible to identify in his work a unique and even unprecedented *mélange* of Buddhist, Hindu, Islamic, and Jainist elements. Put another way: Lalon's songs and practices – in a number of instances – embody and enact an interplay among certain aspects of the Buddhist *Shahajiya* path, Gaudiya *Vaishnavism*, and even the *Kartabhaja*, while he also ranges beyond them resisting facile syncretism and eclecticism,' Azfar Hussain, professor of integrative/interdisciplinary studies at Grand Valley State University in Michigan, USA, wrote in 2020 in a column in the *Daily Star*.[10]

'A Muslim is marked by the sign/of circumcision; but how should/you mark a woman?/If a Brahmin male/is known by the thread he wears,/how is a woman known?' Lalon sang.

And it is the profundity of his poetry, the agelessness of his songs that continue to engage not just the artistically bent but academics like Azfar Hussain who, admittedly, 'fail to do justice to the entirety of Lalon's work, massive as it is'.[11]

'Given the extraordinary range and rigour of Lalon's preoccupations, I've hitherto only scratched the surface of his work. But I hope one can at least make sense of some of his concerns that remain relevant to our struggles against all forms and forces of oppression and injustice in a world devastated by capitalism, colonialism/imperialism, racism, and patriarchy, profoundly interconnected as they are,' Hussain wrote.[12]

Simply put, Lalon can be described as the unofficial patron saint of the idea of Bangladesh. He has been portrayed in literature, films, television dramas and in theatre productions. The first biopic of Lalon was *Lalon Fakir* (1973), directed by Syed Hasan Imam. *Lalan Fakir*, an Indian Bengali-language biopic film, directed by Shakti Chatterjee, released in 1978. Allen Ginsberg wrote a poem in 1992 named 'After Lalon', where he warned people against the dangers of fame and attachment to worldly things.[13]

Every year, in Bangladesh and beyond, Lalon festivals are held to honour the mystic saint and songwriter.

On 13 October 2024, discussants at a programme in Rangpur district said the philosophy that the legendary mystic advocated had inspired the masses in the July–August uprising against the Sheikh Hasina government. The programme was titled 'Why Lalon Fakir Is Important for Us' and was held at the Public Library Auditorium in the district. Moderated by writer-publisher Dipak Kumar Roy, the programme also featured performances of Lalon songs by Lalon artistes Sohag Rahmat, Neelratan, Titu and president of Rangpur Lalon Academy, Abu Naeem.[14]

A month later, a festival on Lalon was cancelled. It was planned in the city of Narayanganj, about 16 kilometres southeast of Dhaka city, in the latter half of November 2024.

The two-day event was called 'Tolerance Festival'. More than 10,000 people had attended the event the year before and listened to musicians promoting Lalon's philosophy, a mix of Sufism and other faiths, which had angered some Islamic hardliners.

So, in November 2024, the authorities did not want to take a chance.

Narayanganj deputy commissioner of police Mohammad Mahmudul Hoque told the press that city authorities had not approved the programme due to concerns about potential violence after assessing security risks.

'This area is a stronghold of groups with opposing views,' Hoque was quoted as saying.

Festival organizer Shah Jalal said it was the first time he had had to cancel such an event.

Abdul Awal, a committee leader of the Hefazat-e-Islam, a coalition of Islamist organizations with significant influence in the area, had led marches earlier that month demanding the cancellation of the festival.

'We cannot allow activities that contradict the true spirit of Islam,' Awal had said. 'In the name of celebration, they promote indecency, with women singing and dancing, gambling, and the smoking of weed,' he alleged.

Lalon's followers, ascetic 'Baul' singers who wander on foot from town to town singing and begging for alms, have been branded heretics by Islamists for a long time. But Lalon festivals have continued, drawing huge crowds. 'The cancellation of Lalon Mela is a bad omen for all of us,' cultural activist Rafiur Rabbi told the press. 'It is disheartening that the government is yielding to majority pressure. Does this mean minorities will no longer have a voice?'

The interim government's cultural affairs advisor, Mostofa Sarwar Farooki, a famous film-maker and screenwriter, said they were doing what they could. 'Sheikh Hasina's fall and her fleeing the country created a vacuum that led to a series of incidents, but we have managed to regain control,' he said.[15]

Two months later, sometime in mid-January 2025, we met a Lalon singer in Kolkata's New Town area. The man had made a living in Bangladesh singing the fakir's songs and enthralling thousands all his adult life. Now he was in India on an extended medical visa and said he had no plans to go back to his country immediately.

'I am a practising Muslim and I sing Lalon songs professionally. I see no contradiction in doing both. If there is one core theme to Lalon's teachings, it is tolerance. What else explains the abiding interest in him from all around the world? But in today's Bangladesh, Lalon is cancelled and so are we, his followers,' the forty-something singer told us, bitterness dripping from his voice.

But the interim government's cultural affairs advisor has said the government has 'regained control' over the situation. 'Mostofa Sarwar Farooki is lying. His own wife had faced flak for playing Sheikh Hasina in the Mujib biopic. [Farooki is married to Nusrat Imrose Tisha, who played Hasina in Shyam Benegal's 2023 film *Mujib: The Making of a Nation*.] But nothing will happen to her apart from some online trolling as Farooki is now part of the interim government. But for people like me, it's over,' he said.

So, how bad is it for 'people like him'?

'Living in the interiors of Bangladesh and being known for being a Lalon singer? A machete can come down on your neck any time for not being Muslim enough.'

Not Muslim Enough

'We have never been Muslim enough for Bangladesh,' Sharmin Sultana Chaiti told us over the phone from Dhaka. 'My organization, the Hizbut Touhid, was founded in 1995 at Korotia village in Bangladesh's Tangail district with the sole aim of reforming religion of its radical elements,' Chaiti said.

'Hizbut Touhid is an apolitical, reformist movement to speak up against wrongdoing, warmongering and any form of repression in the name of religion. Can you believe that for this and this alone, for the last thirty years we have been targeted, faced a ban as a militant body and been subjected to the wrong end of the law?' she asked.

Chaiti told us two powerful sections had been targeting them: those who used religion as business and those who suffered from and spread Islamophobia. 'Both are equally dangerous. On 24 February 2025, at Pirgacha subdistrict in Rangpur, our leaders and workers were attacked during a programme. This happened at the insistence of the Jamaat-e-Islami. They ransacked six houses belonging to our people with the slogan: "Hizbut Touhid's address is the address of the Christians, bring them down, burn them to the ground",' she said.

Chaiti alleged that the Jamaat has a problem with the Hizbut Touhid as their members have not gone to madrasas. 'According to the Jamaat, you cannot talk about Islam if you have not studied in a madrasa. For generations, these merchants of faith have misinterpreted Islam and targeted the powerless,' Chaiti said.

Has the situation become worse now?

'It has. There is no one to stop the Jamaat,' she said.

Mubashar Hasan, author of the book *Islam and Politics in Bangladesh: The Followers of Ummah*, wrote in *The Melbourne Asia*

Review: 'It [Bangladesh] is a Muslim country with over 89 percent Sunnis, yet it thrives on heterogeneity. Within this context, political secularism has Islamic influences but many Muslims remain divided as to what constitutes "pure Islam" and preferences for music, dress, and symbols are a source of contention about what Islam is and isn't.'

With the fall of the Sheikh Hasina government, the societal divide on what constitutes 'pure Islam' has widened. And it is not just Sufis, Ahmadiyyas or Lalon followers but even Sunni Muslims, whose behaviour is not 'Muslim enough', who are the target of Islamist ire in post-Hasina Bangladesh.

As an associate professor of English literature in a private university in Dhaka told us on the condition that we would not disclose his identity: 'In Bangladesh, the Shias, the Sufis and the Ahmadiyyas were always the Other Muslims. It was not as if there was no discrimination before. But it was a debate, often heated, sometimes violent, that would eventually reach an amicable solution towards coexistence. Today, as a Sunni Muslim who is vocal about a liberal, democratic society that should pick and choose some Western values, I am an "othered Muslim". Like the Shias, the Sufis and the Ahmadiyyas, there is little hope even for someone like me.

'You know what I want to say to the Islamists trying to interpret for me my own religion?' he asked us.

'What?'

'Well, I would simply quote from the Quran, verse 2:190:

'And fight in the cause of Allah against those who wage war against you, but do not aggress, for Allah certainly does not love the aggressors.'

13

Can Cinema Save Bangladesh?

The distance between Dhaka and Magura is around 176 kilometres. And it is in faraway Magura, a southwestern district in Bangladesh that falls under the Khulna division, that Shamin Hasan Dhumketu dreams of becoming Shakib Khan and bringing the good old days back to Bangladesh.

We met the ten-year-old boy in a village pandal in 2023 during Durga Puja celebrations in Magura. His infectious smile and cocky comebacks had made us laugh and befriend him. He had said he was trying to grow his hair long like Shakib Khan had in his new film, *Priyotama*.

'Sumon is devastated after his brother dies and he goes away to a distant city,' Dhumketu told us excitedly.

'Who is Suman?'

'Such fools you are. Sumon is Shakib Khan's name in *Priyotama*,' little Dhumketu chided us for not having any idea about Khan's latest blockbuster. He then went on to narrate the story of the film that involved the hero's romance with a politician's daughter and the tragedy that followed.

Devotees who had come for a darshan of the goddess Durga at the village pandal could barely conceal a smile seeing a little boy trying to imitate Shakib Khan's mannerisms. The incident had left us marvelling at how easy Hindus and Muslims in that village were around each other's religious festivals, even as we read reports of attacks on Durga Puja pandals elsewhere in Bangladesh.

What also dawned upon us in that village pandal was the unifying power of Shakib Khan's cinema. It was Ashtami, a day of deep reverence for Durga devotes who perform various rituals to honour the power, courage and compassion of the goddess. Not just us, some Hindu devotees at the pandal were also taken in by this young boy's Shakib Khan imitation, as they stood around him to prompt and at times correct his storytelling. Clearly, they were Shakib Khan fans too!

Dhumketu had won our hearts that day and we had been in touch with the boy through the tumultuous events of 2024, calling him on his father's phone, asking him if he was safe and what was next from the Shakib Khan stable.

In between we got in touch with Shakib Khan too.

Shakib Khan is the undisputed king of Dhallywood, Bangladeshi commercial cinema's answer to Bollywood. He debuted in 1999, with the romantic action film *Ananta Bhalobasha*.

In 2000, his films *Hira Chuni Panna*, *Phhol Nebo Na Oshru Nebo* and *Bishe Bhora Nagin* were superhits. The hits continued and by 2005, fans and critics knew he was an unstoppable force. By 2007, he was being referred to as a superstar. But it was after *Priya Amar Priya* in 2008 that his value skyrocketed – he started asking for the highest remuneration ever for a Bangladeshi actor: 80 lakh taka.

Priya Amar Priya is the highest-grossing Bangladeshi film of the 2010s and the fifth-highest of all time. At the time of its release, it smashed many previous box office records. But its collection of 15 crore taka was eclipsed by Shakib's biggest film, *Priyotoma*, the highest-grossing Bangladeshi film of all time. The 2023 movie raked in 41 crore taka at the box office.

Khan's moniker, 'Bangladesh's Shah Rukh Khan', is not just used by fans but it is an image Khan has carefully crafted over the years. Among the many properties he owns, the most talked-about house is named Jannat, in an echo of Shah Rukh's Bandra house, Mannat. Shakib's eldest son's name is Abraham Khan Joy, similar to Shah Rukh Khan's youngest son, AbRam Khan.

In many films, Shakib Khan has styled himself on Shah Rukh Khan, most recently for Dhumketu's favourite film, *Priyotama*. Bangladeshi entertainment channels reported that Shakib Khan's hairstyle, which Dhumketu was trying to copy when we met him at the Durga Puja pandal in Magura, was a copy of Shah Rukh Khan's hairstyle in his 2023 action thriller, *Pathan*.[1]

We had not been able to sit across Shakib Khan and interview him, but he agreed to a phone interview around February 2024.[2] Sheikh Hasina had just come back to power for a historic fourth term in office a month before, on 7 January. Shakib Khan had become the director of health and beauty brand Remark and cosmetics brand Herlan, and spoken to us about his dreams of becoming a brand ambassador for Bangladeshi cinema in India. An excited Khan had hoped his pan-Indian film, *Dard*, with Indian actors Sonal Chauhan, Payel Sarkar and Rahul Dev, which was set for release in Bengali, Hindi, Tamil and Malayalam at the time, would make him a big success in India as well.

It didn't.

By the time *Dard* released in India on 28 February 2025, anti-Hasina and anti-India sentiment had flooded Bangladeshi cyberspace. This would first manifest itself in the 'India Out' campaign, mirroring similar campaigns in the Maldives, led by Bangladeshi social media influencers calling for a boycott of all Indian goods, and eventually in the anti-quota campaign by students that would snowball into the campaign against Sheikh Hasina that led to her government's fall.

But when we spoke to Shakib Khan at the beginning of February 2024, neither we nor Khan knew of the storm that was coming to hit Bangladesh and how it would affect relations between our countries.

What would Shakib Khan had told us about the future of the India-Bangladesh relations if he knew what was going to happen to Bangladesh in the July Revolution?

During our interview that day, Khan was upbeat not just about partnering with India on cinema, but taking Bangladesh's cosmetics industry to India and beyond.

On comparisons with Shah Rukh Khan, Khan was humble. 'Shah Rukh is not just an Indian superstar, but a global icon. He has made all Asian actors proud by conquering the world with his acting prowess and star power. I love him and respect him, but I do not consider myself Bangladesh's Shah Rukh Khan,' he said.

But yes, the idea of spreading his arms like Shah Rukh and embracing the whole wide world in the warm embrace of universal brotherhood was an idea that had appealed to Shakib Khan.

When we asked him about his politics, Shakib Khan expressed no desire for jumping into the electoral fray. Instead, he said he wanted peaceful coexistence between India and Bangladesh. He stressed the fact that he had a strong nationalistic trait and his ambitions for gaining popularity outside his country would never come at the cost of his own people.

Some of Dhaka's hard-nosed film critics had told us soon after our interview that the capital city's cultural elite, while not oblivious to Shakib Khan's superstardom, did not quite give him the respect he deserved as an artiste. 'Because he is a darling of the masses, his movies are often cheap imitations of Bollywood movies, and it is the garment workers, the rickshaw pullers, the so-called lower classes, who have made him the Shah Rukh Khan of Dhallywood,' one of them said.

Bangladesh's movie industry has, over the decades, suffered from the shutting down of many single-screen theatres due to a drastic dip in footfall, and has been plagued by piracy issues. It is mostly reliant on Eid and festival-centric big-ticket releases. With the fall of the Hasina regime, 2024 turned out to be one of the toughest years for the industry.[3]

On 17 June 2024, the day of Qurbani Eid, Shakib Khan's *Toofan* released and became a big hit even as protests began by students to demand the reform of quotas in government jobs.

Soon after, the cinema industry came to a grinding halt. Film shooting and movie screenings stopped, and several cineplexes and cinema halls were vandalized on 5 August.[4]

Anti-India sentiment peaked in Bangladesh.

In October 2024, in an interview, Shakib Khan said that eventually, all things settle down. 'I'm not overly concerned about these issues. If any real problems arise, the leaders of both nations will find solutions. As Asians, I believe we should strive to live together in unity,' he said.[5]

When asked about anti-India sentiment in the country, Shakib explained, 'Bangladesh continues to send Hilsa fish, our cricketers play there, and diplomatic talks are ongoing. As neighbours, we should coexist peacefully, and that's what I observe.'

Khan said negative comments are exchanged from both sides, and while fluctuations in relationships are natural, cinema would heal differences.

Ruman Ganguly, special correspondent for the *Calcutta Times* supplement of the *Times of India*'s Kolkata edition, has been following the magic of Shakib Khan from the other side of the border. 'They compare him to Shah Rukh Khan, but Shakib Khan's stardom in Bangladesh is akin to Rajinikanth's. I saw a big crowd go mad outside the Acropolis mall in South Kolkata when Shakib Khan had come to promote his film *Toofan* in July 2024.

'You know, I have been writing on cinema for almost three decades. It does have the power to heal. Especially during bad days. The likes of you who talk politics all day often overlook the soft power of cinema,' Ganguly smiled.

The OTT Revolution

If Shakib Khan's persona and cinema have been winning hearts and trying to bridge the widening gap between Bangladesh and India, the country's OTT revolution has tried to look within, discard the candyfloss and hug the cactus.

'Big cinema has made me who I am. I do not feel the need yet to do only-for-OTT films. In Bangladesh, my films are released in theatres first and OTT later. I am for the big picture,' Khan told us.

But the big picture often misses the harsher truths.

Since its launch in Bangladesh in 2021, Bangladeshi OTT platform Chorki has been showing such truths, boldly going where few dare to tread. From a wife unapologetically prioritizing her sexual desires, to a mother smuggling drugs hidden in her private parts, to a man helplessly in love with his cousin's wife, the platform has pushed boundaries with its morally complex characters and raw stories told with finesse.[6]

Chorki's series and films have defied conventions, ignited controversies and set new standards for hyperlocal content with crossover international appeal. Its action-packed series *Shaaticup* (2022) has been called the 'Bangladeshi *Narcos*' and for the gritty thriller *Guti* (2023), it released a promo cleverly referencing elements from *Breaking Bad*.

In March 2024 at a tony continental eatery in Dhaka's plush neighbourhood Gulshan 1, we met film-maker and Chorki's young CEO Redoan Rony for an interview over dinner.

Like Shakib Khan, Rony had told us of his dreams to bring the two Banglas, Bangladesh and West Bengal, together. Chorki, along with Dhaka-based Alpha-I Studios and West Bengal's film production and distribution company SVF, was collaborating on two big films, the big-budget thriller *Toofan* and *Domm*, which Rony was to direct. 'But we will not stop at that,' Rony had said confidently. 'We will make originals and OTT series that will make the global market sit up and take notice. And soon enough, we will venture into other languages and markets both in India and outside.'

Hoichoi is the biggest Bengali-language streaming in India, but Rony had boasted that Chorki has been making serious cross-border inroads since its launch in Bangladesh just over two years prior. The secret sauce behind its success? Shows that shatter stereotypes of what Bangla content can be. Its stories mirror the realities of life in Bangladesh without sacrificing plot, pacing or production value.

For Rony, the courage to tell such stories in a Muslim-majority country came from the conviction that Bangladeshi stories should be told by Bangladeshi platforms, and not by Netflix and Amazon.

'Foreign OTT platforms sell us quality content. But they cannot smell the earth, breathe the air, and enter the heads and hearts of Bangladeshis like we can,' he had said.

Rony is a film-maker himself, and has directed numerous successful shows and movies in Bangladesh, including the National Award–winning *Chorabali* (2016), even launching his own short-lived OTT platform, Popcorn Live, before helming Chorki. Over the years, he has seen Bangladeshi audiences change.

'Chorki was started with the belief that the urban audience in Bangladesh has become mature enough to see the kind of content that we produce,' he told us. 'We were happily amazed to see that not just the urban but the suburban audience took to our shows even before Chorki completed a year.'

Before the 2024 upheaval in Bangladesh, Chorki didn't shy away from controversial themes, uncomfortable visuals or subtle political commentary. Its shows, spanning genres from horror to thrillers and family dramas, became talking points both in Bangladesh and West Bengal.

For instance, the 2023 Eid release *Myself Allen Swapan* sent shockwaves across Bangladesh and became the platform's most streamed content so far. The series featured a middle-class homemaker called Shayla (played by actress Rafiath Rashid Mithila) who ends up placing her sexual and financial needs above conventional morality. Caught in the middle of a game of cat and mouse between drug lords and government agents, Shayla discovers that an imposter has been sharing her home and bed – her husband's twin, a wanted criminal. But rather than recoiling in horror, Shayla accepts him for the passion and financial stability that was missing in her marriage.

Shayla was written like no other female character in Bangladeshi cinema or OTT before. We had an opportunity to speak to actress Rafiath Rashid Mithila, who told us it was a challenging role to play, but one she had thoroughly enjoyed.

'Chorki is changing the narrative within Bangladesh and outside. The brand has come to be known for telling stories others won't dare to attempt. Playing Shayla brought me some hate on social media. But a significant section of the audience and critics loved Shayla and *Myself Allen Swapan*,' she said.

Rony told us women characters had been shown a certain way in Bangladeshi cinema and OTT. 'They have mostly conformed to a set stereotype. With *Myself Allen Swapan*, we wanted to alter the gaze, write a woman character who thinks for herself and her emotional, sexual, and financial needs,' he said. When it became the highest streamed content from Chorki, Rony said the criticisms and the social outrage didn't hurt anymore.

Criticism and critical acclaim have both been constant companions throughout Chorki's journey. In 2022, for example, the thriller-drama *Nikhoj* stirred controversy. It follows a woman searching for her father, who vanishes after being taken away by men claiming to be the police. But the family of photojournalist Shafiqul Islam Kajol, a victim of enforced disappearance, claimed that *Nikhoj*'s portrayal was insensitive.

In an open letter, Kajol's son Monorom Polok said that the series seemed like 'paid content from those in power' and had 'utterly disgusted' his father. At the time, Rony defended the show, maintaining *Nikhoj* was fictional and any resemblance to Kajol's case was coincidental.

Nikhoj was streamed when Sheikh Hasina was firmly in her seat and forced disappearances had become a major controversy that plagued her administration. It was after her fall on 5 August 2024 and the installation of the interim government that Aynaghar, a clandestine detention centre run by the Directorate General of Military Intelligence, would be discovered in Bangladesh.

After *Nikhoj*, the 2023 release *Guti* ignited much social media debate for its complex portrayal of a woman called Sultana (played by actress Azmeri Haque Badhan). An affectionate mother who moonlights as a drug smuggler, Sultana is depicted inserting condoms filled with drugs into her body. Despite criticism for this aspect, *Guti* got a subtle endorsement from Indian film-maker

Anurag Kashyap, who shared its teaser as a story on his Instagram handle, complete with fire emojis. Another big talking point was Chorki's innovative promotion featuring photos of lead actors in yellow lab coats, reminiscent of the iconic characters Walter White and Jesse Pinkman from *Breaking Bad*.

Amid all the bouquets and brickbats, Rony emphasized the importance of earning audience trust over time. 'People need to believe that when we write stories and flesh out characters, we are not looking at doing business by creating controversies. We are simply trying to tell stories honestly about people and situations that we see in society but do not often talk about in public.'

This approach floored film-makers and audiences in West Bengal too. Prasun Chatterjee, director of the internally acclaimed film *Dostojee*, had told us later that Chorki is the best among all Bengali OTT platforms.

'I am not saying other Bengali OTT platforms are not doing good work. But Chorki has maintained a consistency in quality content that should be a yardstick for everyone working in this space,' Chatterjee had said.

Chatterjee, known for his own work in channelling the power of local stories, added that Chorki stands out for its deep understanding of Bangladeshi society and culture. This is evident in several productions, such as the narco-thriller *Shaaticup*. Set in the underbelly of Rajshahi, it features the regional dialect and a local cast, all presented with what a reviewer called 'stylistic swagger'.

'It didn't go down well with the audience,' Rony had smiled, but noted that this was part of the business and not a reflection of the Bangladeshi audience's capacity to handle offbeat themes.

'There is some content that will do well and some that won't. The Bangladeshi audience has matured over the years and has become really smart and demanding,' he added. 'The fact that we continue to grow is proof of that. When the content we produce is seen outside the country, it also breaks the stereotype of Bangladesh as a conservative country.'

Walking a tightrope between artistic freedom and self-censorship is a reality for storytellers across the world, and it was no different for Chorki. But Rony insisted that evening that experimentation was in Chorki's DNA because of its parent company, Transcom Group, a large business conglomerate with a portfolio spanning beverages, pharmaceuticals, electronics and media. Transcom also owns two of Bangladesh's major newspapers, *Prothom Alo* and *Daily Star*.

'Our newspapers have pushed the boundaries of journalism, the papers have employed the best, brightest, and most fearless journalists in the country. Being part of the same family, there is a lot of expectation from us at Chorki,' Rony said proudly.

However, he acknowledged that film-makers, universally, need to be aware of limits based on their sociopolitical and commercial contexts. 'The current government or the ones before have never said, "You can show this but not that." But even as we experiment with storytelling, we have to be smart about how we go about our business,' he said.

That evening, as our dinner conversations simply refused to end, Rony had put forth his big plans for 2024. For one, he wanted to upgrade the Chorki app with better tech and a more user-friendly interface. He also wanted to go back to directing at least one film himself every year.

'I want to explore ideas and partnerships with other regional film industries in India, apart from Bengal. To make our content truly global,' he had said. 'Cultural fabrics differ, but emotions are universal. Film-makers and artistes have been targeted, harassed and jailed across the world for telling stories, but hey, what's the fun otherwise!'

Targeted for Telling Stories

Artistes did get targeted barely a few months after our dinner discussion with Rony in March. But mostly female artistes faced the brunt of mob ire.

On 2 February 2025, *Prothom Alo* wrote an article titled, 'Why Are Only Women Artistes Being Targeted?'[7]

It said one of Bangladesh's leading actresses, Apu Biswas, was supposed to inaugurate a restaurant in the Kamrangirchar area of Dhaka but she couldn't attend the event because of a mob.

Earlier, actress Mehazabien Chowdhury faced similar trouble in Chittagong while actress Pori Moni faced similar harassment in Tangail. All three incidents, the report said, took place within a span of just three months.

'The scheme seems to be the same in each of these cases. A group of people are objecting to the news of the actresses' presence and are foiling the event. The organizers are being forced to exclude the artistes. Informing the police isn't proving very helpful either,' the report said.

While Apu Biswas and Mehazabien Chowdhury chose to skirt the issue, Pori Moni took it on head-on. On 25 January, the actress wrote in a Facebook post, 'How can anyone remain so silent? Feeling deprived of freedom. Why should the artiste face so much obstruction? Feeling insecure. Why aren't we safe in this free country?'

Referring to the incident involving Mehazabien, Pori Moni wrote, 'What are they trying to prove in the name of religion? What more can I say? Shut every medium of entertainment including cinema in this country then. We all would be held responsible for this.'

The officer in charge of Kamrangirchar police station, Amirul Islam, told *Prothom Alo*: 'Pro-Islamists had protested on Facebook. They had stated that they would create chaos if Apu Biswas was invited to the inauguration. I have also found screenshots of such writing on Facebook.'

The targeting of actresses shook the world of art and cinema.

Director Ashfaque Nipun told *Prothom Alo*: 'This type of politics has been going on since long before. This is the politics of stopping any woman who's successful. Some pro-religion political communities are doing [these] out of a sort of insecurity. They are really scared of the concept of liberal women and modernistic society. So they want to subdue that.'

Theatre activist Samina Lutfa said the mob was feeling encouraged by the lack of visible action against it. She told *Prothom Alo* that it was important to ensure that they did not get this encouragement and it was the responsibility of the government to ensure that this stopped.

For Nipun, both state and society have to resist the mob. 'Whether it's an interim government or an elected one, they should keep in mind that such mobs need to be resisted in any case. Women have to be provided with security. Socially, it's our responsibility to resist them without being scared,' *Prothom Alo* quoted him as saying.

How Was It before Yunus?

While the targeting of actresses has become an epidemic of sorts after the fall of the Hasina government, they did not get the respect they deserved even before.

We had spoken to Azmeri Haque Badhon over the phone on 4 October 2023, a day before the Vishal Bhardwaj–directed spy thriller *Khufiya* released on Netflix India.[8]

We had asked Badhon how she felt about the way her character in *Khufiya*, Heena Rehman, was introduced on screen by Bhardwaj. Starring the Indian actress Tabu, the film began with the camera focussed on Badhon's neck as Tabu's voice could be heard in the background: 'Strange, she was. Shrouded like a sin. Obvious like a sacred death. And sometimes, illogical like fate.'

'Playing her lover was a fantasy come true. I like the line "shrouded like a sin",' Badhon had laughed over the phone. 'You know in Bangladesh actresses are not respected. People may not say it on your face, or maybe sometimes they would, but they think of us rather disrespectfully. It doesn't help that I am not only an actress, but I have also lived the kind of life that makes people judge me,' she said.

This coming from the first Bangladeshi actress to have walked the Cannes Film Festival red carpet with a film in the official selection, Abdullah Mohammad Saad-directed *Rehana Maryam Noor*, in 2021, the year Bangladesh turned fifty years old, stunned us.

Badhon told us she was not homophobic, but Bangladeshi society at large was. 'Director Vishal Bhardwaj told me beforehand that there would be a lesbian angle to the story. He asked me if I would be comfortable playing such a role. For me, what mattered was a Vishal Bhardwaj film as my Bollywood debut and the chance to act with Tabu. As far as my role in *Khufiya* is concerned, it is a small but powerful one. In a sense, the entire plot revolves around my character and what happens to her,' says Badhon.

Badhon had told us homosexuality is not a comfortable topic for discussion in Muslim-majority Bangladesh. Eyebrows would be raised and her choice of role for a Bollywood debut would be questioned. But she had told us she didn't care anymore.

Attracted to strong roles, Badhon wants cinema to start conversations around topics that are often brushed under the carpet. A graduate in dental surgery from Bangladesh Dental College in Dhaka, Badhon told us she never got the chance to be a professional dentist because of an early marriage and divorce. While she didn't want to remember that dark chapter anymore, what she wouldn't forget or ever stop being vocal about is the marital rape and chronic depression she had lived with for a part of her life.

'I am naturally drawn towards the kinds of roles like I play in *Khufiya*. Life has taught me that actresses wearing sleeveless blouses and romancing heroes on snow-clad mountains is a big lie. We grew up watching such movies and dreaming of fairy tales. And then came the big crash and the struggle for survival. As an actress today, I want my cinema to look into life as honestly as possible,' she told us.

Khufiya got mixed reviews in India. The Bangladesh press mostly talked about Badhon's big break in Hindi cinema. We saw Badhon next in the news when the anti-quota stir in Bangladesh became a mass revolt against Hasina. Badhon became one of the celebrity faces that joined the protests against the Hasina regime.

Hasina fell, Yunus rose.

Many in Bangladesh cheered.

Badhon was one of them.

In an interview to an Indian news site on 30 August 2024, three weeks after Hasina's fall and Yunus's takeover, Badhon said: 'Right now, I can only trust in Muhammad Yunus and believe that he would be able to give a healthy election very soon. But before that, our society needs a cultural reformation, the nation needs to be rid of its state of decay.'[9]

Ten months later, on 29 June 2025, Badhon wrote on her Facebook page:

> Am I safe in this country? The answer is simple: No. Not at all.
> Every single day, girls and women in this country face abuse, harassment, threats, and injustice.
> And what do we do?
> We endure it.
> We fight back.
> And some ... they don't survive.
> Some lose their lives to this violence.
> Only then – after a death, or a brutal injustice – do people suddenly become 'concerned'.
> There's outrage.
> There are hashtags.
> Then it fades away.
> And we move on.
> This is the reality we've accepted for years. This is not new.
> Now let's talk about me.
> The amount of threats I've received online ...
> The hate speech, the bullying, the harassment –
> Has any action been taken?
> No.

Because in this country, many people believe I deserve it.
Unless I'm murdered, they think it's okay to harass me.
To humiliate me.
To try and silence me.
I had no faith in the system for a long time.
After the July Revolution, I allowed myself to hope.
But I was wrong.
There is no reason to be optimistic in a corrupt, patriarchal country like this.
This is the truth. This is the reality. And we are being forced to accept it.[10]

We remembered what she had told us during our interview in 2023. 'I will turn forty soon. My life started at thirty-five. There was a Badhon before and a Badhon after. Before, I used to live for family, friends, society. The Badhon today lives for herself, free from the shackles of society. If as an actor I cannot choose the type of roles I want to portray on screen, what is the point of being free?' she had asked us that day.

'I have seen the worst of society,' Badhon had told us. 'And came to cinema by chance. Cinema has the power to change how things are. If cinema can't change how Bangladesh is, maybe nothing can.'

We had agreed with her then.

It is now July 2025.

Neither cinema nor politics has changed Bangladesh for the better.

Was Azmeri Haque Badhon wrong about the power of cinema? Or about trusting Yunus to change Bangladesh?

We call Shamin Hasan Dhumketu, our ten-year-old friend from Magura.

'Has your hair grown long like Shakib Khan's?'

'You don't know anything, do you?' the boy chides us. 'Shakib Khan is sporting a new style now. He has shorter hair, a buzz cut. I wear my hair like that now.'

We laugh.

'And how have you been, Dhumketu? Is everything okay in your village?'

The boy is quiet for a while.

'No,' he says, finally. 'But I know Shakib Khan will save Bangladesh.'

14

The Return of Secular Bloggers

Azam Khan can't tell us why Bangladesh committed patricide. Or why he feels his former compadre, YouTuber Pinaki Bhattacharya, sold his soul to France.

Far away from the country of their birth, Khan and Bhattacharya find themselves on opposite sides of the battle for Bangladesh's soul. The two are engaged in a battle of like and dislike buttons, subscriptions and follower counts, even as Bangladesh shape-shifts to turn into something it was not.

Their fellow soldiers, like them, are social media sensations. Azam Khan and his ilk want a secular Bangladesh, the other side spells chaos.

For now, it seems Azam Khan is on the losing side.

If the fall of the house of Sheikh Mujibur Rahman, Dhanmondi 32, to a raucous mob's savage angst on 5–6 February 2025 was a punch to the face, then Bhattacharya's YouTube videos prodding Bangladesh to stamp out the memorial of her founding father was a blow to Azam Khan's gut.

From somewhere in Europe from where Khan can see the mighty Alps, the thirty-five-year-old Bangladeshi sustainable finance associate at a private firm switched between videos of the demolition of Dhanmondi 32 and Bhattacharya's call to violence for several days on his phone on and after 5 February.

'What kind of nation snubs out the memory of her founding father? Especially when that memory is stained by mass murders, deportation and genocidal rape, and that freedom was won after the supreme sacrifice of its people? And to think Pinaki prodded the mob to do what they did on 5 February,' Khan told us over a StreamYard chat.

Twelve years earlier, on 5 May 2013, Bhattacharya had done something similar – tried to convince Khan and a bunch of young, impressionable Bangladeshis to pick up arms not against a memorial but to defend themselves from the armed cadre of the Hefazat-e-Islam Bangladesh.

Khan and his friends had rejected that appeal.

But on 5 February 2025, the mob that gathered outside Dhanmondi 32 took Bhattacharya's suggestion seriously. Bhattacharya, now fifty-eight and a resident of France, is a popular name across Bangladesh through his YouTube channel which has 3.28 million subscribers. His hard stance against Sheikh Hasina and her Awami League government and his criticism of her camaraderie with Modi won him a legion of online followers and haters in Bangladesh and beyond. On 15 October 2022, the counterterrorism and transnational crime department of the Dhaka Metropolitan Police had filed a case on charges of maligning the image of the country under the Digital Security Act.[1] Undeterred, Bhattacharyya carried on his online crusade against Hasina till the fall of her government on 5 August 2024.

Early on 5 February 2025, Bhattacharya put out a video on his channel that immediately went viral and was picked up by news portals:

Dear Bangladeshis, Assalamualaikum. Today, at 9 p.m., mass murderer, fascist and shameless Hasina has expressed a desire to address students. We will give a befitting reply to this display of arrogance. We will demolish Dhanmondi 32. The moment she begins her (online) address, all of you will gather outside Dhanmondi 32 in big groups. Bring bulldozers. If you can't find bulldozers, get hammers, shovels and pickaxes. Dhanmondi 32 will no longer stand. Let us correct injustices of history. Come to demolish the very foundation of fascism. Come with a song on your lips, come shouting slogans, come with your children, come with a smile on your face and revenge in your heart. On the ruins of the memorial of fascism, come to hoist the flag of freedom of our student-citizens. Today, at 9 p.m. let history be written. Let the followers of Abu Sayed follow your path. Come let us finish our unfinished business. Dhanmondi 32 will not stand any more. Student-citizen unity zindabad. Inqilab Zindabad.[2]

On 6 February, news portal *Prothom Alo* reported that the demolishing of Dhanmondi 32 that started the night before (at around the same time that Bhattacharya had suggested) continued till the next morning. 'A huge crowd of demonstrators gathered at Dhanmondi 32 on Wednesday centering around Hasina's address to the nation. At one stage, they set fire to the house of Sheikh Mujib and started vandalising it. Heavy equipment, including bulldozers, were seen being used in knocking down the building around 7 a.m. today. A major portion of the front side of the building has been razed to the ground. Several people, who gathered there, said they do not want to keep any remnants of the autocratic government while many were seen rejoicing when a larger portion of the building was torn down,' the report said.[3]

In our StreamYard chat, Azam Khan said it was uncanny how Bhattacharya's instructions on how to gather and bring down Dhanmondi 32 and *Prothom Alo*'s report the day after, detailing how the attack was carried out, read almost the same.

In exactly three months since, even as India and Pakistan were locked in an armed conflict over the killing of twenty-six Indian tourists in a terror attack in Jammu and Kashmir's Pahalgam, Bhattacharya would use social media to demand the ban of the Awami League, the party he would describe as 'the main political player in Bangladesh that works for India's interests'. On 8 May 2025, Bhattacharya would put out a post on his verified Facebook page saying the time had come to take a definitive step against the Awami League. 'We should do this to give the wounded and dead of the July Revolution their due. Awami League's party offices across the country should be declared citizens' property,' he would write.[4]

Over the next two days, Bhattacharya would exhort his social media followers to gather at Dhaka's Shahbagh junction to demand a ban on the Awami League. The same Shahbagh where he had told Azam Khan and others like him to pick up arms against radical Islamists.

'Hundreds of student activists and leaders of the National Citizens' Party [sic], affiliated to the powerful Students Against Discrimination body – which toppled the Sheikh Hasina government in August last year, are holding a sit-in in Dhaka's Shahbagh intersection demanding a ban on the Awami League,' Bangladeshi local press would report.[5]

On 10 May, the interim government of Bangladesh would ban all activities of the Awami League under the Anti-Terrorism Act. The ban would remain in place until the trial of the party and its leadership over the deaths of hundreds of protesters under the International Crimes (Tribunals) Act is completed, the government would say in an official statement.

We dialled Azam Khan again. Why would such a sizeable chunk of Bangladesh's youth get mobilized by Pinaki Bhattacharya's social media feeds?

'Today's disrupters do not recognize an agent of chaos when they see one. All they see is an ally who would cheer them on as they went around taking secular Bangladesh apart brick by brick. Twelve years ago, we could see through Pinaki at Shahbagh. It is devastating the same Shahbagh would be used to call for a ban on the Awami League and the government would listen to them,' Khan told us.

'Do you remember that day from twelve years ago at Shahbagh?' we asked Khan.

'I do. On that day, both Bhattacharya and I wanted fundamentalism to end in Bangladesh,' Khan told us.

Scent of a Revolution

Shahbagh is a junction between two distinct parts of Dhaka: Old Dhaka to its south and New Dhaka to the north. Standing between the old and the new, Shahbagh has been witness to history's whims. It was developed when the mighty Mughals ruled undivided Bengal in the seventeenth century. Old Dhaka was the provincial capital and the centre of the flourishing muslin industry. By the early nineteenth century, it fell into neglect and decay.

By the middle of the nineteenth century, the Shahbagh area was back in the good books of history as New Dhaka became a provincial centre of the British Raj, ending a century of decline brought on by the passing of Mughal rule.

On 5 February 2013, Shahbagh became a global headline.

A sea of protestors descended on the streets to scream for a secular Bangladesh where a convicted war criminal like Abdul Quader Mollah would be hanged to death for his crimes against humanity and not be allowed to get away with life imprisonment.

The protests were both offline and online with a bunch of influential young bloggers mobilizing support for the protestations at Shahbagh.

Azam Khan was one of them.

As was Pinaki Bhattacharya.

What began with a demand for Mollah's hanging did not stop at that. The protestors wanted all war criminals of 1971 to face the full force of the law, to hang for their crimes against fellow East Bengalis and for siding with the brutal West Pakistan army. 'Mollah was a proud member of the Al-Badr militia during the Bangladesh War of Independence, and was convicted of killing 344 civilians, among many other war crimes,' Khan recalled for us.

As the movement grew in size, both on the streets of Shahbagh and online, it demanded more than the hanging of war criminals. The protestors wanted a ban on the Jamaat-e-Islami Bangladesh from participating in polls, as well as a boycott of all institutions that supported or were affiliated with the Jamaat.

Azam Khan's retelling of the Shahbagh movement took us back to a chilly Delhi winter morning at the Foreign Correspondents' Club of South Asia at Mathura Road.

It was 30 December 2024, and we were at the club to meet a group of Hindus of Bangladeshi origin – now scattered across the globe – who were there to address a press conference for Indian journalists later that day.

One of them, Sushanta Dasgupta, a social activist and entrepreneur from London, told us the Shahbagh movement was about reclaiming the spirit of 1971. 'We spoke truth to power, we pushed for secular values, we pushed back against authoritarianism, religious extremism and the betrayal of our founding principles,' Dasgupta had said in an animated voice that had turned heads at other tables.

The hoarding at the venue of the presser in the club was quite a mouthful: 'The latest situation of the Hindus, other religious minorities, indigenous people, and tribal groups under hostile and pro-jihadist government in Bangladesh.'

At the presser, Dasgupta and others addressed a roomful of journalists from Delhi and called for the setting up of protected, autonomous zones within Bangladesh to save minority communities. Among other demands, the delegation asked for completing the unfinished population exchange from the 1947 Partition, which would facilitate the secure resettlement of displaced minorities.

The next morning, the presser made big headlines in Delhi. Journalist Anindya Banerjee's story on the News18 website screamed: '"Want Protected, Autonomous Zones for Hindus": Global Bengali Hindu Coalition to Yunus'.[6]

But that morning at the club, chatting with us over several rounds of club coffee and hot pakoras, Dasgupta's mind flew back to Shahbagh 2013 and the many impossible dreams he had dreamt for a Bangladesh that would be defined by more than its Islamic identity.

Young and dreamy-eyed for a future free of prejudice, Dasgupta was a proud protestor at Shahbagh. 'Shahbagh wasn't a monolith. Some of us wanted systemic change, others wanted retribution. A deep split emerged between those who trusted the ruling party, the Awami League, and those who feared the movement was being hijacked for political gain. There was also a generational and ideological gap – between those who wanted to preserve Bengali cultural secularism and those more aligned with a rigid nationalist framework,' Dasgupta said.

Dasgupta, Azam Khan and others like them had come under the broader umbrella of the Ganajagaran Mancha, which Bangladeshi journalist Swadesh Roy would later describe as a 'titanic social movement that had helped Bangladesh to ensure a major impact against Islamic fundamentalism'.

Looking back at the events of March 2013 and after, Roy would write on 19 March 2019 that this youth uprising was the maiden one in the subcontinent. It happened through social media, after the 2010 Middle East uprising branded the Arab Spring.

Roy wrote that the nature, stated goal and impact of the Ganajagaran Mancha were opposite to that of the Arab Spring, which had concluded the year before, in 2012. While the Arab Spring wanted to topple autocratic governments, on the streets, the movement gave room to all kinds of protestors, even the fundamentalists. 'The goal and characteristics of the Ganajagaran Mancha were absolutely reverse … [it] was to strengthen the hand of the democratic government, and they did not give any room to any fundamentalists on the street. So, it was entirely a progressive social revolution that became a towering movement against fundamentalism,' Roy wrote.[7]

In their romanticism, many of them could not see what was coming their way.

Machetes, Mayhem, Misdirection

On 15 February 2013, blogger and Ganajagaran Mancha activist Ahmed Rajib Haider was hacked to death near his house in Dhaka's Mirpur area. Rajib, an engineer by profession, wrote against radical groups in Bangladesh. Mild-mannered Haider would use the pseudonym Thaba Baba in blogging communities like somewhereinblog.net, amarblog.com and nagorikblog.com to take on fundamentalists.

Police found seven students of North South University had killed Rajib, provoked by the radical teachings of Ansarullah Bangla Team chief Mufti Jasim Uddin Rahmani.

News portal *BD News 24* reported that on 31 December 2015, Dhaka's Speedy Trial Tribunal-3 delivered its verdict on the case, sentencing Redwanul Azad Rana and Faisal Bin Nayeem Deep to death. Both Rana and Deep were former students of North South University and absconding. The court pronounced different prison terms for six others.

Maksudul Hasan Anik, sentenced to life in prison for killing Haider, had also been fined 10,000 taka. Ehsan Reza Rumman, Nayeem Irad and Nafiz Imtiaj were sentenced to ten years in jail and fined 5,000 taka each.

Ansarullah Bangla Team chief Mufti Jasim Uddin Rahmani was named as the 'instigator' and given five years in jail.[8] It is the same Rahmani who was freed on bail in a case filed under the Anti-Terrorism Act on 26 August 2024, days after the fall of the Sheikh Hasina government.[9]

Haider's killing would change Azam Khan's life forever.

'I felt numb. It was as if a part of me had been hacked with a machete. But hope floats even on the dark waters of despair and we thought it would be the first and last killing,' Khan told us.

It wasn't.

On 27 April 2016, Arafatul Islam wrote in a news report that since Haider's assassination in 2013, five more secular bloggers had been killed. All of them were self-proclaimed atheists and critics of religious fundamentalism. 'Islamist groups claimed responsibility for each of these killings on Twitter, releasing press statements in English and Bengali languages stating the reasons for their deaths. The jihadist organisations have said they killed the activists for their "blasphemous activities",' Islam wrote.[10]

Avijit Roy, Washiqur Babu, Ananta Bijoy Das, Niladry Neel and Arefin Dipon would die dreaming of a secular Bangladesh.

Writing for the Amnesty International website on 9 November 2015, with his name hidden, a blogger said he had stopped going to the office after a machete killed a fellow blogger. 'I was absent for so long, I was about to lose my job. I was the sole breadwinner of my family – the financial impact would have been dire. But what else could I do? My name was on several hit lists published by extremists, yet the police were not willing to protect me. At least that is how I felt after hearing from other bloggers who asked the police for help without success,' he wrote.[11]

For this unknown blogger, and for Khan, Dasgupta and others like them, their normal lives faded away. In the years that followed, many of them left Bangladesh.

'Every time I went out on the street, I had to look back to check if the man behind me was wielding a machete or a knife or a gun to put me down. You can't live like that,' Khan told us.

Khan left Bangladesh in 2016 for a city in Europe which he does not disclose. And yet, muscle memory and the morning newspapers carrying news of fundamentalist attacks against people like him not just inside Bangladesh but across the globe make him turn around even today to check who is walking behind him.

'I underwent therapy. But dark dreams and anxiety are still a part of me. I try to live a regular, boring life in Europe, even though I continue to get death threats online. They tell me they will kill me the moment they can trace me. But till then, I will try to live a little,' Khan said, a smile on his face.

During the weekend, Khan goes to a bar and later to a club to party if the music leads him on. Else, he goes for a walk in the mountains, or rock climbing. In summer, he swims, camps or grills, calling friends over. He tries to pretend his life is normal, even though Bangladesh is again in the throes of madness.

'You know what rankles the most? That some of us lost the way and dived straight into the abyss. Like Pinaki Bhattacharya,' Khan told us.

Prodding protestors to destroy Dhanmondi 32 in February 2025 was not Bhattacharya's only transgression, according to Khan. He was a key figure in the 'India Out' campaign that called for a boycott of Indian products in Bangladesh that began soon after Sheikh Hasina's return to power on 7 January 2024.

Dhaka-based independent journalist Faisal Mahmud had told *Scroll* that Bhattacharya, who fled Bangladesh in 2018 for France fearing government action against him, believed that the 'India Out' campaign was needed to oust Hasina. 'He has no grievances against India, he has grievances against Hasina,' Mahmud told *Scroll* in an interview.

Yet on his YouTube channel, on 23 January 2024, Bhattacharya had posted a video attacking Indian Prime Minister Narendra Modi and his government for constructing the Ram Mandir in Ayodhya on the ruins of the Babri Masjid. While the criticism could have been viewed as opposition to the Modi government's hard push for Hindu religiosity or one questioning the Indian Supreme Court's judgment on the Ram Janmabhoomi–Babri Masjid case, the language used by Bhattacharya in the video that got 811,791 views was a direct call to violence against a foreign head of state. The video ran with the title: 'Go and circumcise Modi.'[12]

Khan told us that while Bhattacharya was free to criticize whomsoever he wished to, his provocative videos amounted to attempts at destabilizing Bangladesh. They also amounted to tacit support to fundamentalists who were out to tear apart Bangladesh's secular fabric, or whatever remained of it.

'Why do you think Bhattacharya's videos get such views? While he trashes the rise of Hindu nationalism in India or Hasina's authoritarianism, his videos appeal to the basest instincts of Bangladeshi youth that have grown up on a potent diet of Islamic radicalization and hatred for other faiths,' Khan said.

On 5 May 2013, Khan alleged that Bhattacharya had offered him and other Shahbagh protestors arms to kill the very fundamentalists he appeals to today. 'We said no. We told him the way forward is dialogue and demand for justice and equality in society. And not a call to arms. Now, he has switched sides and the other side is all too willing to not just bring down Dhanmondi 32, but the very idea of a secular Bangladesh,' Khan said.

So who is Pinaki Bhattacharya and why does he do what he does on social media? We dialled Mufassil Islam in London who knows Bhattacharya from his 'far left days'. For this fifty-five-year-old Bangladesh lawyer, theologian and online activist, Bhattacharya's religion was never a stumbling block for charting out the dos and don'ts of life.

'His father Shyamal Bhattacharya was a respected teacher in their hometown Bogura and instilled in the young Bhattacharya Marx over Manusmriti or any other Hindu text,' he said.

Mufassil said there was a curious connection between the far left, like Pinaki Bhattacharya, among those who had protested at Shahbagh against Jamaat-e-Islami, Hefazat-e-Islam Bangladesh and other Islamic radical groups and these groups themselves.

'While the Awami League co-opted many among the Shahbagh protestors, the party left out the far left from among them. And both of these groups, far left activists as well as the radicals, bore the brunt of the hard power exercised by the Hasina dispensation,' Mufassil told us over the call.

He reminded us of what we already knew. The current Ameer of the Jamaat-e-Islami Bangladesh, Dr Shafiqur Rahman, was a leftist himself in his earlier avatar as a registered member of the Jatiya Samajtantrik Dal.

Even as we tried to wrap our heads around the far left and the radical right coming close in Bangladesh, Mufassil had another shocker for us. Bhattacharya, a physician by profession, got caught in a fake drugs racket that led to the death of children. He had to flee Bangladesh.

'The Jamaat, with its wide network both inside Bangladesh and outside, extended a helping hand. Pinaki dodged the police and the border patrol and escaped Bangladesh. He lodged himself in France by seeking political asylum. His Hindu name came in handy to sell his story to the West,' Mufassil told us.

There are speculations both in Bangladesh and India about Pinaki Bhattacharya's religious identity. Sushanta Dasgupta is convinced Bhattacharya has converted to Islam. 'If you take a hard look at those who comment on his posts and videos, you will find most of them are actively Jamaat members or its supporters. Such endorsement from Jamaat won't come for a Hindu. That apart, I know from common friends that Bhattacharya converted long ago,' he told us.

Whether he has converted to Islam or not, Bhattacharya is a figure of hate and derision for India's Hindu right media outlets. For Kaushalesh Rai, who runs the Hindu Café Foundation, a media outlet catering to the far right, it is immaterial what religion Pinaki Bhattacharya practises. Rai told us over the phone that Bhattacharya aids in the global march of jihadists.

For Akramul Haque, sixty-two, who stayed on in Dhaka despite attacks on bloggers like him and has a garments export business now, Bhattacharya is simply a man with a need for relevance. 'Bhattacharya is a shape-shifter. He has made an about turn as he knows what sells in Bangladesh where illiteracy in a vast majority of the youth drives them towards a radical path and makes them consume his videos in vast numbers, making it a profitable business model for him,' Haque told us over the phone from Dhaka.

The problem with Haque's assessment is that Bhattacharya seems to know how to work the algorithm and not just how to respond to it. He knows when not to speak up even if the topic is trending online. For instance, Azam Khan told us that Bhattacharya had maintained complete silence over attacks on minorities that followed the fall of Hasina, even as news of the attacks made global headlines.

After Hasina, Bhattacharya trained his guns on the Bangladesh army's chief of army staff General Waker-uz-Zaman. In a video on 21 March 2025 with over 15 lakh views on YouTube, Bhattacharya accused Waker-uz-Zaman of being an Indian agent whose sole purpose was to bring the Awami League back into Bangladesh's political arena and restore it to power.

In the same video, Bhattacharya accused the BNP of becoming the new Awami League by speaking up for the 1971 War of Independence, secularism and against radicalism, which are 'Indian narratives forced down upon Bangladesh'.[13]

The bloggers of Shahbagh wanted to use the online space to make Bangladesh uphold the ideals of 1971. Bhattacharya has used social media to take Bangladesh far away not just from Shahbagh and Sheikh Hasina but closer to what Bangladesh was before 1971 – the other half of Pakistan. The scary bit is that he has spanned a lot of mini-mes. One of them is journalist Elias Hossain with 1.2 million followers on his personal Facebook page. Hossain often appears in online talk shows with Bhattacharya and like him is anti-Hasina, anti-India and anti the 1971 narrative.

Hossain is also viciously anti-Hindu.

In a 13 May 2025 post, Hossain warned fellow Bangladeshi Muslims to turn off the national song 'Amar Sonar Bangla' wherever they heard it if they did not want to pray before Hindu gods and goddesses.[14] Hossain is campaigning online to change Bangladesh's national song which he feels is 'too Hindu', written as it was by Rabindranath Tagore.

Political opposition to Hasina is understandable, but why would a physician and a journalist like Bhattacharya preach such intolerance?

Memory took us back to a well-stocked library office at the bungalow of a retired major general of the Bangladesh army who now owns a cluster of private companies. The bungalow was in Dhaka's upscale Gulshan 2 neighbourhood. We had requested an interview and were granted one. It was October 2022 and Sheikh Hasina was in complete control over the political narrative of Bangladesh. Or so we thought.

Over Churchill cigars, single malts and platefuls of snacks, the major general, who requested anonymity, played Tagore songs on low volume as we spoke about the rise of online hate in his country.

'Jamaat is several steps ahead of Hasina's team in shaping narratives. It is not only the leaders and members of the Jamaat or its student wing that she should worry about. The Jamaat has brainwashed an entire generation of young women and men from well-heeled families who got the best of education and are now placed in Bangladesh and beyond as NGO officials, journalists, YouTubers and other working professionals who can shape the narrative,' the major general had warned us.

'Hasina will have nowhere to hide when these people go online to drum up a mass agitation against her,' he had said.

Is Pinaki Bhattacharya one of them?

The major general hadn't answered immediately. He had taken his time, sucked in the smoke gently, closed his eyes to savour the flavour, and then blown out the smoke in near-perfect rings.

'This Bhattacharya guy is there for the taking. What if I tell you that I have a sneaky feeling that he is on the payroll not only of the radical forces, but also a friendly neighbourhood country to keep Hasina in check?'

Which neighbourhood country, we had asked in alarm.

The major general would not answer.

But the answer came from a now viral Facebook reel of Nadia Islam, a feminist writer of Bangladeshi origin, who had a public fallout with Bhattacharya after the end of their 'casual relationship', as she says in the video. 'Pinaki was once an Indian deep state agent who India used to keep Hasina in place, as India was uncomfortable with her rising power in Bangladesh. Not just India, even China was growing uncomfortable with Hasina. Behind the students' movement that led to the fall of Hasina were foreign powers drawing strings,' she said on video.[15]

As night descended on Dhaka and we bid goodbye to the major general, he had prayed again for Bangladesh.

'I am a praying Muslim. May Allah save us from what's coming …'

But what about those who don't pray?

While online protesters of the Shahbagh movement came to be known as the 'secular bloggers', some of them were atheists.

Asad Noor, thirty-three, is one of them. 'I may not be able to write like Salman Rushdie, but I share his predicament for hurting religious sentiments,' Noor told us when we met him in Kolkata in early September 2023, eleven months before the fall of the Sheikh Hasina regime. For an avowed atheist, Noor had joked with us at South Kolkata's Melbourne Café that his friends and fans often say that he looks uncannily like renderings of Jesus Christ.

Noor had no love lost for Sheikh Hasina because it was under her regime that he had to run away from Bangladesh. Noor, who had not stopped writing online even as the Shahbagh movement faced the full force of fundamentalist attacks, had faced the wrath of the law for a battery of charges including hurting religious sentiments.

The Sheikh Hasina government's 'secular ideals' had not been able to save him from harassment. The local police raided Noor's house in Amtali village in the southern Barguna district in Bangladesh in the dead of night on 14–15 July 2020, targeting his parents when they couldn't lay their hands on him. 'On 18 July in the early morning, the police raided the house again and detained Asad's father, Tofazzal Hossain, his mother, Rabeya Begum, two younger sisters (one was a minor at that time), and two other relatives, without any formal charge or warrant. The local police kept the family members in detention for 40 hours before releasing them in the night of 19 July,' an Amnesty International report said.[16]

As a young boy, Noor was sent to a local madrasa to learn Islam. He told us that nobody in the madrasa would tell them to kill Hindus or other minorities, but they wouldn't tell them to not kill them either.

'The grooming happens ever so subtly. You are made to believe everything that Islam teaches you is the word of Allah, everything else is blasphemy. All that is needed after that is a slight nudge and a small boy could become an angry young man with a machete,' he said.

Despite what the madrasas taught him, books took Noor to a world beyond. From 2013, Noor started blogging about what he found problematic around him – the Islamization of Bangladesh's society and polity, and the growing threat to minorities in the country. He had become a part of the Shahbagh movement.

As bloggers like him began to be targeted, Noor relocated to Dhaka in 2014. Dhaka's cosmopolitanism showed him there were other ways of living, challenging the beliefs he had held close to his heart while growing up in his native village even after being part of the Shahbagh movement.

Noor was arrested on 26 December 2017 at the Hazrat Shahjalal International Airport in Dhaka just as he was about to board a flight to Kathmandu. He spent eight months in jail and saw angry demonstrations against him by fundamentalist groups after being released on bail. He was rearrested on charges of peddling drugs, which he claims were false. He was released on bail four months later, after which he decided to leave Bangladesh secretly. That was in February 2019.

Noor has been hiding in India ever since, and met us in Kolkata in September 2023. Just before the fall of Hasina in Bangladesh, Noor sought and found refuge in Canada, from where he has resumed his online writing and video blogging in full steam.

'Bangladesh is being run by fundamentalists. The common man is under attack by the Yunus administration and the student coordinators. The police are attacking journalists who are trying to report the truth around them. Look at their faces. Do they look like cops or Islamic radicals? Remember the bearded cop who opened fire on Abu Sayed [Sayed was a student protestor who died in police violence in the July Revolution]. Let my motherland be free of fundamentalists,' Noor wrote on Facebook on 16 January 2025.[17]

'So, Asad Noor is back?'

'I never left,' Noor told us from Canada. 'Now, from the safety of this Western country and the freedom of speech it provides, I will be more vocal against the rising tide of radicalism that has engulfed Bangladesh. If Rushdie can keep fighting the good fight with one eye, I still have both my eyes intact,' he laughed.

And it is not just jihad against hard religiosity. The bloggers who had shaken up Bangladesh by speaking up for a more equal and just society in 2013 have again logged in to fight the good fight from wherever they are. Asad Noor is not the only one.

During our chat, Azam Khan told us that not everybody among the so-called secular bloggers was or is against religion. 'It was a convenient allegation thrown at us since 2013. Some of us are religious-minded and do not see that as a hindrance in pressing for a secular society then or now,' he said.

In a post on 5 April 2025, Khan drew the attention of his 82,000 Facebook followers to the dire state of Bangladesh's economy and rising prices of food grains. 'Brother, be patient. You have no idea about the fight your fathers and uncles had fought against poverty. Till 2008, all that the average Bangladeshi desired was a plate of rice and lentil. Thereafter, it became rice and fish. And then, he could afford rice and meat. We will go back to having rice and lentil again! I do not talk in the air, brother. In the next six months or before, you will know how you have harmed yourself. So difficult would be your fight with poverty that you will forget the colours on the Palestinian flag, the name of the Indian states that constitute the seven sisters, and the spelling of the Islamic State.'[18]

For Sushanta Dasgupta, being Hindu means fighting for Hindu rights, on X and through his writings, but in no way does he want a Bangladesh that pushes back against any other faiths. 'My fight remains what it was during Shahbagh 2013. I have not given up. I am glad that not just the old ones, many new voices are coming up within and outside Bangladesh to uphold the spirit of Shahbagh,' he told us from London over a phone call.

Since our meeting at the Foreign Correspondents' Club in Delhi on 30 December 2024, Dasgupta had been in regular touch, sharing news items and his views on the goings-on in Bangladesh over WhatsApp.

And Akramul Haque? What does he see today when he looks around him in Dhaka? 'I see the shrinking of cultural spaces, the cancellation of band music from every nook and cranny of Bangladesh. I see playwrights being told not to write about the 1971 War of Independence, to write keeping in mind the sensibilities of the current administration. I see Sheikh Mujibur Rahman's name banned from TV channels. I see minorities being removed from government jobs, being harassed on the streets and inside their homes. I see fear rising from the streets into the air that we breathe. I see revenge being taken for Pakistan's defeat in 1971 and the birth of Bangladesh,' he told us.

'Sheikh Mujib gifted us Bangladesh. Sheikh Hasina took us back to East Pakistan,' Haque lamented.

Is there anything left to save, then?

On 28 March 2025, Dr Imran H. Sarker, spokesperson of the Ganajagaran Mancha, wrote on his Facebook page: 'As long as Bangladesh exists, Bangabandhu [Sheikh Mujib] will. Mujib is the best that Bengal had produced in a thousand years. Who is my leader? Who is your leader? Sheikh Mujib. Sheikh Muijb.'[19]

As disappointed as Haque is with Sheikh Hasina's reign, he is not giving up hope. 'Bangladesh is an idea that is worth dying for, again and again. Inshallah Bangladesh!'

15

No Woman, No Cry

Ruthba Yasmin is trying to reach for the moon. Literally so. She is preparing to become the first Bangladeshi woman to ever set foot on the lunar surface. She has just completed her training for Space Nation's Moon Pioneers Mission.

The Moon Pioneers Mission is a high-fidelity astronaut training experience designed to simulate the challenges of lunar exploration. Hosted by Space Nation, a space exploration training company in Midland, Texas, the company offers hands-on training in space survival skills, lunar rover operation and lunar base operations.

On 16 April 2025, Bangladeshi media reported that Space Nation had revealed a history-making team: a crew of six women and a man. Among them was Ruthba Yasmin, ready to carry both her flag and her vision beyond Earth's atmosphere.[1]

Two days before this news broke, on 14 April, pop icon Katy Perry had rocketed into space with an all-female crew aboard Blue Origin. The singer, along with several other members of a star-studded all-female crew, had left Earth as part of Blue Origin's latest space mission, taking off and landing successfully. Perry had put her pop-star duties on hold to explore the outer orbit for eleven minutes.

'The mission, called NS-31, also included television personality Gayle King and journalist Lauren Sánchez, who was engaged to Blue Origin (and Amazon) founder Jeff Bezos (the two are married now). The crew was rounded out by former NASA rocket scientist Aisha Bowe, bioastronautics research scientist Amanda

Nguyen and film producer Kerianne Flynn. The six women became the first all-female space crew in more than 60 years, Blue Origin has said,' *USA Today* reported on 14 April 2025.[2]

But Katy Perry is not Ruthba Yasmin's inspiration.

That honour belongs to Indian-origin astronaut Sunita Williams, a pioneer who Yasmin believes left her mark not only in spacewalk records but in the hearts of women around the world. 'She has set record-breaking milestones in spacewalks and made extraordinary contributions to ongoing research on the International Space Station,' Ruthba told the press. 'Williams also secured the record for the most cumulative spacewalking time by a female astronaut.'[3]

Growing up in Dhaka, Yasmin had never quite known what it was to be a woman in the modern world or how to defy gravity, literal and societal. It would come as a surprise to her that her experience as a young girl growing up in Dhaka was not that different from girls growing up in other cities around the world when it came to spacewalking.

'Only one in five workers in the space industry are women. And just 11 per cent of astronauts are female,' she said.

But the young Yasmin was not deterred by the skewed ratio.

'It is imperative to acknowledge the countless contributions of women in science and space exploration – such as the NASA women scientists who played a crucial role in the Apollo mission. Amplifying their achievements and fostering inclusivity will pave the way for future generations of women scientists, engineers, problem-solvers, advocates and space pioneers,' she said.

'If I can be the one to make history, it would be a defining moment not just for me, but for the world,' she told the press.

Ruthba Yasmin's story began in Dhaka but her ambition took her far from home, across oceans, to Mount Holyoke College in South Hadley, Massachusetts, where she completed her BA in physics with a minor in mathematics in 2014.

She returned to Bangladesh in 2021, and got a graduate degree in data science from United International University. In 2024, she had a master's degree in electrical and electronics engineering from the University of South Alabama.

Her research centred on space weather – specifically, geomagnetic storms that stir the Earth's magnetosphere and ionosphere. It was a topic that sparked more than academic interest.

'My deep-seated desire to fully utilize my physics degree was the driving force behind my career shift. I developed a fascination with space exploration.'

Yasmin was asked how others like her in Bangladesh could follow in her footsteps.

'Anyone interested in space can take meaningful steps towards joining the field. It starts with a genuine interest in space-related topics and applications,' she said. 'Curiosity, courage, critical thinking, problem-solving skills and your authenticity are key attributes for success in this arena. If you bring these qualities, space exploration is within your reach.'

Ruthba Yasmin's success is being cheered on by not only young Bangladeshis who want to explore space but also by anyone who feels the need to defy gravity and reach for the stars, metaphorically.

Like Asma Ul-Hasan Bristy, twenty-seven, whose journey from a mufassil village in Mymensingh division in the interiors of Bangladesh to the world of ramp modelling and acting in upscale Dhaka had its own set of challenges. Talking to us over the phone from Dhaka on a day it rained on both sides of the border, Bristy said she hoped all young women in Bangladesh would get the chance to realize their dreams.

'But then again, Ruthba Yasmin would not be the first Bangladeshi to be on the moon,' she giggled.

'What do you mean?' we asked, stupefied.

'Don't you follow the news? I thought you guys are journalists!'

Girls, Interrupted

Soon after the death of Naib Amir or the spiritual head of Jamaat-e-Islami Bangladesh, Delwar Hossain Sayeedi, on 14 August 2023, a picture of his face superimposed on the moon began circulating on various social media platforms in Bangladesh.

His followers, quite a substantial number in the country given the outpouring of grief on social media and the size of the crowd that came to his burial at his hometown in coastal Pirojpur district, made the moon picture widely popular on social media, inviting both online admiration and derision.[4]

This was not the first time that Sayeedi's face had appeared on the moon. His supporters had claimed in 2013 that Muslims from Bangladesh to Saudi Arabia saw his face pasted on the moon and it was God's sign that Sayeedi was a true devotee.

'To draw attention of the people who do not use internet, announcements were made through loudspeakers of mosques about the picture, report our correspondents from Chittagong, Rajshahi and Bogra. Besides, many people called the *Daily Star* staff members from different districts to verify if such a moon was really sighted,' Bangladeshi newspaper the *Daily Star* had reported on 4 March 2013.[5]

Sayeedi was the vice president of the Jamaat-e-Islami. He was Naib Amir or the spiritual head of the Islamist party since 2009. His Islamic teachings had attracted a substantial number of followers in his lifetime. To the government of the day (Sheikh Hasina was the prime minister) and the courts of the country, though, Sayeedi was a convicted war criminal who needed to be locked up for life, and in 2013, he was given the death penalty on two counts of crimes against humanity by the war crimes tribunal. He was accused of murder, arson and rape.[6]

'Known as "Deilya Razakar" in 1971, Sayeedi was found guilty of committing crimes against humanity during the 1971 Liberation War ... These include the murder of Bisabali and arson in a Hindu neighbourhood, abduction and rape of three sisters of Gauranga Saha, who was a prosecution witness and identified Sayeedi as the man who had handed over his sisters to the Pakistani army to be taken away as sex slaves. They were returned after three days,' Bangladeshi media reported on 31 March 2015, when the Supreme Court of Bangladesh released the full verdict.[7]

A year later, the death sentence was commuted to life imprisonment.

But before the war crimes tribunal was set up in 2019 to investigate and prosecute suspects for the genocide committed in 1971 by the Pakistani army and their local collaborators, Sayeedi was an elected member of parliament from 1996 to 2008.

'Sayeedi's views on women and minorities were despicable to say the least. He was a convicted war criminal who sided with forces that threaten to disrupt Bangladesh till date. No death should be celebrated, but Sayeedi's hopefully ends a dark chapter in Bangladesh's history,' a Dhaka journalist had told us when the story of his face on the moon did the rounds in August 2023.

So, okay, Delwar Hossain Sayeedi was far from being an honourable man, but his supporters believed that they saw his face on the moon. But what did that have to do with the young Ruthba Yasmin wanting to go to the moon? Why should she or women like Asma Ul-Hasan Bristy be overly worried about the fundamentalist fringe in Bangladesh?

'Because the likes of the late Sayeedi are not the fringe anymore. After the fall of the Sheikh Hasina government, that fringe is now the mainstream and whatever course the politics of this country is taking, women in Bangladesh are having to pay a rather high price,' Bristy told us.

Over the phone, Bristy narrated to us an event that shocked Dhaka during Ramzan in late March 2025. Two girls were smoking at a chai stall when a flash mob gathered around them and started harassing them in full public view in the middle of the day. 'Bangladeshi society is conservative, but few spaces in Dhaka were like small islands of cosmopolitanism where you dared to breathe free as a woman, light a cigarette or hold a lover's hand in the open,' Bristy said. 'But those spaces are now gone. Flash mobs can get to you anywhere at any time for smoking a cigarette, not wearing a hijab, sporting a bindi or a short dress or anything they feel a woman should not do,' she says. 'I don't smoke on Dhaka streets anymore.'

The restrictions Bristy mentioned are not restricted to smoking or wearing short dresses in public – a women's football match was cancelled in January 2025 after protests by students from a traditional religious school damaged the venue. It was the second such incident in as many days.

This happened in the northwestern city of Joypurhat which was due to host a friendly football match between its district women's team and another from nearby Rangpur. A mob of Islamists from the area marched towards the venue. 'There were hundreds of them. The situation worsened, and we had to cancel today's event,' tournament organizer Samiul Hasan Emon told the press later.

The incident caught the attention of global media.

Abu Bakkar Siddique, the headmaster of a local religious school, said he had joined the demonstration with his students and teachers and pupils from several other religious schools.

'Girls' football is un-Islamic,' Al Jazeera quoted him as saying. 'It is our religious duty to stop anything that goes against our beliefs.'[8]

'If schoolgirls cannot even play football in peace, you really think a talented young girl of Bangladeshi origin who had the opportunity to train for moon travel in Midland, Texas, would be able to change the lot of Bangladeshi girls?' Bristy asked us.

We had no answer. She said she had stopped worrying and instead was trying to live her life the best she could. 'It has been raining incessantly since morning. I love rain. My last name is also Bristy, meaning rain in Bengali. Is the weather similar in Kolkata?' she asked.

'It is.'

'I cooked rice, dal, brinjal fry and chicken curry for my lover today. He has come to visit me from India, you know. I destress by cooking and look forward to his visits.'

'Is it easy dating an Indian at a time like this?'

'It isn't. And he is Hindu. But like I said, I have stopped worrying too much these days.'

Bristy told us she was comfortable in her little Dhaka bubble where artistes and free thinkers would lead lives that were unthinkable in the rest of Bangladesh. 'That would be how much of Dhaka's population? Less than 1 per cent. But it used to be the swish set. We would be this mad group that would live free, talk free, not care about the dogmas of society or religion. Now even that bubble is not safe anymore.'

It was not always like this for her. Growing up in her dusty village, Bristy was made to don the burqa, pray five times a day and be ready to marry whoever her family chose for her. 'I am dark-skinned, and though I always loved the way I looked, I was made to feel inferior,' she says. Higher education took her to Dhaka, where theatre caught her fancy and Bristy's life changed. 'I grew confident of myself and my body enough to get myself clicked in attires that would raise eyebrows. But I put them out on my social media feed and even as hundreds of filthy comments and rape and deaths threats came as comments, I landed a modelling assignment simply on the basis of those viral pics. I did not have to look back after that,' she said.

One of those pics had Bristy and another female model embracing each other; in another Bristy is posing as Krishna. 'Nudity for me is art, nudity is my way of showing the world that dark skin is beautiful and young girls should throw away those fairness creams and embrace themselves. As far as posing as Krishna is concerned, the idea of the photoshoot was to show that Krishna is Radha and Radha is Krishna,' she said.

Bristy had moved away from organized religion. She told us she was not a believer anymore. 'The burqa is also gone for good. Though I believe not wearing the burqa or the hijab is not the only sign of freedom from patriarchy. You can don the hijab and be modern. But it should be a choice. In Bangladesh, for almost all women who wear it, it isn't a choice.'

In the time since Hasina's fall, Bristy has graduated from modelling to acting and her OTT series *Bohemian Ghora* will release in June 2025. It is the story of a truck driver with seven secret wives across Bangladesh who thinks an eighth wife will bring him luck. Instead, chaos begins.

'It is fun to act, but I want to move out of Bangladesh now. Who knows, maybe my ramp experience and dark skin tone will take me to Milan Fashion Week. The West appreciates what we cannot. But my heart will bleed for Bangladesh always and for what's happening to women around me who are not as lucky as I have been so far. Or Ruthba Yasmin has been,' Bristy rued.

Bristy said models and actresses were always looked down upon in Bangladeshi society, unlike male actors. 'Truth be told, people think of us as "educated prostitutes", but today in Bangladesh even the ordinary woman is not safe on the streets or inside her home,' she told us.

Quoting data from the Bangladesh Mahila Parishad from January to June 2025, the *Daily Star* wrote that 481 cases of rape against women and girls were reported in Bangladesh, with 345 of the victims being children. This figure is nearly as high as the total number of rape cases reported throughout all of last year, which was 516, the organization said.[9]

The Solution?

The number of rape cases in Bangladesh in the period between August 2024 and July 2025 took an almost epidemic turn. Between January and April 2025, 87.56 per cent of reported rape victims with known ages were children aged zero to eighteen – nearly nine out of ten victims – according to the data from Ain o Salish Kendra, a nonprofit based in Dhaka.[10]

Of 342 rape cases reported during this period, age data was available for 201 victims. Of them, 176 were minors: forty were aged between zero and six; sixty-five between seven and twelve; and seventy-one between thirteen and eighteen. According to women's rights organization Bangladesh Mahila Parishad's monthly media-monitoring report, 389 rape incidents were reported in the first quarter of 2025, with 72 per cent of the victims aged between zero and eighteen.

Similarly, of ninety-one gang rape cases, fifty-one – or 56 per cent – involved minors.

The report also noted a sharp spike in rape incidents in March 2025, which saw 163 reported cases, including 125 (nearly 77 per cent) involving minors. In April, 111 cases were reported – eighty-three of them (72 per cent) involved children.[11]

Clinical psychologist Ismat Jahan, head of the National Trauma Counselling Centre, confirmed the growing trend to the *Daily Star*. 'Many of our regional centres are seeing more cases [of child rape].'

She highlighted the long-term psychological impact on children: depression, post-traumatic stress disorder (PTSD) and suicidal tendencies.

'Children re-experience trauma repeatedly during investigations and court proceedings. Many lose the ability to trust and later struggle with relationships. Some engage in self-destructive behaviour or risky activities in adolescence.'[12]

In March 2025, leading rights organizations including Ain o Salish Kendra, Breaking the Silence, Manusher Jonno Foundation, Plan International Bangladesh and Save the Children jointly condemned the rise in child sexual abuse in Bangladesh.[13]

And then there is the age factor. In Bangladesh, one in every two girls gets married before reaching the age of eighteen. 'This particular figure has been cited in a recently released UN report. Specifically, 51 per cent of Bangladeshi girls are married before they turn 18. Any girl under 18 is a minor and a child. Therefore, this figure, in reality, refers to child marriage. Globally, Bangladesh ranks eighth in terms of child marriages and tops the list among South Asian countries. In this regard, other South Asian countries are doing much better – with child marriage rates at 10 percent in Sri Lanka, 18 percent in Pakistan, and 23 percent in India,' a report said.[14]

'Child marriage is closely linked to high adolescent pregnancy rates. Girls under 18 have little control over their reproductive health and limited autonomy in making reproductive decisions. In Bangladesh, 53 percent of adolescent girls lack control over their reproductive health. One in every four married girls under 18 becomes pregnant. Last year, 28 percent of adolescent girls between the ages of 15 and 19 experienced physical or sexual violence by their partners.'

Attacks on female models and actresses by radicalized flash mobs, moral policing on the streets targeting women, rise of incidents of rape reaching epidemic proportions, scary stats on child marriage.

What gives?

On 19 April 2025, the Women's Affairs Reform Commission, established by the Muhammad Yunus–led interim government in November 2024 to prepare a report on the possible ways to give women equal rights, restore their dignity and respect in society and reduce discrimination, submitted a report containing these and other detailed recommendations to the chief advisor at the state guest house Jamuna in Dhaka.

After the submission of a copy of the report to Yunus, the head of the Women's Affairs Reform Commission, Shireen Parveen Haque, and other members presented the report in detail at a press conference held at the Foreign Service Academy on 20 April in Dhaka.

'Let the actionable recommendations be implemented through us without delay. Let's set a global example. Women around the world are watching. They will evaluate and draw inspiration from this,' Yunus said on receiving the report.

'The report, titled "Identifying Steps to Eliminate Discrimination against Women in All Spheres and at All Levels and Achieve Equality between Women and Men", included recommendations such as establishing a permanent women's affairs commission, preventing and redressing violence and harassment against women, recognising forced sexual intercourse within marriage as rape in criminal law, reforming existing rape laws to ensure justice for male and female victims, banning the use of misogynistic language and imagery in public communication, and launching social awareness programmes to promote respectful, dignified, and sensitive attitudes toward women,' *Prothom Alo* reported.[15]

'Other key recommendations include abolishing the death penalty, decriminalising sex work, amending labour laws to ensure the dignity and rights of sex workers, withdrawing reservations on two articles of the Convention on the Elimination of All Forms of Discrimination against Women, and ratifying Articles 189 and 190 of the International Labour Organization.

'The report also includes 433 specific recommendations, among them providing six-month paid maternity leave in all institutions, including government agencies, offering paid paternity leave, and establishing childcare centres in workplaces.'

The commission reportedly held a total of forty-three meetings, including thirty-nine consultation sessions with women's rights organizations, development bodies, labour groups, ethnic minority communities in both hills and plains and other marginalized communities. Additionally, nine meetings were held with other reform commissions. These consultations took place across Bangladesh, in Chattogram, Rangamati, Khulna, Sreemangal, Rangpur and Mymensingh.

It is not as if the ten-member Women's Affairs Reform Commission had expected these recommendations to face no pushback once out in the public domain. Commission chief Shireen Parveen Haque told the Bangladeshi press that these recommendations might ignite some controversies, which the commission would welcome, as people should discuss these issues. She added that the commission had made the recommendations after considering the constitution, laws, policies, institutions and programmes, and fifteen specific issues.[16]

Haque also said that some of the recommendations could be implemented during the tenure of the interim government, some would remain for the next government to execute, while some were quite simply the expectations and dreams of the women's rights movement in Bangladesh.

Women's rights activists warned of deepening hostility against women on the ground and urged there was no time to lose.

Local media reports quoted Fauzia Moslem, president of the Bangladesh Mahila Parishad, as saying that misogyny has become public since the mass uprising that led to the fall of the Sheikh Hasina government.

'It was inconspicuous before. Violence was present before, with no political rights for women, no social rights. But a moral policing has been underway since the uprising due to misogyny. You can't wear such dresses, can't walk like this, can't put on tip (bindi), you'll be beaten to death if you play football, houses would be demolished,' she said, echoing the sentiment of Asma Ul-Hasan Bristy.[17]

The Pushback

The 433 recommendations ignited heated debates. Popular Bangladeshi YouTuber Pinaki Bhattacharya called Haque and other members of the commission Islamophobes and said Yunus himself had an inherent bias towards NGOs.

'Have you ever seen Yunus so excited about recommendations from any other commission apart from the women's commission? He has said the recommendations should be printed and distributed as pamphlets. If that happens and people get to read it, government officials will be thrashed on the street,' he said.[18]

Jamaat-e-Islami Bangladesh Ameer Shafiqur Rahman said some of the recommendations made by the women's commission would destroy the values of all religions and that the people of Bangladesh would reject the recommendations. 'Some of the recommendations are clear violations of the Quran and Hadith,' Rahman added.

While such pushback was expected, what drew global attention were the events of 3 May 2025, when thousands of supporters of the Hefazat-e-Islam, a powerful radical group in Bangladesh, rallied in Dhaka to demand the scrapping of the commission, claiming it conflicted with Islamic principles. 'More than 20,000 followers of the group rallied near Dhaka University, some carrying banners and placards reading "Say no to Western laws on our women, rise up Bangladesh",' an Associated Press report said.[19]

Threatening mass agitation, members of Islamist parties like the Jatiya Olama Mashayekh Aemma Parishad warned that the Yunus-led government would face severe consequences and would not get 'even five minutes to escape' if it proceeded with the reforms.

The warning 'won't get even five minutes' was a reference to the forty-five minutes Sheikh Hasina got on 5 August 2024, to leave her country as a mob of hundreds of thousands marched towards her residence, baying for blood.[20]

While the fundamentalist forces reacted the way they were expected to on women-centric reforms that they deemed were anti-Sharia and pro-West, the women of Bangladesh were divided on them.

Feminism for Whom?

In an article titled 'Whose Feminism Is It Anyway? Lessons from the Gender Reform Uproar' published on 5 June 2025, the *Daily Star* argued that if any reform was perceived as a foreign imposition, one must rethink not just the message, but the method as well.

'As women across Bangladesh take to the streets both for and against feminist reform, the liberal feminist movement faces a reckoning. The question is not why some women resist emancipation, but what kind of feminist vision has failed to earn their trust. The sight of hijab-wearing women protesting reforms unsettled many liberal commentators. But dismissing them as pawns of particular groups is unwise as well. Many of them belong to the women wings of Islamist parties, madrasa networks, and community groups. Their presence is vocal, strategic, and moral.

'Their feminist counterparts have failed to make room for them. In Bangladesh, liberal feminism has long been perceived as centring on the secular, urban woman as its ideal. This has created a narrow and exclusionary vision of liberation,' the article said.[21]

'Engaging Muslim women doesn't mean compromising principles; it means recognising their autonomy and understanding that their critiques often arise from historic exclusion. But inclusion must be critical: in Bangladesh, male-dominated interpretations of Islam continue to shape public perceptions of gender and law. The issue isn't the presence of religious women, but the uncritical acceptance of patriarchal authority. We must ask: who benefits when liberatory readings are sidelined?' Tara Asgar and Nur A. Mahjabin Khan wrote in the article.

We dialled Dr Rezwana Karim Snigdha in Dhaka. The associate professor at the department of anthropology, Jahangirnagar University, is an authority on gender justice

We ask her what she makes of these 433 recommendations that have divided Bangladesh and forced both radical mobs and women out on streets. 'There is certainly scope for criticism within the 433 recommendations, but it's important to acknowledge that there are some positive elements as well,' Snigdha said. 'For instance, the introduction of Hindu marriage registration is a step forward, especially considering that Hindus in Bangladesh still do not have formal divorce laws. This is an area where legal reform is much needed.'

Snigdha felt that when it came to recommendations related to sex workers, Bangladesh was not ready yet to fully accept such proposals. 'Personally, I am not against recognizing sex workers' rights, but I think the current recommendations could have addressed the issue of rape victims more effectively. Regarding the 377 Act and marital rape, it's crucial to remember that rape is fundamentally about power, not just about sex or consent. The legal framework must reflect this reality,' she said.

On property rights, Snigdha sees positive potential in the recommendations. 'The Awami League previously claimed they would implement equal property rights for men and women but ultimately refrained from doing so. If, through these 433 recommendations, equal property rights can finally be implemented, that would be a significant and welcome achievement,' she says.

Outside these academic debates, the video of a women's rally on Dhaka's streets has become insanely viral on social media and created a fanbase and also drawn its own share of criticism. The video shows young women walking the streets of Dhaka with placards demanding women's rights. And their slogan? In unison, they shout:

'*Cheye chilam hissa, hoye gelam beshya* [All we asked for was our share and you turned us into prostitutes].'[22]

Wonder what Asma Ul-Hasan Bristy would say to that.

Afterword

Soon after the fall of the Sheikh Hasina government on 5 August, 2024, I was called by the minister counsellor at the High Commission of a Western nation to her official residence in central Delhi. She wanted to have an 'informal but private chat' on the developments in Dhaka.

Apart from the minister counsellor, the head (Foreign and Security Policy) and the second secretary of the High Commission, I found myself in a room with the Diplomatic Affairs Editor of an Indian national daily and a professor of international affairs of a private university in Sonipat who claimed to have a deep knowledge of Bangladesh.

The two other Indians in the room cheered what has been termed as the July Revolution and laid out the many flaws of 'Dictator Hasina' and how the events were her just comeuppance. I pointed out that with the Awami League out of the political equation, my one fear for Bangladesh was the Jamaat becoming the new de facto ruler no matter who came to power next.

I was not wrong.

A year and a month later, I was surprised to find that the former undersecretary-general of the UN and the current Congress party MP from Thiruvananthapuram, Shashi Tharoor, shared my fear.

On 11 September 2025, sharing a news story on X that ran with the headline, 'Jamaat-e-Islami wins Dhaka varsity polls', Tharoor posted that the news may have registered as 'barely a blip' in India, but it was a 'worrying portent of things to come'.[1]

Afterword

When was the last time the results of a university's student union election prompted a prominent politician from another country to comment on it on a social media platform?

I cannot think of any. But these are extraordinary times, when the young and the restless in colleges and universities are taking extraordinary measures to alter the course of political movements and push back against the hollowing out of democratic institutions. No politician can now afford to ignore what college and university students think.

Earlier in September 2025, in Nepal, angry youths had taken to the streets following a social media ban to express their frustration over systemic corruption, lack of jobs and economic disparity. People got killed, buildings were set on fire, the prime minister fled in a helicopter and a new one was put in charge through what is now being touted as a 'Gen Z revolution'.

Exactly a year and a month before, on 5 August, 2024, in a similar students' protest in Bangladesh – the July Revolution – then prime minister Sheikh Hasina had to flee her country in a C-130J Hercules jet and take refuge in India. It was the students of Bangladesh who came on the streets to effect a momentous political change in the country.

And this is why the results of a students' union election for Bangladesh's most famous public university and Shashi Tharoor's tweet on it should be taken seriously.

Tharoor also said in his X post that there was an increasing sense of frustration in Bangladesh with the major parties, the now banned Awami League and the BNP and those who wish 'a plague on both your houses', are increasingly turning to the Jamaat-e-Islami, 'not because these voters are zealots or Islamist fundamentalists, but because the JeI are not tainted by the corruption and misgovernance associated, rightly or wrongly, with the two mainstream parties'.

'How will this play out in the Feb 2026 general elections? Will New Delhi be dealing with a Jamaat majority next door?' he wrote.

Tharoor had reason to be concerned. This was, after all, the first

Afterword

time in Bangladesh's history that the Jamaat's student wing, the Islami Chhatra Shibir, has won an election in Dhaka University.

The last time the Jamaat was associated with the Dhaka University was on 25 March 1971. On that day, the Pakistan Army raided the Dhaka University campus and carried out a planned massacre of 200 students, ten teachers and twelve employees. Armed with heavy weapons such as tanks, automatic rifles, rocket launchers, heavy mortar, light machine gun, Pakistani soldiers encircled Dhaka University from the east (Unit 41), from the south (Unit 88) and from the north (Unit 26).

In the wake of the Pakistan Army action, Bangabandhu Sheikh Mujibur Rahman declared Bangladesh's independence through EPR wireless at 12.30 a.m. on 26 March 1971.[2]

And who were the local collaborators of the Pakistani Army?

Pakistani Canadian oral historian and author Anam Zakaria wrote in a 2019 article: 'In March 1971, using the violence as an excuse, the Pakistan Army intervened to stem the growth of nationalist sentiments in the east. It recruited local pro-Pakistan Bengalis and non-Bengalis, including members of the Islamic organisation Jamaat-e-Islami for its operations against Bengali factions.'[3]

That was 1971. This is 2025. Times change, and political parties often change clothes to swim in shifting currents. Not the Jamaat-e-Islami Bangladesh, which has been steadfast in its vision for Bangladesh.

Professor Mujibur Rahman, central Nayeb-e-Ameer of Bangladesh Jamaat-e-Islami, has publicly declared his ambition to see the country governed by Shariah laws. 'We will implement the laws of the Quran in this country, even if it costs our lives. Once the election schedule is announced, this will become a reality, Insha'Allah.'[4]

At the time of writing this, election schedules have been announced. On 5 August 2025, on the anniversary of Hasina's overthrow, Yunus announced that Bangladesh will hold its next round of elections in first half of February 2026.[5] On an official visit to New York for the eightieth session of the UN General Assembly, he even conveyed to the US that Bangladesh is fully prepared for the next election, and that the interim government is making 'comprehensive preparations' to ensure a free, fair and peaceful poll.[6]

The hitch? The BNP wants its arch rival Awami League to participate in the February polls. The party's secretary general Mirza Fakhrul Islam Alamgir told Indian newspaper *Ei Samay* in an interview: 'Let there be a fair and free election. For saying this, many people are insulting me – calling me an agent of India, a stooge of the Awami League. But why should we repeat Sheikh Hasina's misdeeds?'[7]

The problem is that the Yunus administration has banned all activities of the Awami League,[8] and Bangladesh's International Crimes Tribunal has formally charged Hasina and others with crimes against humanity, including mass murder, related to the violent crackdown on student protests during the 2024 July Revolution.[9] Will the Yunus administration and the Bangladesh Election Commission allow the Awami League to participate in polls?

And if they do, which seems highly unlikely, who will take over the reins of the beleaguered Awami League? On 8 September 2025, BBC Bangla put out a report stating that Hasina has been mulling a family-centric leadership model for her party, like the Congress party in India, which has both Rahul and Priyanka Gandhi in Parliament and Sonia Gandhi in Rajya Sabha.[10]

Citing political sources close to Hasina, the report said that Hasina's son Sajeeb Wazed Joy, fifty-four, who is currently in the US, has become the Awami League's de facto spokesperson. He speaks on Bangladesh politics and the party's take on various issues in the international media.

Hasina's daughter Saima Wazed Putul, fifty-two, the former Southeast Asian regional director of the World Health Organization, has been reportedly handling major internal responsibilities of the party, drafting speeches, planning political programmes and representing her mother in various diplomatic meetings. Hasina's nephew (her sister Sheikh Rehana's son) Radwan Mujib Siddiq Bobby is also expected to play a supporting role to her children.

Bangladeshi journalist and photographer Saqlain Rizve, who covered the July Revolution and whose photograph is on the cover of this book, told me that the Rahul–Priyanka model cannot be applied to Joy and Putul, as a mass uprising never toppled any Congress government in India. 'Hasina was ousted for corruption, enforced disappearances and mass killings. Her children cannot escape that legacy. How will people accept them?' Rizve said.

The BNP has its own problems. The party had been waiting for its acting chairperson and the eldest son of former Bangladesh president Ziaur Rahman and the first female prime minister of Bangladesh Khaleda Zia, Tarique Rahman, to return home ever since the fall of Hasina.

Rahman had been in exile in London since the Awami League's landslide victory in the 2008 general election, citing concerns for his safety and claiming that he was being persecuted by the authorities.

A top BNP leader had told me on condition of anonymity that Rahman feared for his safety in Bangladesh, even though there had been a power shift. But on 6 October 2025, Rahman told the *Financial Times* that he would return to his country to contest the upcoming elections and predicted that his party would win a sweeping majority.[11]

The Jamaat-e-Islami, meanwhile, has reportedly said that elections won't happen without the proportional representation system coming into force, while the NCP has demanded that the existing constitution be scrapped and a Constituent Assembly election be held first.[12]

'One issue after another is being stirred up to obfuscate the issue of national election. Certain parties are trying to stall the election by coming up with all sorts of conditions. Unnecessary and irrelevant debates are being initiated,' Bangladeshi political analyst Maruf Mallick wrote in *Prothom Alo*.[13]

'It is unlikely elections will take place in February 2026,' Syed Badrul Ahsan, one of the most respected voices in Bangladeshi media, former executive editor of the *Daily Star* as well as the former press minister at the High Commission of Bangladesh, London, told me over the phone. Ahsan said that Jamaat would want Yunus at the helm for some more time as it 'spreads its tentacles in the country, Islamizing it, taking it closer to Pakistan and away from India.'

Yunus's 'warm and cordial' meeting with Pakistan's prime minister Shehbaz Sharif on the sidelines of the eightieth session of the UN General Assembly on 27 September 2025 aside,[14] the continuing attacks on the Hindu minority in Bangladesh has riled the Indian government and a section of the Indian population.

Author of bestselling books on Indic knowledge systems Ami Ganatra told me the destruction of Hindu temples in Bangladesh is not just an attack on structures – it's a 'deliberate erasure of civilizational memory. Temples are living links to a rich heritage that once flourished across the region. The desecration of murtis, sacred sites and age-old rituals is a form of cultural genocide – an assault on the identity, dignity and history of a people – an attempt to uproot generations from their spiritual and civilizational roots of the past while also undermining the cultural fabric of the present.'

For Ganatra, what we are seeing in Bangladesh today is more than just hostility towards the already dwindling minorities or their own shared history – it also reflects deep-seated animosity toward India, their closest neighbour and well-wisher.

Yunus has admitted that Bangladesh has problems with India. Speaking on the sidelines of the UN General Assembly, he said Dhaka's ties with New Delhi are strained because India didn't like the students' protests that led to Hasina's ouster, and that 'fake reports' in Indian media have worsened the tensions. He also accused India of providing shelter to Hasina, saying: 'India is hosting Hasina, who has created problems.'[15]

But it is Dr Syed Abdullah Mohammad Taher, Jamaat-e-Islami leader, who travelled to New York with Yunus to the UN General Assembly, whose words have rankled India more. Accorded a grand public reception by the Coalition of Bangladeshi American Association, Taher said: 'At least five million of our young men will wage an independence war against India. Many warn if Jamaat comes to power, India might strike. I pray they do – if India enters, it will wipe away the stigma forced on us in 1971, and finally give us a chance to prove ourselves true freedom fighters.'[16]

Apart from strained ties with India, how has Bangladesh been in the past one year? As we have written in the book, a deteriorating law and order situation, rise of radicalism, corruption charges against the new students' party, the NCP, and curbing of women's rights have shown that the more things change, the more they perhaps remain the same in South Asia. Bangladesh now faces 'its worst financial crisis in decades with all three pillars – the banking sector, non-bank financial institutions, and the stock market – mired in instability'.[17]

One is tempted to ask, what exactly did the July Revolution achieve? It is not for two Indian journalists and one Bangladeshi journalist in exile to diss a revolution that has spilled so much blood. It is the primary duty of the Bangladesh press to show the mirror to Bangladesh.

But where is the Bangladesh press? Mahfuz Anam, editor and publisher of the *Daily Star* and arguably Bangladesh's best-known journalist, writes: 'Perhaps today, compared to anywhere else in the world, we have the highest number of media professionals accused of murder and attempted murder. With a change in power, how did so many journalists become murderers overnight? As a lifelong journalist, I find it a matter of great shame and humiliation.'[18]

Yet, let us choose to believe that the July Revolution had no ulterior motive but to bring democracy back to Bangladesh by replacing an authoritarian leader who had turned Bangladesh into a party state. Until this happens, the revolution will remain unfinished.

Notes

1. Hasina's Day Out

1. *Prothom Alo*, 'PM Hasina Sets Example by Making Ganabhaban a Farmhouse: Secretary', 20 February 2023. https://en.prothomalo.com/bangladesh/wcojjygwgq.
2. *New Age*, '350 Injured as BCL Attacks Quota Protesters', 15 July 2024, https://www.newagebd.net/post/politics/240302/.
3. *Business Post*, 'Clash Involving BCL, around 250 Quota Protesters Injured', 15 July 2024, https://businesspostbd.com/national/quota-protestors-bcl-activists-clash-at-du.
4. *Prothom Alo*, '297 Injured at Dhaka Medical College Hospital Take Treatment', 15 July 2024, https://www.prothomalo.com/bangladesh/lehguy1j3s.
5. www.shohid.info, a website listing the martyrs of the July movement.
6. *Prothom Alo*, 'Govt Bans Chhatra League', 23 October 2024, https://en.prothomalo.com/bangladesh/politics/7gocxbtqu6.
7. *New Age*, 'HC Order to Restore FF Quota Sparks Student Protests', 6 June 2024, https://www.newagebd.net/post/country/237094/students-protest-at-hc-order-on-restoration-of-quota-system-.
8. Ruma Paul, 'Bangladesh Protesters Call for PM Hasina's Resignation as Death Toll Rises to 91', *Reuters*, 5 August 2024, https://www.reuters.com/world/asia-pacific/seven-killed-bangladesh-clashes-protesters-push-pm-resign-2024-08-04/.
9. *Prothom Alo*, '14 Policemen Killed, Over 300 Injured in Attack on 27 Police Stations', 4 August 2024, https://www.prothomalo.com/bangladesh/1ua7ybncib.
10. *Prothom Alo*, 'Mobile Internet Shutdown', 4 August 2024, https://www.prothomalo.com/bangladesh/5h6t8ay1rl.
11. *Prothom Alo*, 'Facebook, Messenger, WhatsApp and Instagram to Be Shut Down', 4 August 2024, https://www.prothomalo.com/bangladesh/glx4sc1frw.
12. *Dhaka Tribune*, 'Student Movement's Long March to Dhaka Moved Up to Monday', 4 August 2024, https://www.dhakatribune.com/bangladesh/dhaka/353677/protesters-reschedule-long-march-to-dhaka-for.
13. Ruma Paul, 'Bangladesh Protesters Call for PM Hasina's Resignation as

Death Toll Rises to 91', *Reuters*, 5 August 2024, https://www.reuters.com/world/asia-pacific/seven-killed-bangladesh-clashes-protesters-push-pm-resign-2024-08-04/.
14. *New Indian Express*, 'Bangladesh Back on Boil; Army Says No Firing', 4 August 2024, https://www.newindianexpress.com/world/2024/Aug/03/bangladesh-back-on-boil-army-says-no-firing.
15. *Prothom Alo*, 'Take the Army Back to the Barracks: Retired Army Officers', 4 August 2024, https://en.prothomalo.com/bangladesh/b744za5u9h.
16. *Prothom Alo*, 'Nafiz Was Still Alive on the Way to Hospital after Being Shot', 13 August 2024, https://en.prothomalo.com/bangladesh/deq62xtoct.
17. *Business Standard*, 'Sarees, Fish & Dior Suitcase: The Looting Spree at Sheikh Hasina's House', 6 August 2024, https://www.business-standard.com/world-news/sarees-fish-dior-suitcase-the-looting-spree-at-sheikh-hasina-s-house-124080600633_1.html.
18. *Business Standard*, 'How SSF Got Only 5 Mins to Leave Ganabhaban', 1 September 2025, https://www.tbsnews.net/bangladesh/how-ssf-got-only-5-mins-flee-ganabhaban-leaving-arms-ammo-930511.

2. The General Who Betrayed Hasina

1. *BD News 24*, 'Former Home Minister Asaduzzaman Spotted in "Kolkata Park", Police Unaware of Exit', 2 October 2024, https://bdnews24.com/bangladesh/eea95a05e5bf.
2. Ibid.
3. Observer Research Foundation, 'St. Martin's Island: A New Flash Point in the Bay of Bengal?', 21 August 2024, https://www.orfonline.org/expert-speak/st-martin-s-island-a-new-flashpoint-in-the-bay-of-bengal.
4. Ibid.
5. *hellaney*, 'The New Great Game', 16 August 2024, https://chellaney.net/2024/08/16/the-new-great-game.
6. *News18*, 'Yunus Backed By Terrorists, Rohingya Corridor Ploy to Sell St Martin's Island: Sheikh Hasina', 11 June 2025, https://www.news18.com/world/yunus-backed-by-terrorists-rohingya-corridor-ploy-to-sell-st-martins-island-sheikh-hasina-ws-kl-9380771.html#google_vignette.
7. *Prothom Alo*, '44 Policemen Killed during Student-Mass Uprising: Police HQ', 18 August 2024, https://en.prothomalo.com/bangladesh/government/r5qrxy04c5.
8. *Samakal*, '"Regime Change" with U.S. Support', 2 July 2025, https://samakal.com/opinion/article/303351.
9. Jeffery D. Sachs, 'Accusations of US Regime-Change Operations in Pakistan and Bangladesh Warrant UN Attention', *Common Dreams*, https://www.commondreams.org/opinion/regime-change-pakistan-bangladesh.

3. Bangladesh Turns Back the Clock

1. *Dhaka Tribune*, 'Tofail Ahmed in Bangladesh's History', 26 October 2023, https://www.dhakatribune.com/opinion/longform/329067/tofail-ahmed-in-bangladesh%E2%80%99s-history.
2. 'February 1969: Revisiting the Agartala Conspiracy Case', *Forum*, Vol. 2, Issue 2, February 2007, https://archive.thedailystar.net/forum/2007/february/feb69.htm.
3. *Daily Star*, 'Agartala Case and February 22, 1969', 22 February 2012, https://www.thedailystar.net/news-detail-223317.
4. *BD News 24*, 'The History of the 1969 Mass Upsurge', 25 January 2025, https://bdnews24.com/opinion/7ea9e685e1ed.
5. United News of Bangladesh, 'Bangabandhu Memorial Museum: Witness to History and Tragedy', 11 August 2022, https://client.unb.com.bd/news/Society/Bangabandhu-Memorial-Museum:-Witness-to-History-and-Tragedy/2690.
6. *BD News 24*, 'Dhanmondi 32, Bangabandhu and Our History', 15 August 2022, https://bdnews24.com/opinion/wvzlvqf9oj.
7. *Daily Star*, 'Bangabandhu Museum on Dhanmondi 32: Torching an Integral Part of Country's History', 7 August 2024, https://www.thedailystar.net/news/bangladesh/news/bangabandhu-museum-dhanmondi-32-torching-integral-part-countrys-history-3671166.
8. *Dhaka Tribune*, 'Bangabandhu's Dhanmondi 32 Residence Demolished', 5 February 2025, https://www.dhakatribune.com/bangladesh/372908/widespread-vandalism-at-bangabandhu-s-residence-at.
9. *Eurasia Review*, 'Bangladeshis Demolish Museum Honoring Ousted PM Hasina's Father – Angry She Spoke Online', 6 February 2025, https://www.eurasiareview.com/06022025-bangladeshis-demolish-museum-honoring-ousted-pm-hasinas-father-angry-she-spoke-online/.
10. Al Jazeera, 'Muhammad Yunus Takes Oath as Head of Bangladesh's Interim Government', 8 August 2024, https://www.aljazeera.com/news/2024/8/8/muhammad-yunus-takes-oath-as-head-of-bangladeshs-interim-government.
11. *ABP Live*, 'Bangladesh to Remove Chapters on Founding Father Mujibur Rahman from Textbooks: Report', 31 December 2024, https://news.abplive.com/news/world/bangladesh-to-remove-chapters-on-founding-father-sheikh-mujibur-rahman-from-textbooks-1741007.
12. *Daily Star*, 'New Textbooks Will Say Ziaur Rahman Declared Independence', 1 January 2025, https://www.thedailystar.net/news/bangladesh/education/news/new-textbooks-will-say-ziaur-rahman-declared-independence-3789096.
13. *Hindustan Times*, 'Bangladesh to Remove Sheikh Mujibur Rahman's

Image from Currency Notes: Report', 5 December 2024, https://www.hindustantimes.com/world-news/bangladesh-to-remove-sheikh-sheikh-mujibur-rahmans-image-from-currency-notes-101733412079824.html.
14. *Economic Times*, 'Bangladesh Faces Taka 15,000 Crore Crisis as Central Bank Halts Circulation of Notes With Bangabandhu's Image', 29 April 2025, https://economictimes.indiatimes.com/news/international/world-news/bangladesh-faces-taka-15000-crore-crisis-as-central-bank-halts-circulation-of-notes-with-bangabandhus-image/articleshow/120723942.cms.
15. *The Hindu*, 'Bangladesh Drops the Title of "Father of the Nation" for Sheikh Mujibur Rahman', 5 June 2025, https://www.thehindu.com/news/international/bangladesh-drops-the-title-of-father-of-the-nation-for-sheikh-mujibur-rahman/article69656870.ece.
16. *Daily Star*, 'The Irregular Forces of Bangladesh Liberation War', 26 March 2019, https://www.thedailystar.net/supplements/independence-day-special-2019/news/the-irregular-forces-bangladesh-liberation-war-1719757.
17. *Diplomat*, 'Bangladesh's Bid to Rewrite History', 26 December 2024, https://thediplomat.com/2024/12/bangladeshs-bid-to-rewrite-history/.
18. Dhrubajyoti Bhattacharjee, 'Charting a New Narrative: Redrawing History and Politics in Bangladesh', *Indian Council of World Affairs*, 26 September 2024, https://www.icwa.in/show_content.php?lang=1&level=3&ls_id=11858&lid=7204.
19. 'H.Res.1430 – Recognizing the Bangladesh Genocide of 1971', US House of Representatives Resolution No. 1430, https://www.congress.gov/bill/117th-congress/house-resolution/1430/text.
20. *Daily Star*, 'Remembering the Barbarities of Operation Searchlight', 25 March 2019, https://www.thedailystar.net/opinion/perspective/news/remembering-the-barbarities-operation-searchlight-1719859.
21. *Smithsonian*, 'The Genocide the U.S. Can't Remember, but Bangladesh Can't Forget', 16 December 2016, https://www.smithsonianmag.com/history/genocide-us-cant-remember-bangladesh-cant-forget-180961490/.
22. US Department of State, 'U.S. Consulate (Dacca) Cable, Dissent from U.S. Policy Toward East Pakistan', *The National Security Archive*, The George Washington University, 6 April 1971, https://nsarchive2.gwu.edu/NSAEBB/NSAEBB79/BEBB8.pdf.
23. *Indian Express*, 'Mujibur Rahman Downsized, India's Role in Bangladesh Liberation War Cut: Dhaka Rewrites Textbooks', 28 February 2025, https://indianexpress.com/article/india/mujib-downsized-indias-role-in-liberation-war-cut-dhaka-rewrites-textbooks-9860332/.
24. *Prothom Alo*, 'We Must Not Forget 1971: Mirza Fakhrul', 24 December 2024, https://en.prothomalo.com/bangladesh/politics/84hnysz64u.
25. *Daily Star*, 'Sectors & Armed Forces of the Liberation War 1971', 23 March 2008, https://archive.thedailystar.net/campus/2008/03/04/feature_sectors.htm.

26. Anthony Mascarenhas, *Bangladesh: A Legacy of Blood*, Hodder & Stoughton, 1986.
27. Mumtajuddin Patowary, *Pathyapustake Muktijuddher Itihas Bikriti*, Jatiya Grantha Prokashan, 2004.
28. *Daily Star*, 'Caretaker System Abolished', 1 July 2011, https://www.thedailystar.net/news-detail-192303.
29. *Dhaka Tribune*, 'Jinnah's Death Anniversary Observed in Dhaka with Urdu Songs, Poetry', 12 September 2024, https://www.dhakatribune.com/bangladesh/dhaka/358179/jinnah%E2%80%99s-death-anniversary-observed-at-national.
30. *ThePrint*, 'ISI Delegation Visits Dhaka: How Region Is Witnessing a Geopolitical Shift', 23 January 2025, https://theprint.in/world/isi-delegation-visits-dhaka-how-region-is-witnessing-a-geopolitical-shift/2459042/.
31. *Times of India*, 'Concerned over ISI Team's Visit to Bangladesh: Army Chief General Upendra Dwivedi', 20 February 2025, https://timesofindia.indiatimes.com/india/concerned-over-isi-teams-visit-to-bangladesh-army-chief/articleshow/118396480.cms.
32. Al Jazeera, 'Pakistan Pulls Closer to Post-Hasina Bangladesh Amid Shared India Concerns', 17 January 2025, https://www.aljazeera.com/news/2025/1/17/pakistan-pulls-closer-to-post-hasina-bangladesh-amid-shared-india-concerns.
33. *Dhaka Tribune*, 'ISPR: Six Member Bangladesh Military Delegation Visits Pakistan', 20 January 2025, https://www.dhakatribune.com/bangladesh/foreign-affairs/371379/ispr-six-member-bangladesh-military-delegation.
34. *Daily Star*, 'Yunus Calls for SAARC Revival in Talks with Pakistan PM', 25 September 2024, https://www.thedailystar.net/news/bangladesh/diplomacy/news/yunus-calls-saarc-revival-talks-pakistan-pm-3712241.
35. *Dhaka Tribune*, 'Bangladesh, Pakistan Agree to Strengthen Bilateral Relations', 19 December 2024, https://www.dhakatribune.com/bangladesh/foreign-affairs/368559/bangladesh-and-pakistan-agree-to-strengthen.
36. *Economic Times*, 'Second Cargo Ship from Pakistan Reaches Bangladesh in as Many Months', 23 December 2024, https://economictimes.indiatimes.com/news/international/world-news/second-cargo-ship-from-pakistan-reaches-bangladesh-in-as-many-months/articleshow/116574544.cms.
37. *Swarajya*, 'Why a Pakistani Ship's Arrival at Chittagong Sends Out an Ominous Signal to India', 14 November 2024, https://swarajyamag.com/world/why-a-pakistani-ships-arrival-at-chittagong-sends-out-an-ominous-signal-to-india.
38. *Daily Star*, 'Bangladesh Demands $4.52b, Apology from Pakistan', 16 July 2025, https://www.thedailystar.net/news/bangladesh/diplomacy/news/bangladesh-demands-452b-apology-pakistan-3873841.
39. *Dhaka Diplomat*, 'Government to Replace Foreign Secretary Jashim within

Days, Says Advisor Touhid', 21 May 2025, https://www.dhakadiplomat.com/foreign-ministry/3757.
40. *BD Digest*, 'Did the Foreign Secretary Resign Over the Humanitarian Corridor Issue, or Was He Forced?', 22 May 2025, https://en.bddigest.com/did-the-foreign-secretary-resign-over-the-humanitarian-corridor-issue-or-was-he-forced/.
41. *Daily Star*, 'Dhaka, Beijing, and Islamabad Talk Trilateral Cooperation', 16 July 2025, https://www.thedailystar.net/news/bangladesh/diplomacy/news/dhaka-beijing-and-islamabad-talk-trilateral-cooperation-3922241.
42. *Global Times*, 'China–Bangladesh–Pakistan Trilateral Mechanism Boosts Regional Growth', 25 June 2025, https://www.globaltimes.cn/page/202506/1336965.shtml.
43. Observer Research Foundation, 'A China-Led Trilateral Nexus as India's New Challenge', 28 June 2025, https://www.orfonline.org/research/a-china-led-trilateral-nexus-as-india-s-new-challenge/

4. Rise of the Razakars

1. CNN, 'Tiananmen Square's Tank Man Photos, May 2019, https://edition.cnn.com/interactive/2019/05/world/tiananmen-square-tank-man-cnnphotos/.
2. *Bangla Outlook English*, 'Tobacco Industry's Targeting of Youth under Fire World No Tobacco Day Press Briefing', 28 May 2025, https://en.banglaoutlook.org/news/235599.
3. *Business Standard*, 'How Abu Sayeed Was Shot and Killed in Rangpur during Clash between Police and Protesters,' 17 July 2024, https://www.tbsnews.net/bangladesh/how-abu-sayeed-was-shot-and-killed-rangpurduring-clash-between-police-and-protesters.
4. *Daily Star*, 'Indian Artistes Pay Tribute to Abu Sayed, Support Bangladeshi Students' Plight', 5 October 2025, https://www.thedailystar.net/entertainment/tv-film/news/indian-artistes-pay-tribute-abu-sayed-support-bangladeshi-students-plight-3659516.
5. BBC News, 'Bangladesh Siege: Twenty Killed at Holey Artisan Bakery in Dhaka', 2 July 2016, https://www.bbc.com/news/world-asia-36692613.
6. Sahidul Hasan Khokon, '8 Chargesheeted in Holey Artisan Bakery Attack', *India Today*, 23 July 2018, https://www.indiatoday.in/world/story/8-chargesheeted-in-holey-artisan-bakery-attack-1294170-2018-07-23.
7. Tiffany Ap and Sugham Pokharel, '"I Was Stunned": Politician Identifies Son as Dhaka Terrorist." *CNN*, 6 July 2016, https://edition.cnn.com/2016/07/06/asia/dhaka-attacker-politicians-son.
8. *Diplomat*, 'Bangladesh's Ambiguity on Religion Has Been Expensive for the Country', 8 September 2020, https://thediplomat.com/2020/09/bangladeshs-ambiguity-on-religion-has-been-expensive-for-the-country/.

9. *Sabrang*, 'Bangladesh: Why Are Madrasas Mushrooming?', 16 January 2018, https://sabrangindia.in/bangladesh-why-are-madrasas-mushrooming/.
10. *ThePrint*, 'How Hefazat-e-Islami Has Become Sheikh Hasina Govt's Frankenstein in Bangladesh', 31 March 2021, https://theprint.in/opinion/how-hefazat-e-islami-has-become-sheikh-hasina-govts-frankenstein-in-bangladesh/631556/.
11. *Dhaka Tribune*, 'Qawmi Scholars Endorse Islamic State under Jamaat Leadership', 21 August 2024, https://www.dhakatribune.com/bangladesh/politics/355490/qawmi-scholars-endorse-islamic-state-under-jamaat.
12. *Dhaka Tribune*, 'Ansarullah Bangla Team Chief Released on Bail from Kashimur Jail', 26 August 2024, https://www.dhakatribune.com/bangladesh/nation/356166/ansarullah-bangla-team-chief-freed-from-kashimur.
13. *Dhaka Tribune*, 'Jamaat leader Azharul Walks Free after Supreme Court Verdict', 28 May 2025, https://www.dhakatribune.com/bangladesh/dhaka/382445/jamaat-leader-azharul-released-following-acquittal.

5. Mujib: The Man, the Myth

1. Deep Halder, 'Shyam Benegal's Hasty Film on Bangladesh's Mujib Won't Help Sheikh Hasina Win 2024 Polls', *ThePrint*, 28 July 2023, https://theprint.in/opinion/shyam-benegals-hasty-film-on-bangladeshs-mujib-wont-help-sheikh-hasina-win-2024-polls/1689813.
2. Shafiq Alam, *Facebook*, 9.22 a.m., 7 March 2025, https://www.facebook.com/shafiqul.alam.71216/posts/pfbid0233b7MQDWmhnGmvPQrPiLpi8FdCtpA5sBUJFmYb28sZSD8Wd16rsuMUxDfFfdAi2El.
3. *Daily Star*, 'Dhanmondi 32 House Ripped Apart', 5 February 2025, https://www.thedailystar.net/news/bangladesh/news/dhanmondi-32-house-ripped-apart-3817356.
4. Sam Dalrymple, *Shattered Lands: Five Partitions and the Making of Modern Asia*, HarperCollins, 2025, pp. 148–53.
5. *Telegraph*, 'Divided or Destroyed – Remembering Direct Action Day', 14 July 2023, https://www.telegraphindia.com/opinion/divided-or-destroyed-remembering-direct-action-day/cid/157755.
6. Faisal C.K., 'The Jamaat-e-Islami and the Undoing of Mujib's Sonar Bangla', *New Indian Express*, 9 August 2024, https://www.newindianexpress.com/web-only/2024/Aug/09/the-jamaat-eislami-and-the-undoing-of-mujibs-sonar-bangla.
7. Abid Hussain, 'Who Were the Razakars and Why Are They Central to Bangladesh Protests?', Al Jazeera, 22 July 2024, https://www.aljazeera.com/news/2024/7/22/who-were-the-razakars-and-why-are-they-central-to-bangladesh-protests.
8. Ibid.

9. Sandip Chakraborty, 'Bangabandhu's Clemency to Pro-Pak People is Creating Problems Now', *NewsClick*, 3 August 2024, https://www.newsclick.in/bangladesh-bangabandhus-clemency-pro-pak-people-creating-problems-now.
10. Mubashar Hasan, 'Religion and Bangladesh's Political Parties', *Diplomat*, 16 November 2023, https://thediplomat.com/2023/11/religion-and-bangladeshs-political-parties/.
11. Sabine Kieselbach, 'A Life in Exile: On the Death of Bangladesh Poet Daud Haider', *Deutsche Welle*, 6 May 2025, https://www.dw.com/en/a-life-in-exile-on-the-death-of-bangladesh-poet-daud-haider/a-72449910.
12. Manash Ghosh, 'Fidel Castro Advised Sheikh Mujibur Rahman against Promoting Pro-Pakistan Officers', *ThePrint*, 27 June 2025, https://theprint.in/pageturner/excerpt/fidel-castro-sheikh-ujibur-rahman-pro-pakistan-officers/2671987/.
13. Henry Hardy Cole and Charles Shepherd. 'Photographs II. General View of the Masjid and Colonnade and III.A, B. Hindu Sculptures', *The Architecture of Ancient Delhi: Especially the Buildings Around the Kutb Minar*, 4 December 2021, https://architexturez.net/pst/az-cf-223745-1638593524; Nishant Kumar Hota, 'Unveiling the "Secular" Sheikh Mujib: The Butcher of Bengali Hindus', *Pragyata*, 24 May 2022, https://pragyata.com/unveiling-the-secular-sheikh-mujib-the-butcher-of-bengali-hindus/; Kallol Bhattacherjee, 'President Kovind Inaugurates Landmark Kalibari Temple in Dhaka', *The Hindu*, 17 December 2021, https://www.thehindu.com/news/international/president-kovind-inaugurates-dhakas-historic-kalimandir-destroyed-by-pak-army-in-1971/article37975699.ece/amp; *Daily Star*, 'PM Urged not to Shift Ramna Kali Mandir', 23 June 2006, https://www.thedailystar.net/2006/06/23/d60623012818.htm; *Mayer Dak*, 'Report – Ramna Kali Temple Destruction: (Part 1 of 3)', n.d., https://web.archive.org/web/20010202153900/http://www.mayerdak.com/ramna1.htm.
14. Daily Star, 'When a Government Refuses to Go, People Accept It until They Don't', 25 January 2025, https://www.thedailystar.net/opinion/interviews/news/when-government-refuses-go-people-accept-it-until-they-dont-3807441.

6. Why Young Bangladeshis Hate India

1. Al Jazeera, 'Cricket: India Beat Bangladesh by 280 Runs to Win First Test in Chennai', 22 September 2024, https://www.aljazeera.com/sports/2024/9/22/cricket-india-beat-bangladesh-by-280-runs-to-win-first-test-in-chennai.
2. *Hindustan Times*, 'Bangladesh "Super Fan" Tiger Roby Beaten up during 2nd Test against India, Rushed to Hospital: Report', 27 September 2024, https://www.hindustantimes.com/cricket/bangladesh-super-fan-tiger-roby-

beaten-up-during-2nd-test-against-india-taken-to-kanpur-hospital-by-cops-report-101727426504086.html.
3. Vijaita Singh, 'India "Pushing Back" Bangladeshis Held without Documents', *The Hindu*, 15 May 2025, https://www.thehindu.com/news/national/india-pushing-back-bangladeshis-held-without-documents/article69575971.ece.
4. *Business Today*, '"Bangladeshi Infiltration...": Amit Shah Roars in Jharkhand, Promises Tough Law to Protect Tribal Land', 3 November 2024, https://www.businesstoday.in/india/story/bangladeshi-infiltration-amit-shah-roars-in-jharkhand-makes-big-promise-to-prevent-transfer-of-tribal-land-to-infiltrators-452368-2024-11-03.
5. Kallol Bhattacherjee, 'Bangladesh Sends Protest Note against Amit Shah's Speech in Jharkhand', *The Hindu*, 24 September 2024, https://www.thehindu.com/news/national/bangladesh-sends-protest-note-against-amit-shahs-speech-in-jharkhand/article68675421.ece.
6. *BD News 24*, 'Bangladesh Politics Heats up over India's Position 2 and a half Months after Election', 22 March 2024, https://bdnews24.com/politics/ot02cnmrtr.
7. Ibid.
8. Priyam Paul, 'When a Government Refuses to Go, People Accept It until They Don't', *Daily Star*, 25 January 2025, https://www.thedailystar.net/opinion/interviews/news/when-government-refuses-go-people-accept-it-until-they-dont-3807441.
9. *Prothom Alo*, 'India Is Responsible for Instigating India-Hatred in Bangladesh', 8 December 2024, https://en.prothomalo.com/opinion/op-ed/bss3xquvxn.
10. Ibid.

7. Good Hasina, Bad Hasina

1. *Livemint*, 'Irked by Sheikh Hasina's Speech, Mob set Mujibur Rahman's House on Fire', 6 February 2025, https://www.livemint.com/news/bangladesh-news-sheikh-hasina-father-sheikh-mujibur-rahman-residence-set-on-fire-dhaka-awami-league-muhammad-yunus-11738804133433.html.
2. *Daily Sun*, 'Sheikh Hasina So Far Receives 37 International Accolades', 17 September 2019, https://www.daily-sun.com/post/424167/budget2025-2026.
3. Ibid.
4. *Champions of the Earth, UN Environment Programme*, 'HE Sheikh Hasina', 22 August 2019, https://www.unep.org/championsofearth/laureates/2015/he-sheikh-hasina.
5. *World Leaders Forum*, 'Sheikh Hasina', September 2015, https://worldleaders.columbia.edu/directory/sheikh-hasina.
6. Osama Shaikh, 'Hasina's Era of Economic Progress and Political Strife', *Daily Sabah*, 22 August 2024, https://www.dailysabah.com/opinion/op-ed/hasinas-era-of-economic-progress-and-political-strife.

7. Md Shafi Mostofa, 'Challenges in Bangladesh–US Relations', *Daily Star*, 7 May 2023, https://www.thedailystar.net/opinion/views/news/challenges-bangladesh-us-relations-3313466.
8. Al Jazeera, 'Sheikh Hasina: A Critical Misstep and the End of 15 Years Ruling Bangladesh', 5 August 2024, https://www.aljazeera.com/news/2024/8/5/sheikh-hasina-a-critical-misstep-and-the-end-of-15-years-of-rule.
9. Ethirajan Anbarasan, '"The Howls Were Terrifying": Imprisoned in the Notorious "House of Mirrors"', *BBC*, 1 September 2024, https://www.bbc.com/news/articles/cdd7nqzj20qo.
10. *Netra News*, 'Secret Prisoners of Dhaka', 14 August 2022, https://netra.news/2022/secret-prisoners-of-dhaka.
11. *Business Standard*, 'What We Saw Was Far from Humanity: CA Yunus Visits Aynaghar at DGFI', 12 February 2025, https://www.tbsnews.net/bangladesh/what-we-saw-was-far-humanity-ca-yunus-visits-aynaghar-1066966.
12. *Business Standard*, 'Case Filed against ex-Bangladesh PM Hasina for Plot to Oust Yunus Govt', 29 March 2025, https://www.business-standard.com/external-affairs-defence-security/news/case-filed-against-ex-bangladesh-pm-hasina-for-plot-to-oust-yunus-govt-125032900348_1.html.
13. *BSS News*, '$234b Plundered during 15-Yr Hasina Regime: FT', 13 September 2025, https://www.bssnews.net/news-flash/311292.
14. *Financial Times*, 'Bangladesh's Missing Billions, Stolen in Plain Sight | FT Film', YouTube, 11 September 2025, https://www.youtube.com/watch?v=usUFFxklzas.

8. A New Messiah?

1. *Daily Star*, 'Bangladesh Standing Tall', 10 December 2006, https://archive.thedailystar.net/suppliments/2006/december/bangladeshstandingtall/index.htm.
2. *Star Weekend*, 'A Triumph Against the Odds', 21 January 2005, https://www.thedailystar.net/magazine/2005/01/03/cover.htm.
3. Muhammad Yunus, *Banker to the Poor: Micro-Lending and Battle against World Poverty*, PublicAffairs, New York, 2023, pp. 20–9.
4. Thanh Tung, 'Grameen Bank at a Glance', *Grameen Bank*, 12 March 2008, https://www.grameen-info.org/grameen-bank-at-a-glance/.
5. BBC News, 'Grameen's Muhammad Yunus in Court for Defamation Case', 18 January 2011, https://www.bbc.co.uk/news/world-south-asia-12213755.
6. *Daily Star*, 'Yunus Unveils Formula', 21 March 2006, https://archive.thedailystar.net/2006/03/21/d6032101118.htm.
7. *Daily Star*, 'Open Letter to All', 12 February 2007, https://archive.thedailystar.net/2007/02/12/d7021201011.htm.
8. Ibid.

9. *Daily Star*, 'Yunus' Second Letter', 23 February 2007, https://archive.thedailystar.net/2007/02/23/d7022301075.htm.
10. *Daily Star*, 'Yunus Floats Party Styled Nagorik Shakti', 23 February 2007, https://archive.thedailystar.net/2007/02/23/d7022301022.htm.
11. *Daily Star*, 'Yunus Writes Letter to All', 4 May 2007, https://archive.thedailystar.net/2007/05/04/d7050401129.htm.
12. *BD News 24*, 'Usurers Up in Arms to Usurp Politics, Hasina Tells Cultural Activists', 17 February 2007, https://bdnews24.com/politics/usurers-up-in-arms-to-usurp-politics-hasina-tells-cultural-activists.
13. *Daily Star*, 'Huge Support for Yunus', 18 February 2011, https://www.thedailystar.net/news-detail-174549.
14. CNN, 'Nobel-Winning Microcredit Bank Comes under Scrutiny', 14 January 2011, https://edition.cnn.com/2011/WORLD/asiapcf/01/14/bangladesh.microcredit/.
15. Agence France-Presse, 'Bangladesh Nobel Winner Yunus Should "Stay Away"', 15 February 2011, https://web.archive.org/web/20120525032942/https://www.google.com/hostednews/afp/article/ALeqM5hSRutw1eN77XQl0Bg550Bt8RUKCQ?docId=CNG.894a7c75aef1b21ccc3d7b40f8d06875.9b1.
16. *Huffington Post*, 'Bangladesh Trying to Fire Muhammad Yunus, Nobel Laureate, from Microlender Grameen', 3 March 2011, http://www.huffingtonpost.com/2011/03/02/bangladesh-fires-nobel-yunus-microlender_n_830176.html.
17. *BD News 24*, 'Yunus Files Writ Petition against His Removal', 3 March 2011, https://bdnews24.com/bangladesh/yunus-files-writ-petition-against-his-removal.
18. *Khaleej Times*, 'Thousands in Bangladesh Protest at Yunus Sacking', 5 March 2011, https://www.khaleejtimes.com/world/thousands-in-bangladesh-protest-at-yunus-sacking.
19. *Business Recorder*, 'Bangladesh Judge Confirms Yunus Sacking', 8 March 2011, https://www.brecorder.com/news/6141/.
20. *BD News 24*, 'US Worried over Grameen Bank Future', 5 August 2012, https://bdnews24.com/bangladesh/us-worried-over-grameen-bank-future.
21. *The Guardian*, 'Microfinance Pioneer Muhammad Yunus Accused of Tax Evasion', 10 September 2013, https://www.theguardian.com/world/2013/sep/10/microfinance-muhammad-yunus-accused-tax-evasion.
22. BBC News, 'Muhammad Yunus Faces Tax Probe', 9 September 2013, https://www.bbc.com/news/world-asia-24021842.
23. *Daily Star*, 'JS Passes Grameen Bank Law', 5 November 2013, https://www.thedailystar.net/news/js-passes-grameen-bank-law.
24. *GMA News Online*, 'Nobel Winner Yunus Convicted in Bangladesh Labour Law Case', 1 January 2024, https://www.gmanetwork.com/news/topstories/

world/892790/nobel-laureate-yunus-convicted-in-bangladesh-labor-law-case-prosecutor/story/.
25. *Daily Star*, 'Yunus Conviction a Blatant Abuse of Justice System: Amnesty', 1 January 2024, https://www.thedailystar.net/news/bangladesh/crime-justice/news/yunus-conviction-blatant-abuse-justice-system-amnesty-3508456.
26. *Dhaka Tribune*, 'Dr Yunus Acquitted, Sentence Overturned in Labour Law Case', 7 August 2024, https://www.dhakatribune.com/bangladesh/353991/dr-yunus-acquitted-sentence-overturned-in-labour.
27. *Daily Star*, 'Prof Yunus Acquitted in Graft Case', 11 August 2024, https://www.thedailystar.net/news/bangladesh/news/prof-yunus-acquitted-graft-case-3674911.
28. *New Age*, 'Bangladesh Interim Govt Chief Yunus under Criticism over Privileges', 9 May 2025, https://www.newagebd.net/post/country/264412/yunus-under-criticism-over-privileges.
29. BBC News, 'Yunus Faces Criticism over Special Privileges', 9 May 2025, https://www.bbc.com/bengali/articles/cnv1yev98qeo.
30. *Dhaka Times*, 'Government's Role Questioned as Bangladesh Records 10 Murders Daily', 13 July 2025, https://www.dhakatribune.com/bangladesh/386330/government%E2%80%99s-role-questioned-as-bangladesh-records.
31. *The Hindu*, 'Post-Hasina Bangladesh Records 230% Increase in Attacks on Journalists, Says Rights Body', 4 August 2025, www.thehindu.com/news/international/post-hasina-bangladesh-records-230-increase-in-attacks-on-journalists-says-rights-body/article69893178.ece.
32. *Dhaka Tribune*, 'BNP's Mosharraf Expresses Disappointment over Yunus's Polls Remarks in Japan', 1 June 2025, https://www.dhakatribune.com/bangladesh/politics/382811/khandakermosharraf-expresses-disappointment-over.

9. Boys and Girls in King's Party

1. Ananya Bhardwaj, 'Probe Ordered into Attacks on Hindus, Says Bangladesh Govt Adviser. "Indians Welcome to Investigate"', 3 September 2024, https://theprint.in/world/probe-ordered-into-attacks-on-hindus-says-bangladesh-govt-adviser-indians-welcome-to-investigate/2250742.
2. *BD News 24*, 'Anti-discrimination Student Platform Accused of Politicisation, Criminal Activities', 2 July 2025, https://bdnews24.com/politics/9296cb1e0e4d.
3. *Daily Star*, 'What Recent Scandals Reveal about Student Activism and Our Politics', 31 July 2025, https://www.thedailystar.net/opinion/views/news/what-recent-scandals-reveal-about-student-activism-and-our-politics-3951561.
4. *Dhaka Tribune*, 'Hasnat: Many Engaging in Extortion Misusing NCP Name',

28 July 2025, https://www.dhakatribune.com/bangladesh/politics/387635/hasnat-abdullah-many-are-engaging-in-extortion.

5. Asif Hawlader, 'NCP: 10 Central Leaders Served Show-Cause Notices in Six Months', *Prothom Alo English*, 10 August 2025, https://en.prothomalo.com/bangladesh/politics/nzrfn5ywfo.

6. *Prothom Alo*, 'NCP Is a "King's Party", 2 of Them in Govt: TIB Executive Director', 4 August 2025, https://en.prothomalo.com/bangladesh/2p98we3f1i.

7. M. Niaz Asadullah, 'Bangladesh's Youthquake', *Nepali Times*, 12 September 2025, https://nepalitimes.com/opinion/bangladesh-s-youthquake.

8. *New Age*, 'Security Forces Escort NCP Leaders Out of Gopalganj, AL Continues Rampage', 16 July 2025, https://www.newagebd.net/post/Country/270248/security-forces-escort-ncp-leaders-out-of-gopalganj-as-al-continues-rampage.

9. *BD Digest*, 'Students Who Used to Tutor Are Now Riding in Cars Worth 5 Crore Taka: Bulu', 11 March 2025, https://en.bddigest.com/students-who-used-to-tutor-are-now-riding-in-cars-worth-5-crore-taka-bulu/.

10. *Dhaka Tribune*, 'Nahid Calls for Consensus to End "Mujibbadi" Politics in Bangladesh', 19 March 2025, https://www.dhakatribune.com/bangladesh/politics/376722/nahid-calls-for-consensus-to-end-%E2%80%98mujibbadi%E2%80%99

10. India's New Headache?

1. *Republic*, 'Indira Gandhi Cultural Centre in Dhaka Burnt to Ashes', 6 August 2024, https://www.republicworld.com/world-news/breaking-indira-gandhi-cultural-centre-in-dhaka-burnt-to-ashes.

2. *Swarajya*, 'Unveiled: The Swift Fall of Sheikh Hasina that Was Scripted by External Forces', 6 August 2024, https://swarajyamag.com/world/unveiled-the-swift-fall-of-sheikh-hasina-that-was-scripted-by-external-forces.

3. *Swarajya*, 'How US "Deep State" and Pakistan Backed an Islamist Radical to Mastermind Regime Change in Bangladesh', 1 October 2024, https://swarajyamag.com/world/swarajya-exclusive-how-us-deep-state-and-pakistan-backed-an-islamist-radical-to-mastermind-regime-change-in-bangladesh.

4. *Daily Star*, 'Students Protest Blaming India for Flash Floods', 22 August 2024, https://www.thedailystar.net/campus/news/students-protest-blaming-india-flash-floods-3684081.

5. *Swarajya*, 'New Delhi Braces for Downturn in Ties with Dhaka as Another Row Erupts over Flash Floods in Bangladesh', 23 August 2024, https://swarajyamag.com/world/new-delhi-braces-for-downturn-in-ties-with-dhaka-as-another-row-erupts-over-flash-floods-in-bangladesh.

6. *Daily Star*, 'Govt May Review Non-Beneficial MoUs Signed with India:

Foreign Adviser', 1 September 2024, https://www.thedailystar.net/news/bangladesh/diplomacy/news/govt-may-review-non-beneficial-mous-signed-india-foreign-adviser-3691921.

7. *Daily Star*, 'Dhaka, Delhi Sign 7 New MoUs to Further Deepen Ties', 22 June 2024, https://www.thedailystar.net/news/bangladesh/diplomacy/news/dhaka-delhi-sign-7-new-mous-further-deepen-ties-3638886.

8. *Swarajya*, 'How Mamata Banerjee's Opposition to Sharing Teesta River Water with Bangladesh Has Pushed the Neighbour Closer to China', 19 August 2020, https://swarajyamag.com/politics/how-mamatas-intransigence-over-sharing-teesta-waters-has-pushed-bangladesh-to-china-thus-endangering-indias-interests.

9. *NDTV World*, 'Muhammad Yunus Says Issues over Water Treaty with India Must Be Resolved', 6 September 2024, https://www.ndtv.com/world-news/muhammad-yunus-says-issues-over-teesta-water-treaty-with-india-must-be-resolved-6502627.

10. *Dhaka Tribune*, '"No More Knee-Jerk Foreign Policy with India"', 7 December 2024, https://www.dhakatribune.com/bangladesh/foreign-affairs/367375/%E2%80%98no-more-knee-jerk-foreign-policy-with-india%E2%80%99.

11. *Dhaka Tribune*, '"No Hindus Will Be Left after 30 Years"', 20 November 2016, https://www.dhakatribune.com/bangladesh/10113/%E2%80%98no-hindus-will-be-left-after-30-years%E2%80%99.

12. https://bhbcop.org/.

13. *India Today*, 'Bangladesh Should Occupy Northeast States if India Attacks Pak: Yunus's Aide', 3 May 2025, https://www.indiatoday.in/world/story/india-pakistan-attack-bangladesh-occupy-north-east-muhammad-yunus-chinese-military-help-2718769-2025-05-02.

14. Al Jazeera, 'Bangladesh to Investigate 2009 Paramilitary Mutiny Massacre', 26 December 2024, https://www.aljazeera.com/news/2024/12/26/bangladesh-to-investigate-2009-paramilitary-mutiny-massacre.

15. *OpIndia*, 'The 2001 Boraibari Massacre: When Bangladeshi Troops Brutally Tortured and Killed Indian Jawans, Mutilated Their Bodies', 18 April 2001, https://www.opindia.com/2022/04/boraibari-massacre-when-indian-jawans-were-killed-by-the-bangladeshi-army-2001/.

16. *India Today*, 'Bangladesh PM Sheikh Hasina Uses Goodwill with India to Downplay Massacre of BSF Troops', 7 May 2001, https://www.indiatoday.in/magazine/neighbours/story/20010507-bangladesh-pm-sheikh-hasina-uses-goodwill-with-india-to-downplay-massacre-of-bsf-troops-776194-2001-05-06.

17. *Daily Star*, 'Ex-BDR Chief Floats Political Platform', 16 April 2004, https://www.thedailystar.net/2004/04/16/d40416011818.html.

18. Sultan M. Hali, 'Resistance against India in BD', *Hindu Vivek Kendra*, 2

March 2025, https://www.hvk.org/2005/0305/14.html.
19. *India Today*, 'Declare Bengal's Independence from Modi Rule, Bangladesh Islamist Tells Mamata', 13 September 2024, https://www.indiatoday.in/world/story/ansarullah-bangla-abt-jashimuddin-rahmani-bengal-independence-modi-rule-mamata-banerjee-bangladesh-islamist-threaten-india-2599079-2024-09-13.
20. Md Raihanul Islam Akand, 'BNP Leader Pintu Released from Jail after 17 Years', *Dhaka Tribune*, 24 December 2024, https://www.dhakatribune.com/bangladesh/368979/bnp-leader-pintu-released-from-prison-after-17.
21. Sushim Mukul, 'Bangladesh Frees Ex-Minister Who Funded POK Terrorists to Bleed India', *India Today*, 24 December 2024, https://www.indiatoday.in/world/story/bangladesh-frees-ex-bnp-minister-abdus-salam-pintu-harkat-ul-jihad-al-islami-huji-terrorism-india-pok-recruitment-arms-2654605-2024-12-24.
22. *Awaz: The Voice*, 'Yunus Govt Releases Jailed Islamist Leader Accused of Arming Anti-India Forces', 16 January 2025, https://www.awazthevoice.in/world-news/yunus-govt-releases-jailed-islamist-leader-accused-of-arming-anti-india-forces-33714.html.
23. Sahidul Hasan Khokon, 'Trucks of Arms Seized at Chittagong in 2004 Meant for ULFA: India's Ex-Intel Officer | Exclusive', *India Today*, 23 February 2023, https://www.indiatoday.in/world/story/bangladesh-defense-intelligence-agency-india-bnp-awami-league-major-general-gaganjit-singh-arms-consignment-2338411-2023-02-23.
24. *Daily Star*, 'Chief Justice Obaidul Hassan Decides to Step Down', 10 August 2024, https://www.thedailystar.net/news/bangladesh/news/chief-justice-obaidul-hassan-decides-step-down-3673696.
25. *Daily Star*, 'Five More SC Judges Resign', 10 August 2024, https://www.thedailystar.net/news/bangladesh/news/five-more-sc-judges-resign-3673871.
26. *India Today*, 'Bangladesh Court Cancels Death for Ulfa Chief Paresh Baruah in Arms-Haul Case', 18 December 2024, https://www.indiatoday.in/world/story/bangladesh-high-court-cancel-death-penalty-chittagong-ulfa-paresh-baruah-chattogram-arms-haul-2004-2651606-2024-12-18.
27. Ritu Sharma, 'India–Bangladesh Row: Pakistani Military Officials Visit Border Region Near North-East; Threaten India's "Chicken Neck"', *The Eurasian Times*, 27 January 2025, https://www.eurasiantimes.com/india-bangladesh-row-pakistani-military-officials/.
28. Abid Hussain, 'Pakistan Pulls Closer to Post-Hasina Bangladesh amid Shared India Concerns', *Al Jazeera*, 17 January 2025, https://www.aljazeera.com/news/2025/1/17/pakistan-pulls-closer-to-post-hasina-bangladesh-amid-shared-india-concerns.
29. *Arab News*, 'Pakistan PM, Bangladesh Chief Adviser Agree to Expand

Bilateral Ties at UNGA Sideline Meeting', 25 September 2024, https://www.arabnews.com/node/2572751/pakistan.

30. *Daily Star*, 'Settle Issues of 1971 to Take Forward Ties', 20 December 2024, https://www.thedailystar.net/news/bangladesh/news/settle-issues-1971-take-forward-ties-3780086.

31. *How Does Law Protect in the War?*, 'Bangladesh/India/Pakistan, 1974 Agreement', n.d., https://casebook.icrc.org/print/pdf/node/20809.

32. *Daily Star*, 'Bangladesh Demands $4.52 Billion in Financial Claims from Pakistan', 17 April 2025, https://www.thedailystar.net/news/bangladesh/diplomacy/news/bangladesh-demands-452-billion-financial-claims-pakistan-3873646.

33. Ayesha Farid, 'Foreign Secretary Md Jashim Uddin's Sudden Exit: Diplomacy, Dissent, and Strategic Discord', *BD Military*, 20 May 2025, https://www.bdmilitary.com/analysis/geopolitics-diplomacy/foreign-secretary-md-jashim-uddins-sudden-exit-diplomacy-dissent-and-strategic-discord/1173/.

34. *Times of India*, 'Report: Bangladesh Foreign Secretary to Be Replaced after "Defying" Yunus', 22 May 2025, https://timesofindia.indiatimes.com/world/south-asia/report-bangladesh-foreign-secretary-to-be-replaced-after-defying-yunus/articleshow/121326801.cms.

35. *Daily Star*, 'Türkiye Pledges Support for Bangladesh's Defence Industry Development', 8 July 2025, https://www.thedailystar.net/news/bangladesh/diplomacy/news/turkiye-pledges-support-bangladeshs-defence-industry-development-3935031?.

36. *Nordic Monitor*, 'Erdoğan Uses Turkish Intelligence Agency MIT to Silence Critics, Threaten Foreign Nations', 4 August 2025, https://nordicmonitor.com/2025/08/erdogan-uses-turkish-intelligence-agency-mit-to-silence-critics-threaten-foreign-nations/.

37. *Moneycontrol*, 'Turkish Funding for Bangladesh's Jamaat-e-Islami Poses Threat to India: Intel Sources', 10 June 2025, https://www.moneycontrol.com/explainers/explained-why-turkish-funding-for-bangladesh-s-jamaat-e-islami-poses-threat-to-india-article-13106238.html.

38. *Economic Times*, 'Turkey's Deepening Role in Bangladesh Adds a New Layer to India's Security Calculus', 8 July 2025, https://economictimes.indiatimes.com/news/defence/turkeys-deepening-role-in-bangladesh-adds-a-new-layer-to-indias-security-calculus/articleshow/122312478.cms?from=mdr.

39. *Financial Express*, 'Yunus Stirs Controversy, Calls Bangladesh "Guardian of the Ocean" and Targets India's Northeast — Here's What He Said during China Visit', 31 March 2025, https://www.financialexpress.com/world-news/yunus-stirs-controversy-calls-bangladesh-guardian-of-the-ocean-and-targets-indias-northeast-heres-what-he-said-during-china-visit/3794639/.

40. Jaideep Mazumdar, 'Outrageous Act: Bangladesh's Border Guards Cross Over into India, Try to Stop Construction of Mandir' *Swarajya*, 6 December

2024, https://swarajyamag.com/states/outrageous-act-bangladeshs-border-guards-cross-over-into-india-try-to-stop-construction-of-mandir.
41. Jaideep Mazumdar, 'A New Pakistan-Bangladesh Nexus, Spurred By China, Could Spell Trouble For India', *Swarajya*, 27 September 2024, https://swarajyamag.com/world/a-new-pakistan-bangladesh-nexus-spurred-by-china-could-spell-trouble-for-india.
42. Jaideep Mazumdar, 'Swarajya Exclusive: Bangladesh Is Turning into a Playground of External Powers, and That'll Have Adverse Consequences for India', *Swarajya*, 28 April 2025, https://swarajyamag.com/world/swarajya-exclusive-bangladesh-is-turning-into-a-playground-of-external-powers-and-thatll-have-adverse-consequences-for-india.
43. Jaideep Mazumdar, 'Here's the Bold New Strategy that New Delhi Needs to Craft with Regard to Bangladesh', *Swarajya*, 2 November 2024, https://swarajyamag.com/world/heres-the-bold-new-strategy-that-new-delhi-needs-to-craft-with-regard-to-bangladesh.
44. Jaideep Mazumdar, 'India Must Draw Clear Red Lines for the New Regime in Bangladesh', *Swarajya*, 14 September 2024, https://swarajyamag.com/world/india-must-draw-clear-red-lines-for-the-new-regime-in-bangladesh.

11. A Hindu Homeland

1. BBC News, 'Bangladesh Alleges "Separatist Plot"', 22 December 2001, https://news.bbc.co.uk/2/hi/south_asia/1725254.stm.
2. BBC News, 'Uproar over Sexual Assault in Bangladesh after Video Spreads Online', 30 June 2025, https://www.bbc.com/news/articles/c2k1qkxe1k3o.
3. *Prothom Alo*, 'Bangladesh Sees 2,500 Incidents of Communal Violence in 330 Days', 10 July 2025, https://en.prothomalo.com/bangladesh/g3cfs04xvc.
4. Deep Halder, 'Sedition Case against Bangladesh Hindu Leader Sparks Outrage. "Placed Saffron Flag above National Flag"', 1 November 2024, https://theprint.in/world/sedition-case-against-bangladesh-hindu-leader-sparks-outrage-placed-saffron-flag-above-national-flag/2337733.
5. Deep Halder, 'Fresh Protests in Bangladesh after Hindu Monk Jailed in Sedition Case, Attacks Rported on Temples', *ThePrint*, 27 November 2024, https://theprint.in/india/fresh-protests-in-bangladesh-after-hindu-monks-arrest-over-sedition-attacks-reported-on-temples/2375754/.
6. *Dhaka Tribune*, 'Chinmoy Krishna Denied Bail in Five Cases', 24 July 2025, https://www.dhakatribune.com/bangladesh/court/387245/chinmoy-krishna-das-was-denied-bail-in-five-cases.
7. *India Today*, 'India Calls for Fair Trial of Jailed Hindu Monk Chinmoy Das in Bangladesh', 3 January 2025, https://www.indiatoday.in/india/story/india-calls-for-fair-trial-of-jailed-hindu-monk-chinmoy-das-in-bangladesh-2659316-2025-01-03.

8. Hindustan Times, 'Bangladesh: Advocate Ramen Roy Defending Chinmoy Das "Brutally Attacked, in ICU", Says ISKCON', 3 December 2024, https://www.hindustantimes.com/india-news/bangladesh-advocate-ramen-roy-defending-chinmoy-das-brutally-attacked-in-icu-says-iskcon-101733183391667.html.
9. *News18*, '"CAA by Itself Serves Nothing": Why I&B Ministry Adviser Wants Act Amended', 26 January 2025, https://www.news18.com/politics/caa-by-itself-serves-nothing-why-ib-ministry-adviser-wants-act-amended-9464397.html.
10. Sourav Roy Barman, '"Break up Bangladesh," Says Pradyot Joining Sarma, Sanyal in Slamming Yunus for "landlocked" Remarks', *ThePrint*, 1 April 2025, https://theprint.in/politics/break-up-bangladesh-says-pradyot-joining-sarma-sanyal-in-slamming-yunus-for-landlocked-remarks/2573835/#google_vignette.
11. Ibid.
12. *NDTV*, 'Himanta Sarma Shares Map With Bangladesh's "2 Vulnerable Chicken Necks"', 26 May 2025, https://www.ndtv.com/india-news/assams-himanta-sarma-shares-bangladeshs-map-with-2-chicken-necks-weeks-after-muhammad-yunus-comment-8507728.
13. BBC News, 'Bangladesh Alleges "Separatist Plot"', 22 December 2001, https://news.bbc.co.uk/2/hi/south_asia/1725254.stm.
14. *Uttar Banga Sambad*, 'Rajganj | The 6 Districts of Bangladesh Should Be Split into Independent States! Bengal Army Appeals to Protect Hindus', 1 October 2025, https://uttarbangasambad.com/bongo-senas-appeals-to-make-bangladesh-6-districts-an-independent-country.
15. Kallol Bhattacherjee, '"July Proclamation" on 31 December to Bury Mujib-Badi 1972 Constitution: Anti-Discrimination Students Movement', *The Hindu*, 30 December 2024, https://www.thehindu.com/news/international/july-proclamation-on-31-december-to-bury-mujib-badi-1972-constitution-anti-discrimination-students-movement/article69040639.ece.

12. No Country for Other Muslims

1. *Daily Star*, 'Shrine Comes under Attack in Gazipur', 14 September 2024, https://www.thedailystar.net/news/bangladesh/crime-justice/news/shrine-comes-under-attack-gazipur-3702461.
2. *Daily Star*, 'Attackers on Religious Sites, Sufi Shrines to Be Brought to Book: CA Office', 14 September 2024, https://www.thedailystar.net/news/news/attackers-religious-sites-sufi-shrines-be-brought-book-ca-office-3702761.
3. Laleh-Naz, 'The Scattered Legacies of Bengal's Sufis', *Daily* Star, 20 November 2023, https://www.thedailystar.net/opinion/views/news/the-scattered-legacies-bengals-sufis-3474101.

4. Ibid.
5. Ibid.
6. *Daily Star*, 'Attackers on Religious Sites, Sufi Shrines to Be Brought to Book: CA Office', 14 September 2024, https://www.thedailystar.net/news/news/attackers-religious-sites-sufi-shrines-be-brought-book-ca-office-3702761.
7. *Prothom Alo*, 'Attack on the Ahmadiyya Community', 6 August 2024, https://www.prothomalo.com/amp/story/bangladesh/xhwusf2vrm.
8. Emran Hossain, 'Bangladeshi Ahmadiyyas Targeted by Hate Campaign', *UCA News*, 9 October 2024, https://www.ucanews.com/news/bangladeshi-ahmadiyyas-targeted-by-hatecampaign/106603.
9. Afzar Hussain, 'Fakir Lalon Shah: Subjects, Sites, and Signs', *Daily Star*, 17 October 2024, https://www.thedailystar.net/opinion/views/news/fakir-lalon-shah-subjects-sites-and-signs-3728936.
10. Ibid.
11. Ibid.
12. Ibid.
13. 'Lalon', *Wikipedia*, n.d., https://en.wikipedia.org/wiki/Lalon.
14. *New Age*, 'Lalon Philosophy Inspires People in July–August Uprising: Discussion', 13 October 2024, https://www.newagebd.net/print/post/247634.
15. *NDTV World*, '"Tolerance" Festival in Bangladesh Cancelled after Islamist Threats', 24 November 2024, https://www.ndtv.com/world-news/tolerance-festival-in-bangladesh-cancelled-after-islamist-threats-7095196.

13. Can Cinema Save Bangladesh?

1. *Iconic Focus 24 TV*, 'Shakib Khan Imitates Shahrukh Khan in Everything! Imitate | Shakib Khan | Shahrukh | Iconic Focus 24 TV', *YouTube*, 14 May 2025, https://www.youtube.com/watch?v=uzJI_FR_Dxc.
2. Deep Halder, 'Dear India, Bangladesh's SRK Is Coming to You. With Movies and Skincare', *ThePrint*, 3 February 2024, https://theprint.in/feature/dear-india-bangladeshs-srk-is-coming-to-you-with-movies-and-skincare/1951843.
3. *Dhaka Tribune*, 'Film Industry Eagerly Awaits Getting Back to Normalcy', 6 November 2024, https://www.dhakatribune.com/showtime/364439/film-industry-eagerly-awaits-getting-back-to.
4. Ibid.
5. *Daily Star*, '"We Should Coexist peacefully": Shakib Khan on Relations with India', 10 October 2024, https://www.thedailystar.net/entertainment/tv-film/news/we-should-coexist-peacefully-shakib-khan-relations-india-3724781.
6. Deep Halder, 'OTT Chorki Shook Bangladesh and West Bengal with Its Taboo Stories. It Has Big India Plans', *ThePrint*, 30 March 2024, https://theprint.in/ground-reports/ott-chorki-shook-bangladesh-and-westbengal-

with-its-taboo-stories-it-has-big-india-plans/2020618.
7. Makful Hossaion, 'Why Are Only Women Artistes Being Targeted?', *Prothom Alo*, 2 February 2025, https://en.prothomalo.com/entertainment/movies/t4lcfzlyzq.
8. Deep Halder, 'Tabu's Khufiya Lover, Azmeri Haque Badhon Doesn't Fear Homophobia in Bangladesh Anymore', *ThePrint*, 8 October 2023, https://theprint.in/ground-reports/tabus-khufiya-lover-azmeri-haquebadhon-doesnt-fear-homophobia-in-bangladesh-anymore/1794681.
9. Tanushree Ghosh, 'MC Exclusive | Azmeri Haque Badhon: "Sheikh Hasina Pushed Bangladeshi People Away from Bangabandhu", *Moneycontrol*, 30 August 2024, https://www.moneycontrol.com/entertainment/mc-exclusive-bangladeshi-actress-azmeri-haque-badhon-interview-article-12809901.html.
10. Azmeri Haque, *Facebook*, 11.11 a.m., 29 June 2025, https://www.facebook.com/story.php?story_fbid=4240674766211972&id=100008084717587&rdid=Kb2kOexIOvrMYSUo#.

14. The Return of Secular Bloggers

1. *Prothom Alo*, 'Pinaki Bhattacharya Sued on Charges of "Tarnishing Image of the Country"', 17 November 2022, https://en.prothomalo.com/bangladesh/my8d0b300h.
2. Kalbela News, 'Pinaki Threatens to Demolish Dhanmondi 32 | Dhanmondi 32 | Pinaki Bhattacharya | Kalbela', *YouTube*, 5 February 2025, https://www.youtube.com/watch?v=3Hofom3SNOg.
3. *Prothom Alo*, 'Demolition of Dhanmondi 32 Continues in the Morning', 6 February 2025, https://en.prothomalo.com/bangladesh/politics/1fuoxf4ba6.
4. Pinaki Bhattacharya, *Facebook*, 11.22 p.m., 8 May 2025, https://www.facebook.com/story.php?story_fbid=12769969337841518&id=100044215700385&rdid=dd4PKs1kS3jFfGd7.
5. *Daily Excelsior*, 'Hundreds of Student Activists Hold Protest in Dhaka's Shahbagh Demanding Ban on Awami League', 10 May 2025, https://www.dailyexcelsior.com/hundreds-of-student-activists-hold-protest-in-dhakas-shahbagh-demanding-ban-on-awami-league/.
6. *News18*, '"Want Protected, Autonomous Zones for Hindus": Global Bengali Hindu Coalition to Yunus', 30 December 2024, https://www.news18.com/world/want-protected-autonomous-zones-for-hindus-global-bengali-hindu-coalition-to-yunus-9173152.html.
7. Swadesh Roy, 'Ganajagaran Mancha and Its Impact against Fundamentalism', *Bangla Tribune*, 17 March 2019, https://en.banglatribune.com/opinion/opinion/34312/Ganajagaran-Mancha-and-its-impact-against.
8. Liton Haider, '9 Years after His Murder, the Father of Blogger Rajib Is Still Waiting for Justice', *BS News 24*, 15 February 2022, https://bdnews24.com/

bangladesh/9-years-after-his-murder-the-father-of-blogger-rajib-is-still-waiting-for-justice.
9. *Business Standard*, 'Ansarullah Bangla Team Chief Mufti Jasim Uddin Freed on Bail', 26 August 2024, https://www.tbsnews.net/bangladesh/ansarullah-bangla-team-chief-mufti-jasim-uddin-freed-bail-926241.
10. Arafatul Islam, 'Attacks on Activists – Some Facts', *Deutsche Welle*, 27 April 2016, https://www.dw.com/en/increasing-attacks-on-bangladeshi-activists-some-facts/a-19217814#:~:text=On%20February%2015%2C%202013%2C%20blogger,and%20Islam%20on%20social%20media.
11. *Amnesty International*, 'In Bangladesh, Blogging Can Get You Killed', 9 November 2015, https://www.amnesty.org/en/latest/campaigns/2015/11/in-bangladesh-blogging-can-get-you-killed/.
12. Deep Halder, 'Boycott India Campaign, Exiled "Activist", Anti-Hasina Chorus & BNP's Bid to Regain Lost Ground', *ThePrint*, 22 February 2024, https://theprint.in/world/boycott-india-campaign-exiled-activist-anti-hasina-chorus-bnps-bid-to-regain-lost-ground/1975484/.
13. Ibid.
14. Daily Jugnator, 'Elias Hossain Wants National Anthem Banned', *YouTube*, 13 May 2025, https://www.youtube.com/watch?v=VFMF4fMOwuU.
15. Nadia Islam, *Facebook*, 7.26 p.m., 9 May 2025, https://www.facebook.com/story.php?story_fbid=656051433926470&id=100085648561762&rdid=oHEPoaYtXKKaqpio.
16. *Amnesty International*, 'Bangladesh: Authorities Must Refrain from Harassing Family Members of Human Rights Defenders in Exile', 7 August 2020, https://www.amnesty.org/en/latest/news/2020/08/bangladesh-authorities-must-not-harass-family-of-hrds-in-exile/.
17. Asaduzzaman Noor, *Facebook*, 10.15 p.m., 16 January 2025, https://www.facebook.com/story.php?story_fbid=1813598302824237&substory_index=1813598302824237&id=100056809494966&rdid=qsOFeDVu7k9tK39f.
18. Azam Khan, Facebook, 1.44 p.m., 5 April 2025, https://www.facebook.com/story.php?story_fbid=10163577909636803&id=750041802&rdid=lGJCfyRiO8kzslNn.
19. Imran H. Sarker, *Facebook*, 8.18 p.m., 25 March 2025, https://www.facebook.com/story.php?story_fbid=1206030824225375&id=100044554054369&rdid=rpiaP8qlYj7Tb8GR.

15. No Woman, No Cry

1. Nylah Shah, 'Forget Katy Perry, Here's Bangladesh's Ruthba Yasmin Shooting for the Moon', *Business Standard*, 10 June 2025, https://www.tbsnews.net/features/forget-katy-perry-heres-bangladeshs-ruthba-yasmin-shooting-moon-1162851.

2. Anna Kaufman and Eric Lagatta, 'History Made: Katy Perry, Gayle King Go to Space on Blue Origin Flight', *USA Today*, 14 April 2025, https://www.usatoday.com/story/entertainment/celebrities/2025/04/14/katy-perry-gayle-king-lauren-sanchez-blue-origin-space/83046482007/.
3. Nylah Shah, 'Forget Katy Perry, Here's Bangladesh's Ruthba Yasmin Shooting for the Moon', *Business Standard*, 10 June 2025, https://www.tbsnews.net/features/forget-katy-perry-heres-bangladeshs-ruthba-yasmin-shooting-moon-1162851.
4. Deep Halder, 'War Criminal Delwar Hossain Was against Bangladesh. Why Is His Face on the Moon Now?', *ThePrint*, 22 August 2023, https://theprint.in/opinion/war-criminal-delwar-hossain-was-against-bangladesh-why-is-his-face-on-the-moon-now/1724630/.
5. *Daily Star*, 'Lie Worked Well', 4 March 2013, https://www.thedailystar.net/news-detail-271242#google_vignette.
6. BBC News, 'Bangladesh Islamist Delwar Sayeedi Death Sentence Commuted', 17 September 2014, www.bbc.com/news/world-asia-29233639.
7. *BD News 24*, 'Supreme Court Publishes Full Verdict on War Crimes Convict Delwar Hossain Sayedee', 31 December 2015, https://bdnews24.com/amp/story/bangladesh%2Fsupreme-court-publishes-full-verdict-on-war-crimes-convict-delwar-hossain-sayedee.
8. Al Jazeera, 'Women's Football Match Cancelled in Bangladesh after Religious Protests', 29 January 2025, https://www.aljazeera.com/sports/2025/1/29/womens-football-match-cancelled-in-bangladesh-after-religious-protests.
9. *Daily Star*, 'Offenders Now Weaponising AI', 9 July 2025, https://www.thedailystar.net/news/bangladesh/news/offenders-now-weaponising-ai-3935251.
10. Nilima Jahan and Tangila Tasnim, 'Nearly 9 out of 10 Victims of Rape Were Children', *The Daily Star*, 25 May 2025, https://www.thedailystar.net/news/bangladesh/crime-justice/news/nearly-9-out-10-victims-rape-were-children-3902546.
11. Ibid.
12. Ibid.
13. Ibid.
14. Selim Jahan, 'The Cost of Marrying Off Girls Too Soon', *Daily Star*, 27 June 2025, https://asianews.network/the-cost-of-marrying-off-girls-too-soon/.
15. *Prothom Alo*, 'Recommendation for Ensuring Equal Inheritance Rights for Women', 20 April 2025, https://en.prothomalo.com/bangladesh/w5exlnio5j.
16. Shahin Akhter, 'Women Affairs Reform Commission: Equal Property Right Suggested', *New Age*, 19 April 2025, https://www.newagebd.net/print/post/262690.
17. Rumman Turjo, 'Public Humiliation of Women, Misogyny Go Unchallenged in Bangladesh as Violence Spikes', *BD News 24*, 8 March 2025, https://

bdnews24.com/bangladesh/12ab33c4f5a6.
18. DadaVai Pinaki, *Facebook*, 2025, https://www.facebook.com/reel/709537198649191.
19. *AP News*, 'Thousands of Islamists Rally in Bangladesh against Proposed Changes to Women's Rights', 3 May 2025, https://apnews.com/article/bangladesh-women-rights-islamists-rally-114e1acbe56e7be75bc9b5273365a17a.
20. *India Today*, 'Won't Get Even 5 Minutes to Escape: Islamists Warn Bangladesh Govt', 1 May 2025, https://www.indiatoday.in/world/story/bangladesh-islamist-parties-jamaat-e-islami-hifazat-e-islam-yunus-government-women-reforms-sheikh-hasina-2717939-2025-05-01.
21. Tara Asgar and Nur A. Mahjabin Khan, 'Whose Feminism Is It Anyway?: Lessons from the Gender Reform Uproar', Daily Star, 5 June 2025, https://www.thedailystar.net/opinion/views/news/whose-feminism-it-anyway-lessons-the-gender-reform-uproar-3910371.
22. GTV, 'I Wanted a Fight, I Became a Prostitute | Women's Friendship March | Gtv News', *YouTube*, 19 May 2025, https://www.youtube.com/watch?v=cbJJQ2zAErE.

Afterword

1. Shashi Tharoor, *X*, 4.43 p.m., 11 September 2025, https://x.com/ShashiTharoor/status/1966097834845032745.
2. *The Daily Star*, 'The Black Night', 25 march 2015, https://www.thedailystar.net/frontpage/news/the-black-night-73596.
3. Anam Zakaria, 'Remembering the War of 1971 in East Pakistan', *Al Jazeera*, 16 December 2019, www.aljazeera.com/opinions/2019/12/16/remembering-the-war-of-1971-in-east-pakistan.
4. Netrakona, '"Will Implement Laws of the Quran Even If It Costs Our Lives"', *The Daily Star*, 28 August 2025, https://www.thedailystar.net/top-news/news/will-implement-laws-the-quran-even-if-it-costs-our-lives-3973066.
5. Flora Drury, 'Bangladesh Announces Election as Country Marks Year since Ex-PM Fled', *BBC*, 5 August 2025, https://www.bbc.com/news/articles/czd031z5md9o.
6. *The Daily Star*, 'Bangladesh Prepared for Free, Fair Polls in February, Yunus Tells US Envoy', 23 September 2025, https://www.thedailystar.net/news/bangladesh/news/bangladesh-prepared-free-fair-polls-february-yunus-tells-us-envoy-3992321.
7. *The Business Standard*, 'AL, JaPa Should Participate in National Polls for a Free and Fair Vote: Fakhrul Tells Ei Samay', 23 September 2025, https://www.tbsnews.net/bangladesh/politics/fakhrul-wishes-see-participation-al-jamaat-upcoming-national-elections-1243366.

8. *Al Jazeera*, 'Bangladesh Bans Activities of Awami League, the Party of Ousted PM Hasina', 11 May 2025, https://www.aljazeera.com/news/2025/5/11/bangladesh-bans-activities-of-awami-league-the-party-of-ousted-pm-hasina.
9. *The Times of India*, 'Bangladesh Begins Shiekh Hasina Trial on Mass Murder Charges', 3 June 2025, https://timesofindia.indiatimes.com/world/south-asia/bangladesh-begins-sheikh-hasina-trial-on-mass-murder-charges/articleshow/121556006.cms.
10. Shubhjyoti Ghosh, 'Sheikh Hasina to Lead Children in "Rahul–Priyanka Model"', *BBC News*, 8 September 2015, https://www.bbc.com/bengali/articles/cp3q9125qrko.
11. 'Bangladesh's Exiled Opposition Leader Plots Return for Election', *Financial Times*, 7 October 2025, https://www.ft.com/content/3c657f03-2c5b-4d7e-bae6-82e86ef34a88.
12. *The Business Standard*, 'AL, JaPa Should Participate in National Polls for a Free and Fair Vote: Fakhrul Tells Ei Samay', 23 September 2025, https://www.tbsnews.net/bangladesh/politics/fakhrul-wishes-see-participation-al-jamaat-upcoming-national-elections-1243366.
13. Maruf Mallick, 'Election of Proportional Representation Sparks Concern of an AL Comeback', *Prothom Alo*, 7 July 2025, en.prothomalo.com/opinion/op-ed/odjqwslpl7.
14. *The Tribune*, 'PM Seeks Forward-Looking Ties with BD', 26 September 2025, https://tribune.com.pk/story/2568984/pm-seeks-forward-looking-ties-with-bd.
15. Saurabh Gupta, '"Bangladesh Has Problems with India": Muhammad Yunus on Sheikh Hasina, SAARC Revival', *NDTV World*, 25 September 2025, www.ndtv.com/world-news/bangladesh-has-problems-with-india-muhammad-yunus-on-sheikh-hasina-saarc-revival-9341736.
16. 'Hundreds of Lakhs of Youths Will Fight against India: Abdullah Mohammad Taher', *Kaler Kantho*, 27 September 2025, https://www.kalerkantho.com/online/Politics/2025/09/27/1583434?__cf_chl_tk=8CmtnPNh.Xe_a7Y_X3rzAn98Mnsxme4y3LKgpgGXAyI-1758986037-1.0.1.1-hXP99gWcCCOFzQG.A4mClVekjIgH8rZ3S3jhEoUfBPo.
17. Golam Mowla, 'Bangladesh Faces Its Worst Financial Crisis in Decades', *Dhaka Tribune*, 22 September 2025, www.dhakatribune.com/bangladesh/392081/bangladesh-faces-its-worst-financial-crisis-in.
18. Mahfuz Anam, 'Can Justice Be Dispensed in an Unjust Manner', *The Daily Star*, 19 September 2025, www.thedailystar.net/opinion/views/the-third-view/news/can-justice-be-dispensed-unjust-manner-3989176.

Acknowledgements

The way to Dhaka's rebel heart, for us, opened through Blue Door Cafe in Delhi's Khan Market. That is where we fleshed out the idea of *Inshallah Bangladesh* with our editor Swati Chopra. Without Swati sifting through our travel diaries, political interviews and divergent interpretations of what transpired in Bangladesh and guiding us to put it all together as neat chapters, this book would not have been possible.

We would like to thank Rezwana Karim Snigdha, Associate Professor of Anthropology, Jahangirnagar University, Dhaka; Syed Badrul Ahsan, former Executive Editor of *The Daily Star*, Bangladesh; Indian diplomats Veena Sikri and Preeti Saran; South Asia expert and Coordinator of South Asia Centre at Manohar Parrikar Institute for Defence Studies & Analysis Dr Ashok K. Behuria; senior journalist Jayanta Roy Chowdhury; and our friend and scholar Dr Sriparna Pathak, the founding director of the Centre for Northeast Asian Studies at O.P. Jindal University, for patiently sharing their perspectives and helping us make sense of the tumultuous events that changed Bangladesh.

Our deep gratitude to Sharmin Khan Shudha, Suchismita Sanyal and Sourav Sikdar for being beacons of hope in very dark times when it seemed all is lost, a snapshot of which has been the Preface of the book.

There are many we cannot thank in public for sharing with us their experiences in Bangladesh for their own safety. You know who you are and you shall be in our hearts. Bangladeshi Australian political columnist S.M. Faiyaz Hossain cleared up his work schedule to become lead researcher for the book. Journalist Iram Ara Ibrahim gave us the title of the book and valuable suggestions along the way. We thank you all.

A Note on the Authors

Deep Halder is a journalist and author. He has headed newsrooms in leading Indian media outlets like the India Today Group, Dainik Bhaskar and DNA. Currently, he is Contributing Editor with *ThePrint*, writing mostly on Bangladesh and West Bengal. He is the author of the best-selling books *Blood Island: An Oral History of the Marichjhapi Massacre* (2019), *Bengal 2021: An Election Diary* (2021) and *Being Hindu in Bangladesh: An Untold Story* (2023).

Jaideep Mazumdar is a journalist with more than thirty-five years' experience in various Indian media outlets and an author. He writes mostly on eastern and northeastern India, Nepal, Bangladesh and Myanmar. Till recently, he was Political Affairs Editor with Swarajya.

Sahidul Hasan Khokon has over twenty years of experience in print, digital and TV news media in both India and Bangladesh. Till recently, he reported on Bangladesh for the India Today Group. He has authored five books on Bangladesh's 1971 War of Independence and the rise of radicalism. He is currently in India due to Bangladesh's political instability and attack on journalists.